DRIVEN

LEON MANDEL

DRIVEN:

The American
Four-Wheeled
Love Affair

STEIN AND DAY/*Publishers*/New York

First published in 1977
Copyright © 1977 by Leon Mandel
All rights reserved
Designed by Ed Kaplin
Printed in the United States of America
Stein and Day/*Publishers*/Scarborough House,
Briarcliff Manor, N.Y. 10510

Library of Congress Cataloging in Publication Data

Mandel, Leon.
    Driven.

    Bibliography: p. 269
    Includes index.
    1. Automobiles—Social aspects—United States.
I. Title.
HE5623.M33   301.24′3   76-41262
ISBN 0-8128-2076-2

For Dutch and Avie

Contents

Foreword   ix

PART ONE

1: Friends and Enemies: A Five-Dimensional View   3
2: Middletown Transformed   32
3: Before Ford   61

PART TWO
4: Mother City   79
5: The Marketplace: Field of Combat   116

PART THREE
6: Bureaucrats and White Chargers   161
7: Chasing Our Own Tailpipes   192
8: To What End the Highway?   209

PART FOUR
9: 2001: A Continuing Odyssey   237

Bibliography   269
Index   275

Foreword

Two and a half years ago, a young Reno television newsman, Buddy Frank, mentioned over lunch that his station might be interested in regular commentary on The State of the Car. I had survived a long and dishonorable history with the car, beginning with my bolting from college at the start of my senior year and driving across the country because it was in California that cars were being deified. Actually, the car and I go back even further than that. My father told my mother when I was ten that he despaired of my future: undoubtedly I would end up as a car thief. He was close. I became first an automobile dealer, then a dilettante racer, and ended up as an automotive journalist.

KTVN-TV's news director, Ed Pearce, let enthusiasm get the better of his usually immaculate judgment, and I've been talking about cars twice a week at the end of the 5:30 P.M. local news ever since. It remains the only program of its kind in the country. Maybe every other news director in the United States knows something Pearce doesn't.

The station management has given me an absolutely free hand and maximum protection from the firestorm of advertiser complaints. As a result, I have felt free to talk tough about blood on the highway, the dreary carnival-ethic atmosphere of the automobile retail establishment, Detroit ripoffs, Detroit mind-set, Detroit prejudices, Japanese fallibility, German engineering arrogance, British surrender, and the Bolus and Snopes Racing Team ("Anything Worth Doing is Worth Doing To Excess").

I've invited the TV audience to call me at the station and to call me at home, and they have. I can't think of a call that hasn't been enlightening—or at least interesting. I can't remember any failure of civility or intelligence.

What I have discovered from these calls is something I have suspected for years: there is abroad in the land great unease with the automobile. People are ambivalent as hell about the cars they live with. They are irrationally attached to them, they are choking with rage about having to drive them at 55mph, they feel guilty about the poison they have come to believe the car spreads in the air—but not so guilty that they want to pay to do something about it. They know there is something called an air bag, but they are not sure what it is, much less what it will cost. They know that car prices keep going up, but they don't know whether Detroit is using inflation as an excuse to dip into their pockets. They know small cars are of social benefit, but they won't buy them and they take me to task for describing their virtues. The one subject guaranteed to clog my telephone line well into the night is the frequent lecture I give on what bad drivers we all are.

All this is to say that people watch *Cars* on KTVN because it's about something that is of considerable interest. But if they watch with attention, they also watch with many reservations, much prejudice, and committed uncertainty.

This small segment of the American car-owning public knows it is being had, or it is about to be had, or it has been had, not only by the car sellers but by the people who superintend: the highway patrol chiefs, the road builders, the manufacturers, the bankers. They do not know how they have been ravished and they are not at all sure they want to be given the details, but they can't help listening when they're told.

In wider perspective, I have found again and again that when the automobile is defined as a social problem, people are deeply concerned and then astonished to discover they have taken the car for granted for so long without examining the consequences of ownership.

You deserve to know my prejudices. I have always had an irrational fondness for cars. I have become, in recent years, increasingly impatient with my car-loving friends who seem unaware that they are keeping full-grown, undomesticated carnivores for garage pets. Mine are selfish feelings. I look forward to an old age in which I can motor around in lovely, street-worthy and street-safe cars. When no one is looking, I want to be able to get to the ragged edge in a corner, trailing the brake to steer and feeling only moderately guilty at the thought that I am sailing through the turn within an inch of disaster. I want other drivers to know as much about evasive capability as I do. I want the car I drive to offer interior protection against a "second collision." I don't want to be burdened with the feeling that I am despoiling the earth by driving a car that is wasteful of any natural resource; I want an "ethical car."

Simply, I don't want to be irrational about my fondness for cars anymore.

Another conscious prejudice, or at least a footnote: In my experience, the closer you come to the great cities of the East, the less you get a sense of the national view of the car. It is absurd to own a car in New York, so how can New Yorkers, even those with cars, begin to understand the immense portion of the Los Angeleno's life the car occupies? They can't and they don't. Very clearly then, the perspectives here are not Sutton Place perspectives or Riverdale or even Westchester perspectives. They may, in fact, be better understood in the South Bronx where the car is at least coveted. But since the automobile is a national problem of huge consequence, it is therefore also a New York and Boston and Washington problem—particularly a Washington problem. Thus, when urbanites in the eastern corridor clamor for giant expenditures for mass transit at the expense of highways, it would be well for them to understand the almost hysterical and certainly mystical quality of the opposition.

Morton Mintz of the Washington *Post* sets the lesson from which this book is taken. Mintz's Mass Media Proposition (described in the *Columbia Journalism Review*) is: "If it's really important, it doesn't get the attention it deserves, or gets it late, or gets it only because some oddball pushes it." In this case, I appoint myself the oddball. The matters of real importance, Mintz thinks, include, "... the kind of problems that cut close to the lives, health, and pocketbooks of our readers [he was speaking to journalists here, remember], such as the safety of the air we breathe, the water we drink, the food and drugs we ingest, the vehicles in which we travel ...."

If this book's purpose is to discuss something we have heretofore dismissed as being too familiar for real consideration, its point of view is that if we understand the problem we can at least decide the energy we wish to expend seeking the solution. We don't understand the problem; that is we don't understand that the automobile is a large, single, immensely complicated national problem. And so our solution-seeking is scattergunned. This buckshot approach is guaranteed trouble. So we had better decide pretty quickly about the automobile. And the controlling word in the last sentence is "we." We are the car owners. "They" are the car builders and the car bureaucrats. "They" are not us and their solutions are going to be different from ours, perhaps uncomfortably so. We should and must decide how to buy rationally, how to spend our highway or mass transit money, how safe we wish to be, and how much we are willing to spend to be that safe.

But first we need to know a great deal more about the single great problem the automobile poses. We need to ask questions.

This brings me back to the audience of KTVN's *Cars* in order to thank them. I hope they will continue to be interested. Perhaps they might even continue to be tolerant. There are others to thank, too many to name, but some that must be mentioned. From the automobile industry: John Riccardo, George Butts, Bernard Mullins, Jim Stickford, Irv Rubin, Walter Czarnecki, Maurice Mosko, Forrest Faulknor, Jack Flaherty, Kjell Qvale, Andy Regalia, Semon Knudsen, Peter Von Manteuffel, Leo Levine, Gil Carmichael, and Roger Penske. From government: Bobby Boaz, John Borda, Dr. James Gregory, and Roz Parry. From a variety of newspapers, magazines, and television stations: Lee Hirshland, Ed Pearce, Thom Ryan, Walter Frank, Will Chism, Miles Ottenheimer, David E. Davis, Jr., David Abrahamson, Stephan Wilkinson, Pat Bedard, Charles Fox, Brock Yates, Eric Dahlquist, Bob Irvin, and Keith Crain. In worlds other than automotive: Carl Polk, Dr. George Snively, Dr. Peter Talbot, Marijane Kailek, Peter

Vrooman, Joseph W. Eskridge, Dr. John Miller, Virgil Doyle, Anatoly Arutunoff, D. O. Cozzi, David Curry, Duane Elgin, Dave MacMichael, Peter Schwartz, and Arnold Mitchell.

For research on pre-car America, Rick Thompson, a graduate student at the University of Nevada, was invaluable. Mary Matrille slogged through Los Angeles in pursuit of rational statements on the subject of mass transit. If there is violence done in either area, I hold them harmless. Gaye Hansen typed, retyped, and typed the manuscript again, each time to an impossible deadline, not because there was anything wrong with the due date, but because I was kept breathless by the rush of events.

Professor Richard Adams of Lewis and Clark College in Portland, Oregon read the manuscript and offered fine suggestions from his vantage point as a sociologist and closet car buff. Historian Michael Brodhead, who brings wit, warmth, and immense knowledge to the fortunate students in his classes at the University of Nevada, Reno, brought all those virtues and more to his criticism of *Driven*. My colleague, Steve Thompson, one of the new sort of automotive writers, is a man who came into the world a professional and whose professional eye was penetrating and far seeing in his reading of the final draft; I am grateful. Tom Lankard, Chief of California's Office of Traffic Safety, read and criticized the manuscript from the point of view of an enlightened safety expert who likes cars but prefers people and thinks something can be done to make the world habitable for both. His authoritative comments were of immense help.

Particular thanks to my cousin, Tom Mandel, who is co-author on the futures section. He is a futurist at Stanford Research Institute but his contributions to *Driven* were far greater than his job title or his family ties might suggest. He has influenced the whole manuscript, not the least through enthusiasm and unfailing support. His specific professional contribution has been immense.

To Jacques de Spoelberch, who is as good an editor as he is an agent (very good indeed), but nonetheless a better friend, my thanks.

I am indebted to the editors of *Driven*—Michaela Hamilton and Patricia Day of Stein and Day. Much of whatever is good about this book is good because they were its editors.

Finally, a book publicist once said to me she couldn't call to mind a single author who had been married any length of time. Writers are too full of themselves to allow anyone else into their lives, she said. I've been married twenty-four years, all credit due my wife, Olivia. For her patience, her love, her encouragement, inadequate thanks.

—LEON MANDEL

January 11, 1977
Reno, Nevada

Part One

"When you start adding up the time you
spend in a car, not just behind the wheel
but the time looking for parking places,
and paying parking tickets, and getting
the damn thing serviced, and getting it
maintained—all that shit—I'd just
much rather have the time at my disposal
to use as I see fit."

—DAVID MILLER, futurist
and former car owner

1 : *Friends and Enemies:*
A Five-Dimensional View

I

Winston L. Anderson, Jr., at this moment drinking bourbon and coke, is about to sell his Jaguar V12 E-type roadster. It is his second such car and his fifth Jaguar in about the same number of years. He is not selling his Jaguar because he doesn't like the car. Winston L. Anderson, Jr. loves the Jaguar; it's just that he loves the Porsche he is about to buy more. At this time, in this place, Winston L. Anderson, Jr. is not such an oddity as he might seem. For he is drinking that bourbon and coke in the tower restaurant at the Los Angeles International Airport, having taken off early from his job to drive here to discuss the automobile. He is young, short, dark, and although he seems subdued, a very definite aura of energy surrounds him. It is a mystery how he manages to be almost deferential and at the same time exude that feeling of coiled forcefulness.

Car-crazy Angelenos are common—their city is, after all, the car capital of the nation; nor is it strange that Anderson should be talking about owning imported cars. In California—particularly Southern California—foreign cars take up 40 percent of the market as opposed to about 14 percent elsewhere. Anderson is saying that he keeps a car for only about eight months. Ten at the most. He can afford to buy expensive cars because he has been able to make money on every Jaguar he has ever owned. Shrewd buying. Shrewder selling. Anderson is openly an upward striver; he looks forward to a continuing increase in his income. There is no chance, Anderson seems to be suggesting, that he will revert to the old, make-do, Jaguar-owning days ever again. Porsche today, custom coachwork Lagonda station wagon tomorrow, next month ... what?

Whatever it is, Anderson will try to drive it with a *little* more restraint than the Jaguars, in which he has gotten six tickets in the past two years. "I drove 100 mph every day I owned a Jaguar for about four years." Then he began to get tickets. He remembers every one he's ever gotten. Are they no deterrent? Not to a man who loves driving fast and is confident of himself and his car. "It's just purely a thrill to go fast." It's also a question of coordination between man and machine, to be able to drive to the capability of a car that is safe at 100mph. There is still more justification: "Although I'm a very fast driver, I'm not what you would call a very careless driver. My high-speed driving comes at 6 A.M. on open freeways and there is nobody else around. Further, I have a certain inhibition about being too fast, too abandoned, so that I could never become a racing driver."

It helps that Winston Anderson has confidence in his fellow freeway driver. He does not think kindly of drivers from other states, but he has high regard for the skill and care of his fellow travelers on the great ribbons that wrap around Los Angeles.

Perhaps one reason why he enjoys freeway driving is that it is on the San Bernardino, the Santa Ana, and the San Gabriel that he was stopped by the California Highway Patrol and *not* given tickets for driving 100mph.

"Those things happened during the first two years I was in Los Angeles. I had my surgical greens on and I was going to the hospital." He told the highway patrol he was on an emergency call each time, and each time they cautioned him about *other* drivers on the freeway who were not as competent as he was—the presumption being that as a doctor he was skilled in handling a car and aware of the hazards of high-speed driving.

Yes, this is Dr. Winston L. Anderson, Jr., senior surgical resident at Los Angeles County Hospital, responsible for treatment, on his shift, of all injured persons who come into Emergency, one fifth of whom have been hurt in automobile accidents. How can he tell without a report that these traumas are auto-caused?

Well, they either fell off a 25-story building or they were in a car wreck. I mean, they look like they have just had the hell beaten out of them. They are the most difficult patients to manage because they've got so many parts of their bodies involved in their injuries. They present terrible problems. Treating one part, trying to make it well, often makes another part worse. For example, you've got a person who's, let's say, hit a pole. Okay, they've crushed their chest up against the steering wheel and they have fractured some ribs. They come in and their spleen is ruptured and they are bleeding in the abdomen so they need fluid to keep them alive. But because of the bruise to their lungs, you want them to have as little fluid as possible since an injured lung will take fluid and will put it in a place from which the body won't remove it easily and will destroy the ability of the lung to exchange oxygen with the blood.

Dr. Winston Anderson takes a small sip of his drink and says slowly and carefully, "Next to medicine, I probably contemplate automobiles more than anything else."

What in hell is going on here? This man sees death and injury caused by the automobile every day and every night. On his way to his job in the emergency room of Los Angeles County Hospital, he drives 100mph. Is he ready to be committed? Not really. Dr. Winston L. Anderson, Jr. is simply an American car lover, aware and unaware; intellectually reasonable, but emotionally invulnerable; pragmatic about the dangers of driving, but intoxicated with driving's romance.

Our Winston Andersons are recognizable social phenomena. Many come to carmania young, some only later as boredom settles on their lives or as they are pulled into their past by the call of nostalgia. These, and their brethren who feel a need to work with their hands or have a surfeit of money, pass in the real world as perfectly respectable adults. Only at night, in the neon-lit secrecy of their garages, do they turn into wide-eyed fanatics. There are closet car lovers, exhibitionist car lovers, and car lovers who don't know they are car lovers. The immediate example is the surburban housewife who defines her role as wife and mother in terms of the services she performs for the family. Ask for a description of those services and you get a travelogue: My Day in the Car.

More people pay to watch motor racing than any other sport except horse racing. When someone discovers how to breed a race driver who is as honest as a horse, motor racing tracks will have pari-mutuel windows and draw the biggest crowds in the country. Not many veteran auto-racing observers expect to see the day.

Within the car culture there is an infinite number of subcultures: There are the van people and the off-road people, the racers and the rallyists. There are people who show cars as others show dogs and there are collectors who hoard rare and expensive cars as they would Old Masters, in pursuit of capital appreciation. There are even some Winston Andersons who drive for the pleasure of driving, going nowhere in particular, but simply inhaling the fragrance of the road. Some people autocross (a kind of obstacle course test), and some climb hills against the clicking of a stopwatch.

Car restoration for the sake of working with one's hands is not just popular but profitable. Often there is a side benefit of no mean worth: the restored car of forty years ago can be a better automobile than any available new in showrooms.

Mainly, the automobile has remade leisure and brought endless opportunities for conventional recreation that mobility affords. The car is a device to push away horizons. There is no simpler, cheaper, better transportation for vacationing than the automobile in its variety of forms. Station wagons, campers, motor homes spew out families from every town in the country as the spring thaw sets in. Places inaccessible by train, bus, or airplane are easily reached by car. Nothing has made the vacation so important and universal and analgesic to our lives as the automobile. To take a family of four across the country and back by car costs a fraction of what it might by any other means. If the railroad bound the country together, the automobile has converted it into a vast amusement park. The Pontiac Bonneville station wagon vacationer is not necessarily a car lover, but as you wander across the spectrum of car-as-leisure people, you come closer and closer to a distinct group with clear views and attitudes. They do not seem to be a large minority, but their voices are heard, however faintly. That is why it is worthwhile to examine this curious extreme, to listen to our Winston Andersons talk.

"I reconcile what might be thought of as my schizophrenia about the automobile by thinking that it isn't really the automobile that is at fault." If not the automobile, what? "Drinking." Dr. Anderson says at least half the auto-injured he treats—more likely 75 to 80 percent—have suffered their trauma as a direct result of alcohol. But even if that explains the broken people who are wheeled into Anderson's emergency room, it does not go very far in explaining Anderson himself. "There is a fantastic defense mechanism in every individual with regard to any self-injury or death. You look at these things and say they can always happen to other people but never to you. I may pride myself on driving fast, but I pride myself even more on not driving recklessly."

If Dr. Winston Anderson does not consider that the victims he treats in that huge emergency room in that enormous hospital in the car-death capital of the universe might be pointing their splintered bones in his direction at the time he sponges and sews, stitches and transfuses, he plainly understands that there is some relation between speeding doctor and car-injured patient after the desperate moments of immediate treatment. In every serious case he treats that has involved an auto injury, he later asks two questions of his patients: Had they been drinking? Had they been driving a sports car? Anderson is unconscious of the fact that he seeks self-justification when he asks those questions. He says, incredibly, that of the perhaps three hundred or more *serious* auto accident injuries he has treated, not one—a single one—had been incurred in a sports car. Can it really be that this man, who is introspective enough to admit his attitudes are irrational, is unaware that he is pleading for a cloak of invulnerability? Promise me you were not hurt in a sports car, he begs his patients. And they promise him. "Simply incredible" that none of these three hundred has been injured in a sports car, he admits. "Simply incredible." But true.

Winston Anderson's final rationalization, his last line of defense, lies somewhere in the mysticism of his trade. "Driving an automobile probably has all sorts of psychological and sexual overtones. It's inherent in the relationship. And it's not logical, it's pure emotion.

"To see what I see in the hospital and then drive the way I drive, I have to be saying to myself that I can't get hurt. And I must believe that." He seems astonished by what he has just said, and rushes to cover. "Maybe that's what makes driving so fast a little bit more exciting. In the back of my mind I know these things can happen." This compact, intense man cannot mean what he seems to be saying—that it is the day-in and day-out sight of trauma that adds spice to his driving. Yet who can better understand such a phenomenon than Winston Anderson?

Indeed he admits his wishes are for anything but death. He is embarrassed to confess this; there is self-esteem at stake, but also romance.

> Yes, I think I would have to admit I'm more reckless than a racing driver. I'm probably playing with my life more than he is with his. I guess part of it is that an automobile gives me a feeling of power, whether it is power of ownership or power of control. But an automobile completes a part of my basic self. Way back in the innermost recesses of my mind I have a genuine fear that when I die it's going to be at the wheel of an automobile.

Ah, glory.

No one has ever claimed that car lovers are rational. But car lovers, to whatever degree, at least know where the car is in their lives. If we were all so aware of the role of the car in our own lives, we would have long ago demanded honesty in the marketplace, a forthright and responsive industry, and a responsible governmental monitoring of the car and the highway.

But we are not all car lovers. To most of us the car is anything but an object engendering affection, any more than a pneumatic drill is to a construction worker or a hammer to a carpenter. To most, the beginning and the end of the car is its usefulness as a tool. We do not philosophize much about our hammers and our drills in America.

II

Why are most of us so indifferent to the car if that indifference is placing us in the polluted, vulnerable, expensive societal ruts the automobile has demonstrably dug in our lives?

Denise McCluggage has a good deal to offer by way of explanation of why women are less than enchanted with the automobile—and by not much extension, why men are, too. She understands the car-dependent wives, and she understands the Denise McCluggages—the women who are car professionals—of which there are very few.

She also understands what seems to be the view of the majority of women: that the car is useful but not a matter for deep concern. McCluggage also thinks it is wrong.

She is a born Westerner, now living in an A-frame with an adjoining studio in Sugarbush, Vermont. She went to Mills College in Oakland, California, was a reporter for the San Francisco *Chronicle*, a racing driver of world reputation, the owner/editor/publisher of *Competition Press*—a motorsports tabloid now called *Autoweek*—and the owner/editor and publisher of a general information weekly in her adopted town of Sugarbush. These days, she paints and is a freelance writer, contributing to such varied magazines as *Glamour* and *Madison Avenue*.

Within the world of automobiles, she is a widely respected journalist, a recognized expert on the taming of the automobile (she did a film for the Liberty Mutual Insurance Company demonstrating the techniques they taught in their skid school), and was a consultant to the State of Vermont on safety and driver training. She is remembered from California to Germany as a tough competitor, and is occasionally asked to drive in competition, particularly in endurance races. She has written a book called *Are You A Woman Driver?*, which is as much of a standard text for both sexes as one is likely to find.

If ever there were a person of catholic interests, it is McCluggage. Luck has it that she is a woman preoccupied by snowshoeing, painting, writing, and other arts; printing, automobile racing, Asian philosophies, sociology, highway safety, driver education. Having done it all, she can now stand aside, a dispassionate observer, and comment with insight but without prejudice.

Denise McCluggage—small, vital, and graceful—would like American women to understand some of their own history as they examine their relationship with their cars. History, biology, upbringing, she contends, have given the American women a unique opportunity to place the car in proper perspective, to ask the right questions about its position in all our lives.

Woman and devices for moving people around have a long and honorable association. "At the turn of the century and well before, it was common that women drove wagons and buggies. It was not unheard of for women in cities to be handling horses. Now I think that's interesting," says McCluggage, "because horses are living creatures and women traditionally have had a kind of cultural attending thing—a mother kind of thing—toward animals and children. This was not only acceptable, then, but within tradition. It was also within tradition that men took care of the wagons.

"So with the coming of the car, there was a continuation of the mechanical association between men and the thing that took people around. But there were no living aspects connected with the car, nothing to attend. So, suddenly, women were not driving cars . . ."

There is more than historical cause and effect here. There is cultural implication as well. "Often things become masculine or feminine because chance may have led one sex to be doing a given act most of the time. So it was with the car. The horse was gone, the attending thing was gone, the man drove the car. So you see, in this case, how the car and the driving of the car assumed a gender association." That gender association was reinforced in the early history of the car by its ownership within the status group of the rich. Cars were playthings, they had not yet become utilitarian, they were still toys—men's toys.

"Now World War I was critical in women's becoming drivers. As usual, as often happens when women are needed for something, it is shown that all of the things they thought they couldn't do they can do very well after all. In the war, women became ambulance drivers and they became very adept at driving." After the war, as farms became mechanized, they were equally adept at driving tractors.

So it was clearly established that there was no inherent reason why women could not or should not drive. There was an early problem with upper body strength: cars had to be started by hand crank, which took not only strength, but strength in explosive bursts, which is biologically incompatible with the way women's parts are assembled. But when the self-starter was invented, any pretext that there was some *reason* for a woman not to drive vanished. Nevertheless, there remained a good deal of prejudice on the subject, and not surprisingly much of the prejudice came not from men but from women. Oddly, McCluggage feels some of that prejudice within herself to this day: "If I see a woman driving a car with a man sitting next to her, I have the same dislocated feeling as I have when I am shown a picture and asked to say what's wrong with it. As I was growing up, the common sight when the family was in the car was of the man driving. Curiously, I can't get away from my own upbringing to take it as a matter of course that a woman should be driving when a man is sitting beside her."

She has already explained her actions in terms of other women and other men. "Highly capable women frightened men [in the early days of the automobile] and that fright was sexual. It was this fear: 'If they are truly equal drivers, what else must they be truly equal in and *then* what could happen?' "

This wise woman allows such comments to go without editorializing; if anything, she will make some effort to understand the prejudice. "The concept, the *act*, of penetration is part of our culture, and I am not sure that biologically there is not a certain basis for the concept of male aggression." The words are a concession to the rapidly crumbling arrogance of her guest, sure of his biological superiority. McCluggage is not an ardent feminist but she raises consciousness about women, about cars, and she does it with compassion.

Clearly, there is no longer any reason why, in real world terms, the man should be captain of the ship, but McCluggage is ambivalent about her feelings as to the role of the automobile in all this. For example, she understands perfectly well the wife in her taxi-driver role. "For most women, the automobile was and is another household appliance, one that sits out in the driveway and, like all labor-saving devices, is a mixed blessing. The existence of that car in the driveway means the woman can choose; she can substitute four wheels for four walls." But that, too, is a cultural imposition. "Many suburban housewives married without knowing how to drive," says McCluggage. "Their husbands taught them for essentially selfish reasons. 'You have to know how to do this,' they said. 'You need to know this so you can spell me on long trips (although he would still be the captain) or you must know how to drive in order to relieve me of certain burdens.' It made living easier for the male. So the wife had a car to use, and then she had a car of her own—as much as it was—but it remained a jitney kind of thing and she remained a servant." McCluggage recites the rationale almost word for word, as one hears it from Dunwoody, Ga. to Belmont, Calif. She can't let her kids out on their own, she owes it to them to give them all the advantages, if she says "ride your bike" or "hitchhike," she is exposing them to terrible danger. So her mother role, her attending role, is shaped in the form of the car.

McCluggage also sees this as the product of the nuclear family. In the old extended family there were brothers and sisters, aunts and uncles and cousins to play with at home; now there is almost no choice but for the child to go long distances to find friends. In a sense, then, McCluggage is saying the woman is partly responsible for her role as a chauffeur—even those who complain bitterly about that role—for certainly wives as well as husbands have opted for the nuclear family. Most surburban women, McCluggage is sure, are not enthusiastic about their jobs as unpaid chauffeurs, but she reminds them they are victims of their own doing. "We cannot pull away from our acculturization," McCluggage says. "It's like MacLuhan said, 'I don't know who discovered water, but it wasn't a fish.' "

The car *can* be an instrument of freedom—"liberation" if you wish—for the woman, but she must understand it to be. It is no more a dynamic to the women's movement than the blanket is to the sexual revolution, thinks McCluggage. "A woman can go out and get into her car and go nowhere as well as she can go somewhere. Now perhaps knowing that possibility exists is liberating. To realize, and indeed sometimes to turn the other way instead of picking up the kids . . . a lot of women still pick up the kids, but an awful lot of women have left home."

As McCluggage put it in a piece she did for *Madison Avenue* called "Machomobile—Move Over":

Women's attitude toward cars has changed in recent years. . . . It's Sisterhood time. . . . Where once a woman might have looked upon a car with the suspicion and disdain due a rival, now she looks upon it with interest. She seeks a new relationship with the car. And since her relationship has not been one circumscribed by tradition (such as the male's "love affair" with it) she is freer to establish a relationship based on her individual needs and preferences.... None of this "somewhere west of Laramie" jive for her. Women are not romantics when it comes to cars.... The woman wants to know what your car does and how easy it is to get it to do it. How much parking space does it need? Will the seats burn her legs when the sun's been shining? Can she get the hatchback to hatch when her hands are full? Are there high sills to lift packages over? Can she cope with a flat tire by herself? Are there pointy things and hard spots for her kids to fall against? Can she really see out every which way? Can she stop quickly and simply when there's a demand for it? How resistant is the car to mauling by its fellows? Are repairs reasonable and readily available?

If McCluggage is right, and certainly she is in this, in what other perspective does the woman place the car than "utilitarian"? "She doesn't need an image-maker, she needs a tool for living." That clearly sums up McCluggage's understanding of most women's view of the car and does as well to explain most men's view of the car. If there is any criticism of what McCluggage has to say, it is that it is sexist. Why should women have the exclusive right to weigh the car on the scale of practicality? You would expect McCluggage to have an answer and she does:

I suppose if one were searching for a biological determination of the differing male and female attitude toward cars, it could readily be found. Certainly the male role in the sex act is as a performer. Potency is a male concern. Traditionally he has been a measurer of length and breadth and a clocker of distances run. He is an impulsive scorekeeper (even consider that word "score"). Is it not natural then that he cares about 0-60 records, horsepower ratings, bore and stroke? (Just *look* at those words!) Performance, after all, is the criterion of his most intimate, ultimate game. Isn't it to be expected that his other interests are colored with the same attitude? Judging from the reminiscences I've heard of boyhood antics, performance with the male appurtenance was important long before puberty— pissing distance being the record in question. The female's anatomy certainly destined her to be no more than a curious spectator at such boys-being-boys sport and, as she grew older, probably less concerned about statistics when it came to automobile performance as well. She does not see the car as an extension of herself, identifying its ability to perform with her own. Being separated physically from a tool of performance, she is separated psychologically as well. Her question is not, "What'll it do?" but "What'll it do *for me?*" Is it useful, will it please me? She is free of those shadowy misconnections that adolescent males make between cars and sex, many of them carrying such hang-ups into their adult life. She has none of those problems. She knows a car is a car, a cock is a cock. What can either do *for me?* A sensible question in either context, I think.

Denise McCluggage leaves it to those men who view cars as objects of utility to justify their judgments in terms other than biological.

III

Dick Lewis would be glad to try. Dr. Richard Lewis is a clinical psychologist specializing in problems of the adolescent. He should be able to tell us something about what there is in the upbringing of a child that rivets his attention on the car and holds it there.

Dr. Lewis sees much value in the adolescent's first encounter— his first *personal* encounter—with the car. "In our culture, the acquisition of a car is the young's first chance to have demonstrated, in a material way, his emergence into adulthood. Very commonly, it is not given to him. He has to go out and earn it. I've seen numerous young people settle down—it's most striking with boys—for the first time to goal orientation when they want that automobile.

"For the first time, they are working for something they really want. Obviously, that has a very positive effect on growth."

The opposite is true as well. "I've wondered what would happen if they didn't have that goal, if they didn't have an opportunity to work for something they really valued? What impact would that have on the adolescent years?" Lewis sits back with the ever-present red-and-white-swirled can of Coke in his hand that marks his addiction, his sandaled feet propped on a flop-down wall desk and muses. "I'm thinking about the number of hours that are spent at least working, at least gainfully employed in making the effort in the job market."

Dr. Lewis may be asking us to contemplate some broad implications in the process by which the young *acquire* their cars; he would do well to suggest further that we think about the attitudes toward the car *after* it is acquired by the work/reward fashion. If a sixteen-year-old works for a summer to get a down payment on a car, or to buy a cheap car, will he cherish it or will he resent it? Either is possible.

Ideally, he will understand that the work has been worthwhile since the goal is of his own choosing and has been realized. But too often he is introduced to a "reward" system that confers an ultimately disappointing end accompanied by a resentment about the means. That resentment—hating every moment of a job filled with drudgery (which is about all a sixteen-year-old can expect to get)—often washes over the car within weeks of his buying it. This resentment seeps into the stream of pleasure he finds initially in the ownership of the automobile and it gradually poisons his feelings toward the car. Certainly that car is going to cost money to operate. If he has made a down payment on a new car, he is going to have to make monthly payments and buy gas and pay for routine maintenance. That means more work. It can mean more resentment. If he has bought a cheap car, there is a very strong likelihood that it is going to require an expensive repair job within a short time after he gets it. He can learn to either do the work himself—a source of byproduct satisfaction—or he can pay out his hard-earned drudge money to someone else to fix it, who is almost certainly kiting the price of repair. Since that happens all too often, it happens equally often in such cases that the work/reward system backfires.

Dr. Lewis may have a first-rate point in thinking of the initial work/reward experience as a potentially fine and positive thing, but unless there is a predisposition to like cars, as distinct from an inherent need to seek escape from an inevitably restrictive (to an adolescent) family, there is as much chance that the work/reward experience will end in long-term bitterness as it will in a long-term romance. The first translates into the car as a necessity; the second into the car as a love object.

So the work/reward system is unpredictable as a forecasting device in telling us whether or not the car is going to become a central object in a person's later life. It doesn't even allow us to make a judgment about whether the car will be prominent enough that he might even devote some time to thinking about it instead of viewing it as an unpleasant given. What could we expect if the driver licensing procedure were as strict as it should be once the work/reward system had produced a car? Nothing but good, in terms of establishing a rational relationship between driver and car from the beginning. As it is, driver licensing for the first time is a rite of passage. "Ritual" is a good word. "Routine" and "rote" are better ones. Despite the agonizing over the acquisition of a learner's permit and then the awful moment of the driver's test, almost no one ends up failing. The lion is slain. But it is a stuffed lion to begin with, long dead. If driver training were what it should be, if driver licensing demanded skills every motorist should possess, the test would take an hour at least and would fail a minimum 50 percent of the applicants. *Then* there would be a work/reward system that would really polarize the country in its view of the automobile and perhaps thereby place it in its proper perspective. Those who were able to drive would understand their cars, take pride in the driving of them, and because of that interest and pride be aware of the tricks of the market, the pressures of the industry, and the prejudices of the government. Those who didn't and wouldn't could turn their rage on strip mining or the Socialist Party or the automobile. At least there would be a driver constituency that had reason to care. Unfortunately, this is a fantasy scenario for the moment.

Instead of institutionalizing Dick Lewis's kind of work/reward theory, extending it to driver education in particular in pursuit of better driving and a more enlightened public, departments of motor vehicles in some states are taking on the role of parent surrogates. The relevant regulation in these jurisdictions says that should a parent wish for *any* reason to ask the department to revoke the license of a minor, the act is done. Dr. Lewis is cautious about making a judgment here because the DMV's act has its roots in common law liability, and you do not upset legal tradition without heavy thought. But he is clear that one of the results is to imperil the independence potential of the ownership of an automobile by the young. There are some parents—particularly suburban parents—who would applaud this inhibiting of the first tentative free flight of the child. Fortunately, they are becoming almost rare.

What is *not* rare is another misuse of the car, depriving it further of its objective identity. This is the manner in which the car becomes the purported cause of action in family arguments. The scene is a familiar one. The child who does not yet own a car asks if he can take the parent's car for the night. The child who owns a car or is buying a car misbehaves and is grounded. The car turns into a disciplinary weapon, a kind of everyday Iron Maiden. Dr. Lewis says, "It isn't really the automobile people are arguing about here. The car is not the true basis of these fights any more than clothes are the true basis of other kinds of arguments. These arguments are really about such things as power, roles, how much independence am I going to give you? How much independence can I get? The automobile may be the focal point, but it really isn't the dynamic."

That is all very well but in the real world people arguing don't stop suddenly and say to each other, "Wait a minute, we're not *really* talking about Chevrolets here, what we're talking about is whether you're going to make a life of your own or whether I'm going to insist that you continue your dependence on me." If it were somehow possible to do that, the automobile could be detoxified as a point of conflict. But it isn't. The world doesn't work that way. No doubt, should the parents and the children magically find themselves in Dr. Lewis's office in the midst of an argument about the car, he could quietly and persuasively point out to them that their disagreement was on a far more fundamental issue than a 3,800-pound chunk of metal. It is sad that, to most parents and most children, the automobile doesn't just *seem* to be the focal point so far as they're concerned, it damn well *is* the focal point.

Nor is there much expectation that the child can put the car into any sort of decent perspective as he goes through the agonizing process of learning to drive from one or another of his parents—usually the father. If money problems lead the hit parade in matters of divorce, driver instruction by parents is often the catalyst in the ultimate alienation of the child. There is just too much emotional content in these encounters, too much reminder that the parent is all-knowing and the child is ignorant just at the point when the child is seeking the very object and the specific knowledge that will set him free. It's a cultural cliché, this overt antagonism that flows from the parent trying to teach the child how to drive. Properly so. It happens all the time. There are two problems here—one emotional, one mechanical. How will I teach my child to drive without banishing him from my house? How will I teach my child to *drive?* Later on, in a discussion of what bad drivers we all are, a single solution to both problems is suggested: revise our driver training system. Teach the teachers how to drive. Teach them how to teach driving.

There is another land mine in the parent/child/car complex— the pure parental reward system. "I'm giving you your car, or I'll lend you the car for the night," can backfire as easily as the work/ reward system. In fact, it can probably backfire more easily. It has none of the content of confrontation with things as they are that the work/reward method does; it has almost all the content of every parental reward experience the child has ever encountered. Again, this occurs at the moment when, in the parent-child relationship, the child is extremely vulnerable.

Work/reward, driver licensing departments of motor vehicles as parent surrogates, parent teaching child to drive, parent rewarding child with use or ownership of a car, car as the focus of a family argument; all these things sap the car of its identity. It isn't an object to be viewed objectively anymore. In these cases, in fact, it starts out being viewed from exactly the wrong perspectives.

There is nothing wrong with viewing the car as a tool. But there is a lot wrong with viewing the car as colored by strong and distorting experiences with one's parents. Unfortunately, that is too often the case. The car becomes the end all of one's life (as in the case of a race driver or a car thief, to take extremes) or it is ignored as a real influence on one's adult years. In either case, a sense of proportion has been lost and the adult, in dealing with the car, is incapable of coming to grips with the difficulties or the advantages the automobile brings to his life. So his decisions regarding the car are irrational and many of these irrational decisions have brought us to our present state of unease and inability to cope with the problems the car has inflicted on society.

These are tentative explanations; they are not solutions. Dr. Lewis, still sucking away at his Coca-Cola, would like us to consider some solutions in terms of "value systems." He means by this that people reward themselves in a variety of ways. They are materialistic. They pursue power. They are producers. They savor the act of living. They rejoice in interpersonal relationships.

Materialistic people might try to understand that the car is a part of their persona. You are your car. Understanding that, you're in a position to make more rational decisions about what you're going to own. If it's really necessary to have a Cadillac Seville, at least recognize the car for what it is in your life. The same mechanism is at work with the power/control people. If their lives are directed at imposing their will on their surroundings, they are likely to choose something on the order of a Corvette or a Jaguar. That is all right, too, so long as they know why. In both cases, knowledge of the reasons for specific ownership is the equivalent of being able to change if Seville ownership or Corvette ownership no longer makes sense.

As for the producing people, cars are less important to them. Their satisfactions come from the manner in which they can enrich society, others, and themselves as a pure result of their ability to contribute. Unless their production is the production of irresponsible cars, they are not likely to be much concerned with personal irrationality in dealing with the automobile. They are likely instead to view the car with objective eyes. Look to the producers, Dr. Lewis seems to be suggesting, as people likely to be making sensible suggestions about how to bring the car back into mainstream America.

The last two categories of reward according to value system: the rewards that come from simply being alive and enjoying sunsets and fresh salads and the rewards that come from the pleasure of the company of others pose no problem to those trying to put the automobile into place. Sunsets and friendships don't get in the way of making sensible judgments about whether more and larger or fewer and smaller cars are the better solution for society.

Dr. Lewis learned something himself a few years back at a Gestalt workshop during which a number of professionals were told to sit in a circle and suppose themselves to be their cars. "Be your car," they were told.

Richard Lewis was a Datsun 240Z (a small sports coupe). "Obviously, a lot of us had projected our personalities onto the car. I remember saying with mine, 'I'm a 240Z, and I really look kind of flashy, and I'm pretty stylish, but I'm also very practical because I was a good buy.' So, you see, we do project a lot of ourselves into our vehicles."

If that is true and if Americans were to sit around in a 215-million-person circle, we might discover that we were all certifiable.

IV

One of the few men who see the car as a broad social benefit and who is able to articulate his views as few others, is a man whose automotive syllogisms are terribly vulnerable. One reason is that he may be saying some important things, but they are suspect because he is speaking within the halls of the automobile industry. He speaks of what the car has brought to minority groups; his opponents translate that into the failure of the mass transit system to serve such groups better as a result of having been emasculated by the automobile. He speaks of freedom of movement; his opponents understand that as an expression of individual selfishness subverting the common good. He speaks of the automobile allowing random living patterns; his opponents imply that this defeats any attempt at rational regulation of society. He talks about the gaiety, even the frivolity, the car can introduce into lives largely filled with drudgery; his opponents talk about a lack of seriousness of purpose to accomplish the greatest good for the greatest number. He mentions the car's ubiquity; his opponents condemn the same ubiquity as wasteful, selfish, a rapine of finite resources, and suffocating. Frank Wylie can't win for losing.

You would not be far off the mark characterizing Wylie as the Archibald Cox of the auto industry. He looks much like Cox. He sports a short, bristling, gray flat-top haircut. He invariably wears narrow bow ties; he looks at you directly and fully when he speaks in his measured, careful phrases. His mind is inquisitive and is ever sorting until he manages to penetrate a problem with simple, elegant words. Cox, the lawyer, speaks for a self-interested constituency; Wylie, the working head of Chrysler's press relations, speaks for the self-interested constituency of his company. He is contemplative. He is placid, but occasionally uneasy. Perhaps that is because his job requires him to dissemble, and Frank Wylie is not by nature a dissembler. Know him long enough and somewhere, sometime, you will come upon a hint, the barest suggestion, of ruthlessness. The men who work for him do not wear kid gloves, and that is on his instruction. Like Cox, Frank Wylie is an advocate. Wylie's advocacy is forever on behalf of the automobile.

> None of us really lives on enough land anymore to wander or to walk across a hill—to be really alone. So I suppose the car represents a great system for having your own little world, a substitute for the country, if you will. You're able to order it the way you wish—the equivalent perhaps of deciding whether you want to climb the hill or not climb it, whether you want to sit down, whether you want to go out or whether you want to look at the sky, watching the clouds, or see the clouds but not watch them. When I am alone in a car I have created a private world. Being alone is rare. It is a lot more important to some people than to others. It is terribly important to me.

This represents so much of the value of owning a car that it is difficult for those who want this country to be auto-independent to attack the argument with success.

One man, one car is no defensible slogan. It represents an insane approach to the conservation of resources of every kind. The attack on the car from this quarter is intellectually immaculate—and unacceptable. For if the car has given the American anything at all, it has granted him privacy. Perhaps he climbs into his car and becomes a different man; there is ample evidence to suspect he does from his behavior on the highway. Perhaps what we understand as automobile-conferred privacy is only a refinement of the historical need to be mobile in a kind of ultimate way. The car owner is McCluggage's ship captain, and he can turn where he wants to turn without rhyme or reason on his path to nowhere. But it is in granting privacy in the midst of a crowd, an apartment in a crowded city, that the car confers many of its most cherished benefits.

All those cars during the rush-hour peaks, spread four lanes wide in a petrified stream on a freeway, are not really inflicting cruelties on their drivers, however much the owners might complain later. Perhaps the commuter train rushing down the median, or the bus steaming along in the diamond lane or the express bus lane, will deliver its passengers home sooner than the cars will. But in the meantime the drivers of the cars are *alone*, quietly renewing themselves in their own particular ways after a day in contact with the world, having had to use the lubricants of forced civility to coexist with their neighbors or fellow workers. "Renewal" in this sense may seem strange usage, but if the person in the next car in a traffic jam is shouting to the world or pounding his fist on the wheel, or singing along with his radio, or if he is simply brooding, it is merely the uninhibited acting out of his anger or joy or frustration in a world of his own in which there can be no reprisal.

Of *course* it makes no sense to transport one man or one woman in a single automobile to the person calculating the cost/ benefit ratio of the trip. But emotions can't be reduced to graphs. Freedom is not one of the elements susceptible to computer modeling. "Being alone is rare. It is a lot more important to some people than to others. It is terribly important to me." To deprive the driver of his car is to propose depriving him of his privacy, of his own world, and to do so on the basis that it will save fuel or metals has about as much impact on the car owner in terms of trying to alter his behavior as a charitable appeal has for research and development to find a cure for wallaby dysplasia. It is simply not compelling in this day in this country.

But used as a part of the argument for mass transit, it becomes a stronger force, for in that case it need not stand alone. If the saving of resources is transmuted into a bulwark of the brief for mass transit, the benefits to the transit dependent add sufficient weight to the case so that it might carry the day. Aluminum doesn't vote. The aged and the young, the black and the woman hold the franchise. They have reason to speak against the car. Says Wylie:

> We have created perhaps America's largest growth industry which we have called "senior care centers." They are nothing more or less

than blighted parking spaces for the parents of the working generation. The old are gradually weaned. They were living with the family. They were dependent on the family in the cases in which they could no longer drive. The next move was from the household to the nursing home. We treat the aged now much as we treat mongoloids: Put them in cages, feed them. To say we have deprived them of mobility is to understate. They are in those places. They can't drive. They have no alternatives.

So long as the aged are not confined, they remain, with other low-income people, transit dependents. But the old are not the only car-affected minority and "car affected" need not be understood in negative terms. It *must*, though, be recognized here as having the unspoken modifier "unduly" attached to it. "Unduly affected." Wylie points out in terms of blacks, for example, "Society had already proscribed certain areas to them in terms of living. But the car, and its buying, was one area where blacks could do as they damn pleased. They could buy anything. Blacks *couldn't* buy any house. Blacks *couldn't* live in any district. So when they bought cars, they also bought another kind of freedom, freedom from restrictions. They bought status. They bought success. They bought a sense of equality."

This is going to be a tough one for the mass transit people. So long as minorities can afford only subsidized transportation, their needs are going to form the public transit advocate's strongest argument in getting legislation for mass transportation and against cars. But when incomes rise, the buying of a car, this sense of equality, this proof of success is going to result. When previously deprived people have money, they buy cars, and cars once acquired are going to be hard to get rid of.

In these senses, talking about minorities is talking about mass transit is talking about doing away with cars. There is a more subtle argument against continuing auto dependence. It concerns itself with futures. Frank Wylie talks about "advantages" now offered by the automobile.

The car made random living and working patterns possible. Somebody suggests a new job and it happens to be on the wrong side of town. The extra money doesn't make it quite worthwhile. It means taking another subway, another transfer, another hassle. I suspect the predominant feeling among the young and not a few of the older people is their increasing unwillingness to be hassled. They have been regimented enough. Not just in the military, but in schools and in businesses. People are trying to get away from just that regimentation.

That is going to be another problem in ridding ourselves of addiction to the automobile. For, should world shortages continue, we are going to find ourselves with a managed economy. That, in turn, means a regimented society. And that, whether or not Frank Wylie or you or I like it, means fewer automobiles. The "realists" are already taking up the cry of regulation of the economy. The simplest example is standby fuel allocation and plans for outright rationing. One can only say to the Frank Wylies, raising their glasses in celebration of what the car has brought us in terms of the way we live and work, "Wait a minute. Perhaps you'd better drink that toast in water; the alcohol in your glass might become too valuable as a fuel."

V

David Miller, the futurist, has performed his welcoming tea ritual on this bright November day in his apartment on Lake Street in San Francisco. Now he is sitting cross-legged on a great mushroom cushion in the middle of his living room floor talking about life without a car. It's been almost ten years since he kicked the habit. As a consultant to large corporations, he found he was traveling so much that he rarely saw his old Chevy Biscayne, a car that was "just wheels," nothing special.

One day he came back from a particularly long trip and had to bail the Chevy out of an airport parking lot for an exorbitant amount of money. When he got home, there was an insurance bill lying in ambush demanding a $300 check for coverage on his car. David Miller looked at the bill and thought to himself, "You know, I could rent a lot of cars and take a lot of taxis for $300." So, forthwith, he tore up the bill, walked downstairs, drove his car to a junkyard and never saw it again. He hasn't owned a car since.

I'd begun to realize that time behind the wheel was bad time. You couldn't read. You couldn't write. You had to fight traffic, using plenty of energy. So I said, "I'm going to try to give this up." I'm sure the junkyard people thought they ripped me off because I wasn't trying to make any money. I was just trying to get rid of my car and I wanted to get shed of it while I was in the mood. I made myself a ground rule that since I didn't have a car, whenever the whim struck me, I would rent one or take a cab. And what happened was that I did do those things quite frequently in the early years. I do it less and less as time goes by. I've gotten adjusted to living without a car.

Some time later, Miller remarried and discovered that, since his wife came complete with a car, he was burdened with an automobile again. He set about, successfully, dissuading his new wife from continuing as a member of the unenlightened car owner's association. Miller was fair about it, no blackmail. "Look, sell it," he said to her. "If at any time you want to buy another, go out and buy one. But sell the one you've got and try doing without."

So David Miller started a new life without a car by making two deals: If he wanted "private" transportation, he would allow himself to rent a car whenever and wherever he wished; if he wanted a cab he'd call one. And if his wife wanted to swim back into the mainstream of car ownership, she was perfectly free to do so. No absolutes, no rigid commitments. An experiment. Thus far, it's worked for almost ten years. How?

First off, both David Miller and his wife were prepared to make some sacrifices. "Trade-off prices," Miller calls them. "Sometimes we end up down on Market Street waiting for a late streetcar home and if we're tired and it's cold, we damned well wish we had wheels. If there's no cab in sight, we're stuck."

And then the Millers made a conscious choice about where to live. "It's not accidental that I live in a city where a car is not an operational necessity. We're trying very consciously to develop a life way in which the car is not a part."

Miller and his wife chose an apartment in a closed ecosystem of a neighborhood. Like New York, San Francisco is a city of neighborhoods. It is a honeycomb of self-contained cells. "I have a fierce sense of love for the neighborhood. There are a lot of independent shops, a variety of neighborhood restaurants, and even neighborhood newspapers." Miller feels that if he wanted to lead his life within an area of perhaps a square mile, he could—except for the continuing trips to Nigeria or Palo Alto or wherever he goes to consult. He has a mail drop downtown and around the corner from it he has his club where he swims daily. It all gives him a feeling of being "terribly, terribly mobile. I don't feel constrained in the least." It is important to understand that although the Millers feel a part of the neighborhood, they also feel themselves to be a part of the city and of the county surrounding. "I didn't do it for the money," he repeats with some sense of satisfaction, "although it does save a lot of money." And he didn't give up the car out of a vague sense of guilt that he was corrupting the environment. "To me, I would never again lose an opportunity to try and reclaim some time from the 'have to' to the 'discretionary' categories of the manner in which I spend my life, time I could turn to good use. When you start adding up the time you spend in a car—not just behind the wheel but the time looking for parking places and paying parking tickets and getting the damn thing serviced and getting it maintained, all that shit—I'd just much rather have the time at my disposal to use as I see fit."

All very well for David Miller. But how are others to arrive at the same level of material asceticism? "I have a friend in Marin County, an independent consultant and a very orthodox guy. Well, he has a sixteen-year-old son who wants nothing to do with the car. It's a hassle, he says. He says transportation is no problem because all his friends are still into that silly trip. Now here's a young chap who grew up in one of the most affluent counties in California, born and bred there, a kid, a teen-ager, and he's not interested in having a car." David Miller suggests that his friend's son is no anomaly. For a thousand reasons—many of them fuzzy environmental commitments but an equal number hard decisions based on cost—young people are doing without cars.

That Miller's friend's son is not an isolated example is borne out by a trip to Eugene, Oregon. Eugene is the fitness capital of the United States. It had 122 miles of bicycle paths at last count. There are so many joggers that the city has invented its own jogging shoe and established its own jogging shoe manufacturing company: Nike. In front of the high schools in Eugene are bike racks that hold as many as 300 bicycles. Sure, there's still street racing down Eugene's main drag, called "The Gut," in muscle cars that date from enchantment with Detroit's youth market. But Eugene has chosen to seek alternatives to the car. It has a blocked-off mall in the center of town. It does not ignore the car, but it does not cater to it either. Eugene *does* cater to the quality of its community life, and to Eugene that means some constraints on the automobile and some encouragements to alternative forms of transportation, primarily those that emphasize human participation.

The sixteen-year-old in Marin is not alone.

David Miller thinks there is another reason cars for the young are on the way out.

I believe that the median family disposable income—real income—is going to be under pressure for the long term. Those big, fat slobby days of the '60s are gone. People are going to have to pay a larger share of their income for housing now. Other forces are going to diminish their discretionary income. One of the first places this crunch is going to be registered is in second and third car ownership and it seems generally the most marginal car in the typical family is the car the kid owns. It has been the last one added to the set, and it is likely to be the first one to go.

Family attitudes are going to have to change with a decrease in family income. Even if the child is earning the money for his own car, increasingly that money is going to be needed for the family itself.

Start with the child, end with the man, David Miller is saying. Whatever the reason, whether it is by choice or by necessity, the young may find themselves without cars. There are two possible outcomes: Either the child will covet an automobile when he is an adult and able to afford one, or he will never have had reason to want one. Anyway, *choice* may be irrelevant, Miller says. If some gloomy predictions about the state of the world's economy are right, few of us will have an opportunity to own a car even if we want one.

There is no going back, David Miller thinks further. The

consumer economy of the post World War II period is done with forever. "It was a basic culture theme from 1946, fueled by the ambitions and the expectations of people whose parents had bitter memories of the Depression. In a world of plenty, these are the people who constituted what we called the Flatulent Consumer Society. There was material affluence, people were discovering more discretionary time. It wasn't accidental that *McCall's* invented 'togetherness'; the mystique of the happy suburban family moving onward and upward to little suburban houses on little green plots in the country though still near the city." But the dream has turned into a nightmare of agonizing commuting, of astronomical prices for land in suburbia, of tacky sameness. There is a discordant sound to *McCall's* once warm and lovely words these days. A poll of suburbia might find the least popular word in the house is "togetherness."

"Well," says David Miller, "you know these people who used to rejoice in the suburbs have been forced to become realists enough to be able to say 'that was a good trip, but it had some high prices. It was like Chinese food that was satisfying and didn't last.' Even if they don't say it, even if they don't feel it, the trip is over anyway. It's simply less and less possible, and we're going to feel more and more inhibited about flatulent consumer behavior as well, so what next? "

David Miller doesn't know, but he sees some signs. So far as they point to the direction the automobile is going to take, Miller believes the Chevette and the Rabbit, the Honda Accord and the Ford Fiesta to be the cars of the future. "The Beetle (Volkswagen's longest model run car) was the leading edge of a thing just beginning to develop. It was the first car Americans adopted that didn't say a damn thing about the status of its owner. Partly, of course, it was a cult thing. But still, it was the beginning of a movement ..." Except that in the middle of its sales cycle, the Beetle became the status darling of the know-nothings, Miller is right. Detroit has already dropped the annual model change. It has dropped the biannual model change and gone to a temporary three-year cycle. Ahead lie cycles of far longer duration. Ford's Maverick is a case in point. It ran a virtually unchanged model for seven years. Because of its original acceptance as a pure transportation module, it's a status thing that the VW Beetle rid us of. There are Cadillac Seville owners who spend almost $15,000 for a name, but there are far more Ford Granada owners who spend a third that for a car. Without question there are as many Granada owners who could afford Sevilles as there are actual Sevilles in private hands. Goodbye status, hello utility. "The suburban game is closing," is the way Dave Miller puts it.

Miller understands the car lease to be another indicator of people's willingness to discard the automobile as an almost human appendage. "It used to be that the car was just like the house. You know, you might have a goddamn mortgage on it and no equity, but it was important to have the title; leasing a car is relinquishing title, it is relinquishing that mythical, nonsensical claim to 'ownership.'" Miller does not mention that leasing brings with it, in fact, all the burdens of ownership. His point is that someone who leases has at least rid himself of the notion of ownership. "In some sections of this society, people are beginning to ask, 'what does this do for me?' as opposed to 'What does it mean as a symbol?'" Astonishing to hear that echo three thousand miles from Sugarbush, Vermont where Denise McCluggage used almost the same words to describe the new woman's attitudes about the automobile. But Dave Miller wasn't talking about Gloria Steinem when he unconsciously parroted McCluggage; he was talking about you and me.

Will there at least be a farewell party for the car? "A structure like the automobile in society appears to be immortal almost until its last years of life," says Dave Miller. "And then it disappears very quickly." We tend to overestimate the importance of things to our lives, he is telling us; we tend also to underestimate the speed with which technology rushes replacements to fill the vacuum.

We will awaken one morning in about thirty years to find the car as scarce as a five-plumed blue whale.

There are futurists who agree with Miller. There are also some who are saving money right now to buy their A.D. 2031-model Rolls-Royces.

VI

Agree or disagree with Winston Anderson, Denise McCluggage, Dick Lewis, Frank Wylie, or Dave Miller, at least give them this: they are aware of the pervasive effect the automobile has on American society. They are giving much thought to the manner in which the automobile affects their lives. Few of the rest of us can say the same.

Our problem is that most of us don't think the automobile presents a difficulty with which we have to deal. It is not that we don't know the car's kill rate. Nor how our days are shaped by our addiction to the automobile. We even have some vague idea of the car's cost—individual and societal. But we have concluded that the automobile in America is a domesticated animal. It is so familiar a sight that we find it hard to believe we are faced with the silhouette of a predator when we look upon it.

Our problem solvers aren't much help. A group here examines the car as a polluter of the atmosphere; a group there looks at it as a menace on the highway. Here an economist, there a physician, everywhere a specialist. It simply won't do. We have been looking at a single phenomenon, one poisonous fruit, as though it were a scattering of grapes. It is not. It is a single problem of enormous complexity. It is so complex that our senses are overloaded and our research community as well. The first reaction causes us to look away toward something more pleasant or more susceptible of solution. The second results in a chain of little solutions which do not coincide with other little solutions. Thus we can cut down pollution from the car—we understand very well how to do that— but we say we cut it down at the expense of fuel economy. Or we reduce the size of cars at the cost of their safety. Or we ban the car from the inner city to the detriment of those who need to travel around inside it because we provide no substitutes. Or we spend money on freeways and put off investment in mass transit.

There is no answer to taming the car so long as we continue to ignore the creature itself. No matter how familiar the object seems, no matter how expert Americans think themselves about the car, it remains a fact that we are an ignorant people when it comes to dealing with the single American manufactured object that most affects our lives.

We don't understand the people who build it, much less how they go about it.

We don't understand state and federal legislation that governs its use. Most of us don't even know what the legislation is.

We don't know how to buy and maintain a car.

We don't really know why we do it in the first place.

Whether the work done to bring the automobile into rational perspective by our social scientists is reasonable or not, we can't tell. We don't know what they're doing. Are efforts to reduce its ferocity effective? We can't make the judgment. Not one in a hundred American car owners has ever heard the expression "Second Collision." Is the government really on the right course in regulating car design so that over the next decade cars will be more economical to run? Most people aren't aware that the government has such a program.

We don't even know how to drive. Worse still, we don't know that we don't know how to drive.

The answers exist, most of them anyway. They are not going to mean much, however, until and unless we recognize that they are solutions to a single, if difficult and complicated, question. It is the question the automobile raises that we'd better get around to examining before we're all run over. All of which is to say we've got the solutions in front of us, but what's the problem?

2 : *Middletown Transformed*

This trip is a pilgrimage. A little more than fifty years ago, a group of social scientists did a cultural biopsy on a community they called Middletown, and their work became a classic. By the time they had finished their study, it seemed to Robert S. Lynd and Helen Merrell Lynd that a frozen section of Middletown did indeed meet the mandate of the subtitle of their book, that it should be "A Study in American Culture."

"Middletown" was Muncie, Indiana. It is a city that talks to us as much about the car—then and now—as any town in America. The Lynds' study began in January 1924 and lasted eighteen months. When the book was written and finally published, its preface was dated June 1928.

Robert and Helen Lynd understood their first task to be one of choosing an appropriate community. It had to be representative America, and it had to be susceptible to study, which is to say it could be neither outsized nor diverse. With these broad criteria, the Lynds were able to focus sharply on what they considered desirable characteristics for any town they might choose. They wanted a temperate climate. Middletown should also be bent over with social and economic growth pains. It had to have existing industry and all that industry implied in the mid '20s. It should be in the Middle West, "that common denominator of America."

But there were also some things Middletown *couldn't* have or be. It couldn't be dominated by one industry. It couldn't be a college town, since that would mean it would be denied its own distinct local artistic life. It couldn't have any "peculiarities," which the Lynds defined as "acute local problems which would mark it off from the mid-channel."

Reading all this as *Middletown's* early pages unfold, you come to a two-level understanding of what you are soon to encounter in the rest of the book. First, the Lynds would chronicle the great movement of their times, the population shift from farm to city. There is much talk about Muncie in 1890 and frequent comparisons with that tranquil period in Indiana. More important, both for the Lynds and the reader, there will be a nice sense of what "Middletown" really meant in the first quarter of this century in America. Certainly the Lynds were writing for their contemporaries, but it would probably please them to be aware of how striking their study is to an observer swimming fifty years downstream.

Clearly, a contemporary Middletown would not be defined by the Lynds' criteria and, in fact, those criteria themselves seem astonishing a half century later. The Lynds' 1924 Middletown would be very much "off from the mid-channel" in the *last* quarter of this century.

Although the Lynds made frequent mention of the automobile in *Middletown* and in their later book, *Middletown in Transition,* their emphasis on the car appeared in a peculiar place in the books. *Middletown* and the subsequent book were divided into six parts: Getting a Living, Making a Home, Training the Young, Using Leisure, Engaging in Religious Practices, and Engaging in Community Activities. Granted there is frequent mention of the car in all parts and granted that the study took place in the year and a half from the beginning of 1924 to the summer of '25, yet it seems astonishing that the Lynds should have decided that among all those categories, the distillation of what the automobile meant to Middletown should fall not just under the broad category of Using Leisure, but under the chapter in that part entitled

"Inventions Re-Making Leisure." What engenders that astonish-
ment is the Lynds' own recognitition that a good part of
Middletown's economy was based on the automobile even then.
(They go into an extended description of the tediousness of an
automotive assembly-line job in Muncie in "What Middletown
Does for a Living".)

We now know that during the very months of their study in a
town they picked as typical of America, the American automobile
market was becoming saturated. That is not to say Detroit would
not find ways of *oversaturating* the market, but by 1928, the year
of the date of *Middletown*'s preface, car ownership in this country
had reached a point which automotive economist Emma Rothschild points out would not be attained in Great Britain until
1966. A country with one car for every five people should have
reflected that engorgement in the image of its typical town. True,
the Lynds were observing things as they were. But they were
engaging in prediction as well, as the title of the "Inventions Re-
Making Leisure" chapter says quite clearly. However, the Lynds
did not seem to be aware they were watching the beginning of a
revolution that would have an effect on every aspect of their
study. They did not seem to understand they were virtually
standing on the running board of the instrumentality of that
revolution, an instrumentality that would rush them, Middletown,
and the rest of the nation into an entirely foreign social landscape.

Since the Lynds published *Middletown in Transition*, the
results of a study done almost a decade after the original work,
nobody has gone back to Muncie to discover what has happened
to a city the Lynds defined as representative of America, except
for a brief visit from a television newsman in the late '60s.
Certainly no one has gone back with a view to discovering
something about the manner in which the little idyllic city of the
Lynds had been affected by the great automobile revolution.

That is the "why" of this journey.

Muncie is in Delaware County, about an hour and fifteen
minutes northeast of Indianapolis at 55mph. There is close to five
miles of two-lane road as you turn off the four-lane highway and
approach Middletown, a road the people of Muncie view with
embarrassment, but not sufficient embarrassment to settle an

internal argument which has been going on for years on a right of way for a new, wider road. It is a flat trip.

While Muncie might not like its two-lane road (complete with a little community named Middletown along it), it comes as a relief even after so short a trip on the antiseptic interstates. A two-lane road at night is filled with surprises. It demands attention to the work and the pleasure of driving. It dares a driver's skill, lying in wait with unmarked side roads, S-bends, and pickups running dark like ships in a wartime convoy. The sign on entering Muncie proclaims it to be "Modeltown, America."

The city's Chamber of Commerce has a four-page, institutional-green handout on 120-pound paper that tells you all you want to know about Muncie, except what it's like. Boiled down, the chamber's statistics say that Muncie is compact, that the city is close to Chicago but closer to Cincinnati and closest to Indianapolis, that fewer than 100,000 but more than 50,000 persons live in Muncie, and that nine-tenths of the population of the city/county (Muncie/Delaware) are white. The Chamber claimed that as of January 1974, unemployment was 4.6 percent. Of the employed, "manufacturing" accounted for something under 20,000 persons, "commercial" for something over 20,000. About half again as many as in either category worked in something called "non-manufacturing" and about half as many as in either category (10,000) worked for the government. Remember the figures.

We are being told a number of important things about Muncie, but we need to understand rather more than the figures tell. A good place to start is with the Lynds. Recalling that their study was much concerned with the population shift from farm to city, the number of people working in manufacturing, service, and government is striking. Equally remarkable is how sharply the breakdown of the manufacturing and non-manufacturing employment statistics points to the contrast between today's Muncie and yesterday's. Remember the Lynds chose Muncie because, among other things, it was *not* a one-industry town and because it was a town *not* dominated by a university. The chamber's figures say that almost half the people in the "manufacturing" category in Muncie work for Warner Gear (a subsidiary of Borg-Warner),

Delco Battery (General Motors), and Chevrolet-Muncie, which builds transmissions, axles, and steel forgings for GM. In terms of industry, Muncie is a car-manufacturing town. The Chamber's brochure also says Muncie's largest employer is Ball State University, which in the spring of 1976 had an enrollment of 17,000.

So much for the Lynds's idyllic Middletown. As for the Chamber's rosy view: 1974 was an awful year for the automobile business, and it is inconceivable that wholly-owned subsidiaries of the great Detroit companies could have maintained anywhere near full employment (long-term layoffs in the industry reached above 200,000). In fact, a young Chamber of Commerce executive casually mentioned an unemployment figure for 1974 of over 10 percent. He said Muncie's rate was the highest in the state.

The hothouse atmosphere of Academia and the single-cylinder clanking of a car-building town were influences the Lynds did not need to contemplate, but those combine into the influence Muncie feels today. Nor can the Lynds be criticized for failing to foresee the two other segments of significant employment in Delaware County and in Muncie: service and government.

In terms of the automobile, then, the Lynds probably should be given low marks for dismissing it largely as an entertainment device. But they could hardly be held responsible for not seeing that its service and aftermarket (the supply, manufacture, and installation of replacement parts) appendages would loom so large in Muncie's life half a century later.

Even more unlikely would have been their ability to look into a future in which the government on a federal, state, and local level would be hiring large numbers of people to regulate and then monitor the regulation of the automobile.

II

Lamar Ziegler, Muncie's traffic engineer, bulges in his chair in a curious little one-story pink building down from the courthouse, speculating about his problems and how they began. He says that when Muncie first started there were two theories on how to build its streets. One theory was that the streets should be wide enough to allow a team of horses to come into town, deliver the goods brought in by the farmer, gee all the way around in the middle of the street, and go back out on the same road it came in on. Fol-

lowing that plan meant big blocks since there was no reason to
have to turn around them. Unfortunately for Muncie, the second
theory prevailed. Early builders created streets so narrow they
might be European—just wide enough to allow the horse and
wagons to pass, and short, compact blocks. This worked accept-
ably until the coming of the automobile, when the lack of space
for parking and constant stop and go traffic made Muncie a
driver's nightmare.

Ziegler thinks there might be 55,000 to 60,000, perhaps even
65,000, cars in Muncie city. "If you can drive in Muncie, you can
drive anywhere, they say."

Ziegler is a cheerful man, careful to give credit to what seems
to be a phantom predecessor. In fact, while his office existed prior
to Ziegler's appointment, Ziegler seems to be Muncie's first traffic
engineer.

Ziegler, Richard Heath, Muncie's police chief, and the Chamber of Commerce claim Muncie is built in concentric rings and
that each ring is represented by a road, although some of those
show only as orange smears on plastic-covered maps of the city to
indicate they have yet to be built.

If that is the official image of Muncie, it is because that is how
Muncie would like to see itself. Orderly. There is a suggestion of
care and thoughtfulness, of tranquillity and steady growth in such
a community self-image, as though the town had spread by man's
will in accordance with God's order of the universe.

Chief Heath and Engineer Ziegler's scheme is easy to follow.
Muncie's first circle—its downtown cluster of buildings—is
bisected by a short and brand-new pedestrian plaza, which may or
may not help Walnut Street merchants but has played hell with
street racing near Muncie Central High School.

The ambience of downtown Muncie is not much of a match for
the artistry of the new mall, for the center of the city leaves an
after-image of dirty brick and stone, of buildings slumped
haphazardly together as though for mutual support. If Muncie
sparkled in 1924, luring the farmers of central Indiana to its big
city ways, it gives off the aesthetic effluvia of an old New England
mill town today.

Surrounding downtown, in Muncie's second circle, are houses
so unprepossessing they might have been built during the Lynds'

later study and not painted since. An arbitrary turn into a random residential street begins with a view of large forty-year-old houses perched on perhaps a quarter acre of land and blending almost unnoticeably into somewhat more modest three-bedroom dwellings of slab or brick. "For Sale" signs appear as the street becomes a curious midwestern transplanting of what seem to be British row houses, many of them with peeling paint and front porch stairs askew. It is not striking that all these houses are of different sizes and conditions; it is striking that despite that, they seem so alike.

The suburban circle of the young does not yet surround Muncie but threatens to. Soon a trip into Middletown will be as flavorful as a trip down any part of Santa Monica Boulevard in greater Los Angeles. Here are the shopping centers and the tracts.

In this manner, driving in widening circles, with the traffic engineer's triple orange rings in mind, it is possible to accept the Zieglerian/Heathean view of Muncie as an orderly city, growing in a traditional fashion: docile houses surrounding aging business center, themselves about to be swallowed by an oppressive, constricting ring of ready-built suburbs. The city's leadership only reluctantly admit that Muncie has no master plan for development.

The Lynds discovered how startled Muncie was to learn that a fresh eye saw the town in a dimension totally strange to its own self-image. In *Transition*, they quote a speaker at a Chamber of Commerce dinner: "One thing that was resented in *Middletown* [by the community] was that, with all the dispassionate laboratory analysis and all the microscopic study ... the Lynds used everything but a stethoscope. Had they used a stethoscope, they would have had a far different report to write. They would have depicted the influences that made it vital—[Middletown's] heart."

What would one discover about Middletown in 1976 with a stethoscope instead of the anatomical chart which hangs on the traffic engineer's wall? Better even than a stethoscope, what if one were to carry that common machine used to diagnose the heartbeat of an automobile, the oscilloscope, along the path its viewscreen showed the city's pulse to beat strongest?

The shape on the display of this oscilloscope is a backwards "L" with little squiggly circles along the horizontal. It charts a very different journey through Muncie than that around the widening circles of the traffic engineer's route. But like that one, it is a trip that can be taken only by automobile.

This trip begins in an enclave at the top of the "L," a haven of turreted and mullion-windowed houses just beyond the faceless, shapeless campus of Ball State University. In that enclave, the streets are wide and gracefully curved. Set far back from them, the houses seem to represent not mere wealth, but age, stability, elegance, and power. They are much varied: Norman, colonial, neo-Georgian, but they have in common that if Muncie's social structure has a kingdom of heaven, it is here. Here is where Middletown's automobile dealers sell their very large, wood-decaled station wagons in pairs with Cadillac Sevilles and Continental Mark Vs. Here, even in January, with their leaves long since blown away, the trees surrounding the houses and their great lawns give privacy. There is little traffic around these houses, and what there is moves at a stately pace.

The immediate encounter with Muncie after leaving that quiet enclave is with the university campus. Ball State buildings occupy perhaps five blocks on each side of a broad avenue which nonetheless seems not even so wide as the narrow roads of downtown. That is only partly because the avenue is clumped with busses and cars and criss-crossed by students wandering every which way across it. The real feeling of compression comes from the oppressive commercial feeling of the buildings, all of which seem to be echoes of the same structure. There is not much difference in walking through the Chrysler Highland Park plant, with its purposeful office buildings, or driving down Park Avenue in New York, with its constant repetitive Lever Houses and Seagram's buildings, than driving through Ball State University.

Further down the "L" is a community of Muncie houses typical of Lamar Ziegler's second circle; then a small jog caused by confronting the White River; and another small jog back through downtown via a street lined with Mom and Pop submarine sandwich shops; and then junction with the base of the "L"—Madison Street. Madison is the main route from one end of town to the other. Whatever it used to be in the Lynds' time, it is now—beginning with a Travelodge—a collection of the commercial jetsam of the American franchise mania. Along this five-mile route are chain gas stations: Amoco, Arco, Clark, Shell, Marathon,

Texaco, and Standard; quik-stop food palaces: McDonald's, Downy Flake Do-nuts, Foster's Hamburgers, Colonel Sanders Kentucky Fried Chicken, Ponderosa Steak House, Pizza King, Mac's Hamburgers, and the Treasure Chest of Sweet Fixin's. Raintree Muffler 500 shops is represented on Madison. So is Schwinn with a large bicycle dealership. Photo-T has a quick-in, quick-out franchise as does the Rider Truck Rental System; Mary Carter paint company is here as well.

A logical end to Madison would come with the Holiday Inn at the far side of this longish chain of familiar, dreary names, but down just a few blocks is a shopping center and farther along on Route 67, which is Madison's name so far as the State of Indiana is concerned, is an industrial sector in which Westinghouse has its Large Power Transformer Division and the area in which the new Delco plant is to be built.

There are two more lists to come from this drive along the base of the "L" and before the curlicue meanders that follow, and as they show on the oscilloscope/stethoscope, the blips and beeps the names generate are revealing.

Businesses deliberately *not* mentioned, but which nonetheless punctuate the jerry-built franchise façade on the flanks of Madison, are some of Muncie's used car dealerships.

John Moldovan, the sleek, slender young man at the Chamber of Commerce, had given some feel for those dealerships when he talked about Muncie and the Muscle Car—those survivors of the '60s performance era when Detroit decided that what America wanted and needed were cars with flared fenders, fat tires, wings on their deck lids like the racers on the late model Grand National stock car circuit in the Southeast.

There they were, at Midway Motors, East Side, Big Jack's, and Suburban Motor Sales: Chevrolet Nova Super Sports 350s, 396 Chevelles, Camaros, Pontiac Grands Prix, Mustang Hatchbacks, Oldsmobile Cutlasses and many of them—it seemed in numbers way out of proportion—had special magnesium wheels, chromed exhaust tips, headers, and fat tires. They were General Motors cars almost without exception, most of them with some kind of go-fast accessory, many of them with what seemed as many go-fast accessories as could be stuffed in or on them. And they were big

American cars with the exception of one tiny grouping of a Gremlin, an Opel (one American-built, the other an American captive import) and a Volkswagen Sirocco. That was surprising only until a search through Muncie's yellow pages and then a disbelieving second and third search revealed that the town had not a single foreign car dealership; this in a year when about 16 percent of the new cars sold in the United States were built elsewhere.

Muncie's used car dealers are very clear in their own minds about the American craze for performance, or the *appearance* of performance. They also seem quite sure that oil embargos are things of the past, and that Americans are unwilling to give up big cars. They share the same delusion as the public they serve, or the same narrow focus. For embargo or not, there is going on in the world an inexorable diminution of fossil fuel reserves.

On the other hand, Big Jack, Midway Suburban, and their fellow used car dealers do not misunderstand Muncie's sentiments about imports if the bumper sticker on the back of a downtown '65 Falcon is any indication; "Get US Moving, Buy An American Car," it read, and to Muncie, with its dependence on its two GM plants and its Warner Gear facility, this is no idle sloganeering.

Just beyond the Holiday Inn on Madison is a shopping center with a large Hook's drug store in its center, and inside the store is a magazine rack which says as much about Middletown/Muncie and the car as the GM plants and the orange circles on the map in the traffic engineer's office. This list, this blip on the oscilloscope, is a compilation of auto or auto-related magazine titles, and it puts any comparable selection in car Nirvana, Southern California, to shame. Along one whole section of the long rack are examples of these magazines: *Mechanics' Illustrated, Popular Science, Dirt Bike, Road and Track Annual Buyers' Guide, Chopper, Popular Cycling, Cycle Magazine, Cars, Road and Track, RV Van World, How to Build a Street Rod, '76 New Car Buyers' Guide, Truckin', VW High Performance and Accessory Guide, Digger* (for the street bike enthusiast), *Cycle Guide, Volkswagen Greats, Motor Trend, Hot Rod, Hot Rodding, Car and Driver, Car Craft, Car-Toons, Stock Car Racing, Rod Ideas, Vans and Trucks Magazine, PV4,* and *Hot Cars.* The second largest segment of special interest magazines has to do with outdoor activity and if you are generous enough to include the *Fish and Seafood Cook Book*, it contains about twelve titles.

That is the end of the "L." Clearly, it is a different dimension from the three circle concept both in geography and perspective. But there is a greater difference still. Lamar Ziegler and Chief Richard Heath think of their town as a smallish, stable community, in its way unique though sharing problems with towns its size across the country.

That is not what the drive on the "L" says at all. In fact, beginning with the enclave of great houses beyond the university, followed by the slab-sided sameness of the passage down the inward-leaning walls of Ball State, coming upon downtown and turning onto Madison to encounter the image of contemporary America, there comes stronger and stronger a feeling of *déjà vu.*

It does not hit until you discover the great factories at the end of Madison. They make the connection and, although it should not be so by now, the connection comes with a jolt.

For the drive on Muncie's "L" is a not-so-rough microcosm of the drive from Grosse Pointe, with its great mansions, down the perpendicular of Jefferson past the car plants and the Teamsters' Solidarity House to downtown Detroit, and then the turn on the base of that particular "L" to Woodward Avenue with its own greater reflection of American commerce, now ridden with the aftermath shambles of two great riots, to the Highland Park and Lincoln plants of Chrysler and Ford.

III

Muncie officials and Muncie watchers from the academic windows of Ball State understand that Muncie residents *seem* content: 86 percent like living there; 79 percent are proud of the city; 69 percent of whites feel race relations are improving (the reverse statistic, almost to the percentage point, is felt by the blacks in Muncie); 62 percent think the labor-management relationship is good and improving; 56 percent of the city's people are very satisfied with their jobs (90 percent of those over twenty-five years of age); 85 percent are reasonably satisfied with the school system; 69 percent generally approve of the way the city is governed; 87 percent are content with city services such as garbage collection and street cleaning; 71 percent give approval to the manner in which the city is policed; 54 percent seem more than reconciled with Muncie's housing; and 83 percent like the Indianapolis-owned, conservative newspapers, both of which, morning and evening, belong to the same company.

Despite all this approval, there is more than a hint that what smugness there is in Muncie is not entirely shared by the people who have to deal with the city's problems.

Not twelve steps from the tuna fish sandwiches sold by the city hall concession stand is police chief Richard Heath's office.

Heath is a bright, bouncy man who wears a uniform and who is surprisingly, almost shockingly, young. He answers questions in a brisk, direct manner.

Richard Heath has some studies of his own. Unlike the Muncie Attitude Study which confirmed all that Muncie boosters thought was good about their town, their police chief's studies tell him he has some reason to be worried. In 1975 Muncie had 210 vehicle property damage accidents, 60 vehicle personal injury accidents, 63 hit and run accidents, and 24 car accidents listed as "miscellaneous." All of those were mutually exclusive and did not include Muncie's four car-related fatalities. While extrapolations of the figures might console Richard Heath in terms of national averages, such extension would be whimsical. No one charged with protection of property and life in a city of 80,000 could be particularly comfortable with 361 serious accidents.

The consequences of Muncie's felonious automotive conduct flow into Lamar Ziegler's territory. They also require that the organization of the police department reflect very serious concentration on the problem of the automobile. Muncie has a traffic coordinator who works with all four shift captains. The town has four radar units and two speed timer units, with around-the-clock surveillance using at least two radar cars at all times. Every officer on Muncie's 127-man force has to take his turn at traffic control duty.

Heath knows, although he would probably not admit it, that this is police duty in the worst sense of the word. It is "police" in the sense of picking up, of keeping things tidy, of intimidation, of hopeless exercise in prevention, of producing revenue and, saddest of all, of draining limited resources from the real job of control of

serious crime. This is Heath's encounter with the national problem
of frustration in dealing with what we are only too happy to
consider the unfortunate but inevitable "negative" aspects of the
automobile.

However Chief Heath might resent the miscasting of his force
into human stop lights, he detests the specific criminal radiations
the car gives off.

To what extent, considering all crime, does the car bring
misdemeanor and felony to Muncie?

Oh, he would say probably 36 percent.

That's a pretty specific figure.

Yeah, he says glumly, 36 percent. Exactly.

Much of that 36 percent is represented by the theft of Citizen
Band radios and tape decks from parked cars, Heath says. Some of
it—not much—is marked down as "joy riding," a misdemeanor.

Accidents and minor crime. Richard Heath is giving us just the
briefest look inside more complexity the car has brought to our
lives. Not the obvious problems represented by injury to a friend
or member of the family, an experience becoming more and more
common to more and more of us. Instead, the terrible legal and
bureaucratic maze we have constructed to try to direct the
automobile into harmless paths—at the very least away from our
vulnerable persons and our emptying pocketbooks.

When Chief Heath reels off numbers of people hurt and killed,
he is echoing in Muncie terms an automotive byproduct one
former Washington official, whose training had been in medicine,
called "America's number one health problem."

Americans are solutionists and given a problem will try to
solve it quickly and in the most complicated and expensive way
possible—probably in consequence of their haste. Thus, once we
finally understood what was happening on our highways, and we
did not understand in terms of legislation until 1966,* we created
an enormous federal and state bureaucracy to cope with the
problem. That bureaucracy, in turn (and by mandate of the
Congress), understanding there were three elements in the safety
problem—the car, the highway and the driver—decided reasonably

---

* If 1966 seems a familiar year, recall it as the year when Britain reached the same degree
of ownership we had arrived at in 1928, which is to say the 1966 legislation was probably
due in 1928 to begin with.

enough that the quickest solutions to the mopping up of blood on the Interstates and in the cities was to act to change the car. It moved straightaway upon the manufacturer. Thus, within a short period of time, the manufacturer found himself with his design department transplanted to Washington and staffed by the federal government. It didn't help much in terms Richard Heath would understand, but it changed the automobile. No more Big Jack performance cars, no more horsepower race, no more "run what you brung" on the highway. And so the car builders turned to dress-up options and luxury and convenience add-ons, both to make the car more attractive as a piece of merchandise and to increase profits.

While in Chief Heath's understanding, three-point seat restraints, collapsible steering columns, side door beams, and the mass of standards Washington imposed on car manufacturers all over the world who wished to sell in the Muncies of America, probably helped to reduce his accident statistics, it is not likely that they helped very much.* But they also may well have brought some of the crime that so bothers Richard Heath. Perhaps if we had been left with snorting horsepower cars, Detroit would not have stuffed all those stereo tape decks in their new Olds Cutlass Supremes and Buick LeSabre Sport Coupes. At least not so quickly. But deprived of that extra per unit profit, Detroit hastened to give itself and its dealers another way of making money.

Muncie's petty thieves are making money from that decision, too, as Richard Heath's statistics show.

At the same time, Muncie's joy-riding problems seem to be telling Washington that if its goal is to excise the pleasure-producing center from the automobile, it is taking on a difficult if not impossible task.

Totally unaware of how clearly he is defining one of Washington's great barriers in neutering the automobile, Richard Heath, Muncie's young police chief, grows even younger and

* The legislation defining them did sweep along with it the establishment of the state agency which provided Chief Heath his statistics, the Indiana Department of Traffic Safety, a microcosm of the federal National Highway Traffic Safety Agency and one of fifty such state microcosms required by the law. In that sense, perhaps, the safety devices brought the problem into focus for police chiefs across the land.

more animated when he begins to talk about his own pleasures involving the car. He has begun his discussion by commenting that street racing in Muncie—that practice of drag racing on city streets—is minimal. As he starts to explain why, the beginnings of a surge of joy seem to lift him from his chair. He is smiling now, both with pride in the solution and because this is the opening he seeks to describe his feelings.

Heath races karts. They are tiny, suspensionless platforms driven by small rear mounted engines, on which the driver sits, inches from the pavement. A typical single-engined kart darts around an artificial obstacle course of a track perhaps half a mile long averaging somewhere near 35mph. But some twin-engined karts are staggeringly fast. In the late '50s and early '60s, when Ferrari was building some very fast sports/racing cars with top speeds of 175mph, a twin engine kart held the lap record at one full-blown, almost three-mile-long road-racing track on which those Ferraris raced. One of the current challengers for the world driving championship began his career in South Africa racing karts. Karts are not to be laughed at.

Richard Heath's fourteen-year-old son works with his father on the kart Heath races. Shortly, he will have his own to race. With his father, he will travel all over Indiana to kart races. Heath can't wait for summertime. Muncie, Heath says, is a motor racing city. MidAmerica drag strip is seven miles north of the town, and with a sanctioned facility, Muncie's kids have a place to compete. Muncie's police, Heath does not say and does not need to, have in MidAmerica a very clear reason to enforce the No Street Racing laws in the city. In cities without some kind of outlet for carmania, police—many of whom were street racers themselves as teen-agers—are reluctant to enforce such laws. In one Muncie-sized western city, not only do the police turn a blind eye to the regular gathering of as many as one hundred cars on an abandoned street at night, but the private ambulance service in the community makes routine runs by the site, not just to be sure that there have been no injuries, but so that its female owner/driver can race against some of the street-hot Chevelles and Mustangs in her ungainly Cadillac ambulance.

Winchester, with its infamous banked oval racetrack for sprint cars (the fierce open wheelers most observers consider to be more dangerous than any other race cars), is twenty-two miles east of Muncie. Terre Haute, where there is a sprint car dirt track, is somewhat farther in the other direction. And of course there is Indianapolis with its two weekends of time trials and its Memorial Day race, a three-weekend orgy which draws an estimated 500,000 persons (Indianapolis Motor Speedway never gives out attendance figures). A good deal of Muncie goes down, says Heath, but many like true aficionados go only to the qualifying sessions instead of to the all-too-often boring 500-mile race. Heath also mentions Indianapolis Raceway Park, site of the largest drag meet of the year, with as many as 1,500 entries, some of them from Muncie.

" 'Why on earth do you need to study what's changing this country?' said a lifelong resident and shrewd observer of the Middle West, the Lynds quote in their second paragraph of "Inventions Re-Making Leisure," 'I can tell you what's happening in just four letters: A-U-T-O!' " It's still happening in Muncie in the late 1970s. If to the Lynds the car meant the literal broadening of horizons, the range of the car as opposed to the range of the horse, the mortgaging of a house to buy a car and therefore the beginnings of a shift away from traditional ways of dealing with money, or rolling houses of prostitution, it only incidentally meant the kind of leisure activity Richard Heath is talking about. ". . . manifestations of Speed are not confined to 'speeding,' " the Lynds said. "Auto Polo next Sunday!" they quote from a contemporary ad. That is as close as *Middletown* is able to come to Richard Heath's understanding of the car as a leisure device, although the first Indianapolis race was held thirteen years before the Lynds began their study.

Middletown does reflect on what effect the car might have on the unity of the family in terms of leisure, but not quite in the way Muncie's police chief understands it. Richard Heath's kart racing in the summer with his son and his winter evenings in the garage working side by side with his boy to prepare the new kart for the upcoming season say a great deal about how the car provides a placid bond of leisure activity. The explosion of auto range that results in the off-road vehicle-motorcycle-dirt-bike-all-terrain ve-hicle-camper-motor-home summer gypsy caravan that crosses and recrosses this nation stuffed full of children and grandparents and ramrodded by a heat- and temper-ridden family head would have stunned the Lynds, and says even more.

If Richard Heath sees Muncie's problems with the automobile in terms of crime, traffic control, and leisure, Lamar Ziegler sees it in an equally contemporary sense, identifying problems in *his* area that affect Muncie in the same fashion they affect the balance of the nation.

He understands that to be really effective in moving those 55,000 or 65,000 cars around Muncie, the city fathers would have to knock everything down and start all over again. It is clear to Ziegler that since the automobile is "the lifeblood of the community," Muncie is prepared to go almost to the limit in accommodating the car, but he *doesn't* understand either where the limit is or how to get there.

He is faced with this dilemma because, so far as Lamar Ziegler is concerned, for Muncie there can be no such thing as mass transit as the great cities of the country understand it; even if there used to be.

The Lynds said this (almost in passing) in their comparison of Middletown in 1924 with pastoral Muncie of 1890: "Everybody in Middletown in 1890 got to work by walking ... Today ... one gets about the city and the country surrounding it by bicycle, fifteen-minute street-car service, regular bus service, and five interurban lines ..."

Ziegler doesn't remember the street cars or the interurbans. In his middle-aged memory and in his files, which can only reflect what his small office has room to store, Muncie's mass transit system has "changed very little" from the '20s.

To Ziegler, Muncie's bus system is immutable. It is there, running eleven fixed routes that feed into the downtown area to a central transfer point, with schedules of thirty-minute headways. It has always been there and always will be, and he hates it. Busses don't work well. They cost as much to run in one year as they cost to buy. In Muncie, the system is privately owned, but because busses are so inefficient in terms of cost, the city has to subsidize the owners.

Unlike Heath, Ziegler speaks jargon. "We've been working on grant applications to provide operational revenues," he says, by which he means that the city has had to buy six new busses recently because the equipment was so worn, and he resents the fact and wants somebody else to pay for the next go around of purchases. As he talks about Muncie's public transportation system, he gets angrier and angrier, to the point where he begins to speak English. There's just too much automobile and pedestrian impact on the busses, he answers to a question of what a model mass system might be. Busses can't get the job done. A bus is ". . . a great, big, long thing that carries forty-five passengers. Every time it accelerates from a stop light, there's this big, black smoke stream that comes up behind it. They all look like they haven't been washed in six months. They always have all their fenders dented in and they're never repaired. You're lucky," Ziegler says in a triumphant peroration to his bill of particulars, "if you see one person, one passenger besides the driver, riding the bus."

Still, for all the redness of his face when he talks about Muncie's busses, Ziegler understands the need for *something*. He calls people who use busses "captive riders" and properly defines them—at least so far as Muncie is concerned—as the very young, the very old, or the very poor. He is aware of and sympathetic to their needs. "Without the bus system, these people would have no other means of transportation." His understanding doesn't help to find a solution.

The Zieglerian syllogism says there will always be the old, the young, and the poor: that therefore there will be a need for public transportation; that public transportation will never pay for itself; that the city will have to subsidize it as a result.

And that there is probably *no* system that will work, not even Dial-A-Ride, a demand/response system that uses mini vans (the typical demand/response system is the taxi). But since public transportation is a community need and the city will have to subsidize it anyway, Ziegler would be just as happy to settle for demand/response. At least it is portal to portal, it doesn't require great, smelly devices that are never full, and it might even cost less than a system using conventional vehicles.

Sitting there, swinging his chair from side to side as he talks about his problems with the busses, he suddenly stops and prepares to make what is certainly going to be the controlling point. Even with its narrow streets and its high automobile population, Lamar Ziegler wants it known that Muncie is an efficient community in which to get around. You can drive clear across Muncie in fifteen minutes at the height of traffic, he says. When the city finally puts its several million dollar appropriation ("We're right on the verge of it") in the "traffic control area" and street construction, it will be even better. It's been a long afternoon, and Ziegler has forgotten his earlier railing against Muncie's narrow streets and its short blocks and the manner in which they combine to make any kind of traffic control almost impossible.

Lamar Ziegler celebrates the car. He will pay lip service to its social wickedness and at the same time *prove* that Muncie could not live without it. Listen, he says, Muncie is still a typical midwestern community. River transportation is not feasible, not even with the White River running through the middle of town. Railroad transportation is declining. In the two industrial parks now being built, the developers are far more concerned about highways and natural gas than they are about railroad access. Muncie is and has to be completely highway oriented. But when Indiana built I-69, I-70, and all the other Interstates, Muncie, unlike neighboring Anderson, was left out. Of course that won't burden the community for long. By the end of the decade, there'll be a four-lane connecting to I-70 to the south. Ziegler is saying outright that without the automobile Muncie could not have had its growth, that if it wishes to continue to grow or even maintain a status quo, there is going to have to be continued reliance on the automobile. Why even 30 percent of Ball State students are commuters.

Yes, yes, yes, of course Ziegler is aware of OPEC, and traffic fatality figures, and inflation, and the cost of the car, and finite resources, but none of that makes any difference because Lamar Ziegler, as representative of the automobile establishment, has two constants in his life. One is the absolute conviction that Americans—at least the Americans the Lamar Zieglers all across the country see and know in Muncies throughout the land—are *never* going to give up their cars. The other is they aren't going to have to. After all, Muncie—all the thousands of Muncies—is in America and in America we have American technology and American technology can solve *anything,* up to and including synchronizing stop lights in Middletown and sorting out the traffic problem.

That's Lamar Ziegler's solution, because he sure doesn't place much faith in the federally required transportation plan. The '66 act required that in a three-year period all urbanized areas over 50,000 have a transportation study. Muncie started a few years late so the study didn't even begin until 1969. The $750,000 project was to be split into three, one-year increments. What Lamar Ziegler has now as a result of that is his map with the plastic overlay and the orange smears. He clearly knows why that's all he's got, and he's anxious to explain. They left the local people out of it, he says. State Highway in Indianapolis was the contractor, and State Highway has a bad habit of very slow turnaround. Three years were used up in the process of negotiating the contract. There were other delays in reviewing the negotiations and reviewing the reviews. And of course there were those slow turnarounds. Maybe by 1977 or 1978 or 1979, Muncie will have a genuine Transportation and Land Use Study, but Lamar Ziegler is clearly not very optimistic.

He knows such a plan is indispensable, but he also knows that implementing it will be expensive. Muncie's double ring road system does not show on Ziegler's map because his map does not go to the year 2000, and it is only then that everyone involved estimates it will be completed.

In the meantime, he has his forecasts and his faith in American technology. Some contentment, too, since even in the height of traffic, according to Muncie's traffic engineer, it takes only fifteen minutes to cross town.

Well, not exactly. It is close to an hour in the 8 A.M. snow from the Holiday Inn on Madison to the sociology building at Ball State.

Here, if anywhere, should be the people who understand what the car has done to the people of Middletown. Here, if anywhere, are the people who should understand Middletown's new problems, deposited over the years in the town square by the arrival of more and more cars.

Dr. David Morris is hearty and forthright. He has in common with Richard Heath and with few of his colleagues that he not only speaks English but uses his words carefully and with style.

Although he confirms that Muncie is indeed a Standard Metropolitan Statistical Area (SMSA), an urb, it is a *small* urb and part of a dynamic surrounding. Projections are clear that the great migration to large cities is continuing and will continue to continue; howevever, there is another simultaneous migration beginning, really the third of this century: First (as the Lynds descended upon Muncie to observe) came the movement from the farm to the city; after World War II there was a great flow to suburbia (while the movement to the city went on unabated); now there seems to be a great movement out of the suburbs *and* out of the cities and into the small communities of the nation—the SMSAs of 50,000 or somewhat more. Dr. Morris is being very careful now in his definition. An SMSA is a unit specified by the Bureau of Census. Morris says an SMSA includes at least the county in which the inner city of a minimum 50,000 population can be found. Here is the significance of that careful differentiation: the city has its geo-socio-political boundaries. In many people's minds, says Morris, that is the definition of "urban." But it is no longer true, since the SMSA *includes* the county (one might say, in Muncie's case, the countryside) that surrounds it. Morris says it this way: "Urban, for all practical purposes, can include a city plus vast territories surrounding it which are not a part of its political sphere of influence. Therefore you may find that you can have—by census definition—multiple county units if they are linked to the life of that central city of 50,000 or more."

Now we can understand the concept of SMSA and population shift in terms of movement in and out of a city, but still within the SMSA. We also understand the migration as being one *away* from large urban areas and into small SMSAs. And we understand it further as movement out of the central portions of those small SMSAs and into genuinely rural areas, which nonetheless qualify as "urban" since they are "linked to the life of the central city."

Some further points about this third migration. A study done in 1974 by the Stanford Research Institute (SRI) for the National Science Foundation, *City Size and the Quality of Life,* analyzed people's attitudes toward city size. These are its conclusions:

—There exists a strong and pervasive preference for smaller scale living ...

—There exists considerable dissatisfaction with large urban environments relative to small town-rural environments.

—The preference for smaller scales seems to be a long-standing one . . .

—These preferences are not simply nostalgic yearnings—a larger percentage of the young (under thirty . . .) indicates a preference for smaller scales.

—These preferences are not simply a part of any American myth that views the good life as being found in the country—the polls showed markedly increasing satisfaction with place of residence as scales decreased.

—Two localized studies in the states of Wisconsin and Washington suggest that, although many people prefer a smaller scale of living, they would like to live within commuting distance of a large city.

—These preferences also extend to support for a national distribution policy that would limit population growth in larger urban areas and stimulate growth in smaller towns/rural areas.

One more reference to the SRI report. It cites a conclusion of the Commission on Population and the American Future as saying that a clear majority (53 percent) of a sample of the American population wanted to live in a rural or small town atmosphere.

(The Institute adds a caveat about its report: "It is important to point out that this report has a policy bias," which bias was the need to give hard number support to what SRI perceived to be the wish of the American people to pursue the third migration.)

Clearly these are forces at work in Muncie, but where Stanford Research sees the nation, Dr. Morris sees Middletown/Muncie. This is not to say his scope is so narrow that Muncie is his only concern—far from it—but his view is skewed by the place in which he lives and teaches. Thus to him the best candidates for small urban growth are the college towns with their satellite cultural facilities and their willing, motivated, and educated labor forces to man our new service economy.

Whereupon futurist David Miller's words about another population trend come to mind:

. . . in 1970, the census itself identified some ten SMSAs outside the major metropolitan areas that had been experiencing unusually rapid growth. . . . I think that's what's happening here. To the extent that's right, we are going to re-invent a sort of [he stumbles a bit, searching] *condensed* and *compact* small town, a more autonomous one . . . that will probably, except as it has suburbs around it now, not duplicate the suburban pattern around older cities because of this new environment and land use ethic and counter growth ethic.

We can infer from this a very new kind of community coming into existence, with a new kind of population, new shapes to its surrounding areas, and new priorities. And we can see the automobile in all of these misty outlines. Much of the third migration is by car; movement in and out of the city/county units is by car. Cars and their derivative pick-up trucks have thus not only moved into cities, increasing the mobility of their inhabitants, but (with yet another derivative, the tractor) they have affected the 'rural parts of the nation as well. It is not too strong a statement to say that the three migrations—particularly the second to the suburbs—was largely predicated on automobility.

As for David Miller's new suburbs, what are they to be like? If we are going to see suburbs whose shape and purposes have been changed by this "new environment and land use ethic," will they nonetheless be the creation of the car and therefore totally dependent upon it? Will they be "suburbs" at all?

These are some of Muncie/Middletown's problems in the late '70s as understood and dealt with by its managers and thinkers, all of whom believe that the automobile is the town's life blood. Why is it taken for granted in Middletown that the city could not exist without it? What would happen if we concluded, as a result of a combination of the car's kill-rate, its ravenous appetite for finite resources, the deadly cloud it gives off that we could no longer afford the automobile as a social device? What are the questions Muncie is not asking itself about how the town would live if the car were legislated away?

IV

Muncie's managers, and the thinkers whose professional landscape is cluttered with the automobile, think Muncie lives in the present; in fact it lives very much in the past.

The great automobile depression of 1974–75 may have brought disagreeable unemployment statistics to the Muncie's Chamber of

Commerce computers but, as we have seen, the Chamber chose to ignore them and the depression has left no deep scar upon the community. Muncie's auto workers know theirs is a cyclical business. They have been through many of those cycles, but their lives have been buttressed in the later ones by United Auto Worker union-won SUBs (supplementary union benefits), designed precisely to see them through the dark period of layoff. Muncie's plant managers as well as Muncie's auto workers do not understand that the depression was the result of a consumer revolt.

Muncieites are dimly aware that cars are going to change somewhat in the future, but they don't know how nor how soon. No one in Muncie seems to have read the provision in the so-called Compromise Energy Bill (now known as the Energy Policy and Conservation Act) signed in January of 1976 by President Ford that, through the device of mandating minimum fuel consumption, is going to alter the shape of cars as they have never been changed before. Police Chief Heath, as one example, does not understand that the town's big-car values and all they symbolize in terms of growth are already things of the past, even though he should be able to recognize, in the introduction of the '77 cars, the beginnings of this radical change in our automobiles.

Introspective Muncie, in the person of Dr. David Morris, does not seem to recognize the impact of the automobile on the city's social institutions: its family structures, its leisure habits, its schools. Ball State's urbanologist is only casually concerned with the role of the car in increasing the magnitude and accelerating the speed of social change as represented by the women's movement, the composition of the work force, the changeover to a service economy.

Muncie's automotive brain trust is not much concerned with the shortage of raw materials in the world.

The people who think and talk about the future of the automobile in Muncie feel certain the city can resist to the end any attempt by government at any level to interfere in its citizens' private lives, particularly that part of private life which centers on the automobile.

They speak as if the years since the 1966 act had never been, as if the government were still outside the automobile industry instead of within it.

Dr. Morris is a midwesterner who grew up with the car, who always depended upon it as Muncie/Middletown now so clearly does, and who found the questioning of its worth so startling that he might have been asked whether he really needed the blood that ran through his veins. He says, "[We're] involved in other important social issues . . . the demise of the big city . . . the whole issue of race and minorities . . . crime . . . the effects of suburbanization." Doesn't he realize that in his contemplation of the great urbs and their problems he must deal with the car?

The "demise of the big city," if Dr. Morris means that literally, would come as some surprise to Stanford Research Institute which predicates its report on *City Size and the Quality of Life* by citing a long-term trend for big cities to become bigger. The numbers are on SRI's side. In 1940 there were twelve cities with populations of a million or more; in 1970 there were twenty-nine such cities. Jerome Pickard's population projection for the year 2000 in his report for the Commission on Population Growth and the American Future, says that by the end of this century there may be such great cities and they might contain as much as two thirds of the nation's population.

If, however, Dr. Morris is talking about "demise of the big city" in the sense of the deterioration in the quality of life, he is talking in good measure about the automobile, whether he understands that or not. Those cities are going to get larger and proliferate because much of the migration to them is by car. The overcrowding in those cities that leads to pathological social behavior such as violent crime, stratospheric divorce rates, mental illness, suicide, and alcoholism could be largely relieved if the automobile could exist in big cities to be used only as a leisure escape device. Whether it can or cannot is a matter for much study.

Erosion of the quality of life surely includes assaults on the environment. Here the automobile has been properly identified as an urban criminal for years. The National Center for Air Pollution Control said flatly in 1968: ". . . air pollution is strongly correlated with population and is an unavoidable consequence of the agglomeration of people, cars, and industry. . . . clean air for very large cities is inherently difficult to attain." As for noise pollution, Stanford Research Institute says, "Since average work trip length increases with city size ... it seems reasonable to assume that people spend more of their time making and being exposed to transportation noise in bigger cities. It also seems reasonable to assume that unacceptable levels of exposure to noise in areas adjacent to urban freeways is more likely to be concentrated in the bigger cities where freeways tend to converge." The authors based their conclusions on a 1972 Environmental Protection Agency report on noise.

But what would happen, according to Dr. David Morris, if the federal mass transit Utopians came along and took the car away from Muncie?

"We would be up that proverbial creek in a leaking boat."

In Muncie, the car is taken for granted. Especially the *big* car. Chief Heath has reluctantly decided to try intermediate-size cars for half his police fleet to replace the old standard-size ones. Already Heath has discovered that the cars he bought as "intermediates" are as big as the new large cars. In one year, "standards" had lost one thousand pounds and a foot in length. By 1980, *compacts* will have become the standard-size car built in this country.

Since these are federally mandated changes, and since the Big Three auto manufacturers—GM, Ford, and Chrysler—will have spent some $6 billion among them converting their lines to conform with those changes, and since those enormous companies must make an equally enormous push to sell the new small cars they have spent so much money to design and build, Muncie's car plants and car economy will likely steam along at an only slightly decreased rate for the balance of this decade.

There is then the prospect, very real in the minds of those studying the problem of the economy, that it will crash. The automobile industry will have entered and ended its final cycle, at least in the terms Muncie auto workers understand such things.

Projections for the early '80s from a broad community of futurists tell us there is an apocalypse coming. But discounting "apocalypse" and substituting "severe downturn" in forecasting the economy, other factors threaten the automobile which Muncie does not see. As arbitrarily chosen indicators of what Muncie might confront in the next decade there are first these conclusions of a consensus (Delphi) study by the Center for Futures Research of the Graduate School of Business at the University of Southern California: 83 percent of the participants in the polled group considered that the earliest occurrence of the next severe economic depression would be 1978; 78 percent thought there would be some form of retail rationing of oil and natural gas reserves before the end of the 1970s.

More telling is data from the U.S Department of the Interior which says that by 1985, of the thirteen basic raw materials required by an industrial economy, we will be reliant on other nations for more than 70 percent of seven of them.

Perhaps Muncie does not recall the fuel embargo. Perhaps Muncie does not think such embargos can extend to other critical materials. Perhaps Muncie does not think of such things at all. Surely, however, Muncie's citizens must be able to see the spoor of the automobile, and they should not find it difficult to realize that where the automobile fouls, the federal government follows. Pollution, in fact, is no stranger to Muncie.

"A small river wanders through Middletown, and in 1890 when timber still stood on its banks, White River was a pleasant stream for picnics, fishing and boating, but it has shrunk today to a creek discolored by industrial chemicals and malodorous with the city's sewage." Thus, in 1924, the Lynds were aware of man's incredible swinishness. When it comes to blotting out the sky with noxious gasses, 1976 Middletown didn't seem more concerned with the mess it was making than it did during the Lynds' study. Dr. Morris points with some justice at what he calls "the rapid disaffection with the whole environmental movement in the period of eighteen months or so when the Arabs turned off the tap. Social movements can occur (and subside) very quickly in this country."

Morris's boss, Dr. Whitney Gordon, the head of the Department of Sociology at Ball State, is even more explicit. Indianians (and by extension he is suggesting all Americans) are pragmatists, he says. Hard-headed. Down-to-earth. "They will say, 'Look, maybe in Chicago pollution is an issue ... but goddamn it, our area's not that smoggy so why are you slapping on these flat-footed, broad indictments as if they were coming out of the Court of Louis XIV to the French settler somewhere in the boonies in Canada?' "

That is likely just what citizens of Middletown *will* tell the federal government when push comes to shove. Then Dr. Gordon makes an even more cogent point: "They will count the particles [of noxious emissions], you know, in the atmosphere. They will do their homework, and they will say, 'Except for two counties in the State of Indiana, you have legislation that oppresses five million people. Now that's just not right.'" He sits across from a round table in his crowded office with a bright, eager look and puts forth two premises he wishes taken for granted: First, if the people of Indiana say it's just not right, the federal government will agree with them and withdraw any order to reduce emissions; second, that things as they are will continue to be.

In short-term projection, Whitney Gordon is right about the federal government. It has already postponed more stringent emissions control regulation, although more as a result of industry pressure than popular unrest. Still it *has* rescinded other federal constraints (mandatory motorcycle helmet laws are the immediate example) purely in response to public resistance. There is an argument that if car prices rise enormously and the industry makes a case that the jump is due to unreasonable emissions requirements, a howl will come up from car buyers that will intimidate the Congress when the next round of clean air legislation is debated.

Dr. Gordon, though, is more sanguine than the world warrants in his second expectation. Many cities, including Muncie, have *already* banned cars from downtown or parts of downtowns. The consumer revolt has *already* shown that it can have an effect on the numbers of cars on the road. Material and labor costs have *already* moved auto prices so high that new car buys are affected.

To Lamar Ziegler these are mysterious ebbs and flows of unseen tides. "Air pollution? I've read and seen some studies, and I'm afraid I don't remember the results. We're not in the best category, we're not in the worst category, we're somewhere in between. It's not a serious problem." To Ziegler, the environment is "air" and air quality doesn't worry him.

Richard Heath and Muncie's police force have a difficult enough time coping with things as they are. They can't waste energy contemplating what might happen if they become required to police new mandatory seat belt laws or staff vehicle safety inspection programs or form a New York replica transit patrol to man a giant new mass transportation system.

John Moldovan and the Chamber of Commerce don't begin to comprehend what the end of the autoindustrial age might mean to Muncie employment statistics.

Shock, violent change, upheaval, earthquake in Middletown/Muncie would be the consequences of any *significant* replacement of the automobile as Muncie's chief transportation module. If the economists are right about an economic apocalypse, if the environmentalists' arguments about the rape of the land prevail, if the government succeeds in relegating the automobile to leisure-use status the repercussions in Middletown will go off the Richter scale.

For in that case what happens to McDonalds, Colonel Sanders, Two-Guys Auto Supply, Raintree 500 Mufflers, Holiday Inn, shopping centers, and Chevrolet-Muncie transmission plants, and to the 15 percent of American workers in the interchangeable urban modules around the nation that are duplicate Muncies who are employed in the auto and auto aftermarket industries?

What happens to us all? And how did we manage to find ourselves here in the first place?

3 : Before Ford

One state west of Indiana and less than a century before the Lynds' descent upon Muncie, George and Jacob Donner set out for the longest and most famous luncheon appointment in American history.

The very fact of the trip makes the point. The extraordinary nature of the Donner Party's members adds a view overlooked too long about why we are now inundated with 119 million motor vehicles. Both speak to us about our auto-irrationality.

When George and Jacob Donner, brothers, set out for California from Springfield, Illinois in 1846, George was sixty-two and Jacob sixty-five years old. They did not have to go. Their motives were very much like ours: they simply wanted to go, and movement had become a way of life.

By any standard, the Donners were successful men. George had moved a great deal, from North Carolina progressively westward to Illinois. Uprooting was nothing new for him.

Jacob had another reason for the trip to California, one equally familiar to today's migrants. He was ill, and California represented a relief from both farming and the harsh Illinois winters.

Historian George R. Stewart, whose *Ordeal by Hunger* includes diaries and letters written by the survivors, which give the definitive account of the journey, lists a third member of the party as James Frazier Reed, forty-six, who in Illinois "had prospered as a merchant, railroad contractor, and manufacturer of furniture, but lately had suffered some reverses in business." To Reed, California meant another chance, as it has meant for generations since. For his invalid wife, Margaret, it promised an opportunity to regain her health.

The other members of the Donner party were not so wealthy as Reed or the Donners, but they were not indigents by any means. For the most part they were successful merchants and farmers.

The point is a simple one: the California trip was arduous and few if any of the Donner party needed to make it.

George and Jacob did not survive the winter camp at Truckee Lake in the Sierra, joining the total of five dead on the journey before reaching the lake, and thirty-four dead while in camp or in the mountains trying to cross to safety, and a final fatality after reaching safety. Forty-seven survived, the last of whom, the infant, Isabella Breen (at the time of her death Mrs. MacMahon of San Francisco), died on March 25, 1935.

Only the Reeds and Patrick Breen lost no members of their families. Of the survivors, many figured prominently in the growth and prosperity of their new settlements: the Breens, the Reeds, Donners (children), and Murphys are important in local history.

The Donner legacy is a telling one for no reason other than as a most unfortunate dramatic example of the indefinable American need to *move* somewhere, anywhere. Theirs was the grand tragedy of social and geographic migratory habits and mobility of the American experience. Frederick Jackson Turner and, perhaps more significantly, George W. Pierson, have told us how important that mobility has been in our development.

Both were historians, both changed historiography in terms of understanding the American experience. In a very real sense both were talking about the manner in which the automobile would be accepted, although they had no thought of doing so. When Turner stood to give his paper to the American Historical Society at the Chicago World's Fair in 1893, he was to introduce a thesis that pervaded the teaching of history in this country in subsequent decades, and that all unwittingly opened the understanding of how and why we came to embrace the car as though he were writing some future preface to an as-yet unwritten and undreamed of charter of the Motor Vehicle Manufacturers' Association.

He spoke before an audience that had dwindled because of the heat and humidity of a summer's day, July 12, after having spent the entire preceding weekend preparing his paper. Of the almost two hundred historians who had begun the day, many had departed weighed down by the four papers given before his (including subjects so sparkling and diverse as "English Popular Uprisings in the Middle Ages" by Dr. George Kriehn and "Early Lead Mining in Illinois and Wisconsin" by Dr. Reuben Gold Thwaites.)

Turner's "Significance of the Frontier in American History" did not play well at all. Not many people credited it on merit, much less news value. The Chicago newspapers, which lavished praise on "Early Lead Mining . . .," gave it almost no mention.

Simply, Turner said, "The existence of an area of free land, its continuous recession, and the advance of American settlement westward, explain American development." The frontier, Turner said, mandated mobility, produced individualism and somehow (it was here that he was most vulnerable and most frequently and successfully later attacked) "promoted democracy." It decreased the American dependence on the Old World which meant the advancement of our own industrial independence.

The point to be made is this: It is no good trying to explain our acceptance of the car by beginning with the cost of the Model T, the enshrinement of Henry Ford the Original as a great American hero, or the car as a suddenly discovered rolling bedroom. A great deal of what we know of the settling of this country and the shaping of the American character tells us that a description of the automobile was as good as written into the American manifest destiny.

The American Historical Association waited until 1971 to take the automobile seriously and along with it its pioneer historians, James Flink and James Rae. But we should understand that the roots of the car go deep in our history, for Frederick Jackson Turner provided, on that hot day in Chicago, a beginning insight into how ready we would be to accept the automobile when it finally came along, and a later critic, Professor George W. Pierson, fiercely disclaiming the frontier thesis as an end-all explanation, gave us a broader and more useful understanding. "What made us and kept us different," Pierson wrote,

> was not just the wildness of the North American continent, nor its vast empty spaces, nor even its wealth of resources, powerful as must have been those influences.
>
> No. It was, first of all, the M-Factor: the factor of movement, migration, mobility. Colonization was one part of it, immigration, another; the westward movement itself was a fraction, but only a fraction of the whole. This whole began with many old-world uprootings. It gathered force with the transatlantic passage. It flooded on to the farmlands of the mid-continent. But increasingly it meant movement also *away* from the frontier, from farm to town, from region to region, from city to city. Individuals, families, churches, villages, on occasion whole countrysides have partici-pated—and continue to participate.

And so we have the introduction of the M-Factor. If we wish to understand this strange swirl around and about the country, if we want to reconcile Stanford Research's seemingly contradictory statements about movement from city to suburb, from countryside to city, from city to city, from suburb back to city, from suburb and city to SMSA, we could do far worse than to pay attention to George Pierson's M-Factor.

If we consider this M-Factor in the light of our economy, Pierson asks,

> ... what will we find? An economy in which transportation has loomed extraordinarily large—witness the railroads, the automobile age, the airplane industry ... witness also how our myths of how prairie schooners and pony express, paddle wheelers and the long whistle of the trains, Ford cars and the *Spirit of St. Louis* have entered into the folklore of our people.
>
> For Americans, it has been said, the automobile restates a national principle, since, after all, the settler was the first auto-mobile. In the U.S., a mile is something to put behind you.

Pierson is telling us that in the M-Factor we find the key to the American character.

Automotive historian John Rae, quoting R. L. Heilbroner, nails it down nicely. Heilbroner was musing on the impact of the car in this M-Factor framework.

> Yet these reflections on the impact of the automobile still fail to do justice to its quintessential contribution to our lives. This is its gift of mobility itself—not mobility as a dollar-spreading device or a mechanical substitute for personal movement, but as a direct enhancement of life, as an enlargement of life's boundaries and opportunities. This is so enormous, so radical a transformation that its effect can no longer be measured or appreciated by mere figures. It is nothing less than the unshackling of the age-old bonds of locality; it is the grant of geographic choice and economic freedom on a hitherto unimagined scale.

Early, constant, pervasive mobility; the wish to move, the *need* to move. If we are to understand how deeply rooted mobility is in the American character we have only to look at the rude if not downright primitive conditions travel imposed on our ancestors.

Our first roads were paths worn by animals, later preempted by Indians, in turn evicted from them by settlers. One such path, from the upper Potomac to Pittsburgh was widened to twelve feet by General Braddock's forces in order that they could transport wagons and artillery to attack Fort Duquesne and drive the French from the Ohio Valley in 1755. Part of that path we now know as the Cumberland Road.

Farm wagons were our earliest vehicles, followed by devices called stage wagons which were lighter than the all-wood farm wagons because we had advanced our knowledge of ironworking.

Coaches were imported, very expensive, and at first used only by the rich or (familiarly enough) by officialdom. By the mid 1700s, Massachusetts had about seven pleasure carriages for every one thousand persons. New York was only somewhat more mobile.

Two accounts of travel—one in 1810 by a Briton and another in 1892 in a letter from a former teamster—suggest that life on the road in the nineteenth century took no quantum leaps for most travelers in terms of amenities. Englishman Fortescue Cuming wrote of a trip he had taken on an Ohio national road a few years prior to 1810:

I was shewn to bed upstairs in a barrack room the whole extent of the house, with several beds in it, one of which was already occupied by a man and his wife, from the neighboring country, who both conversed with me until I feigned sleep, in hopes that would silence them, but though they ceased to direct their discourse to me, they continued to talk to each other on their most private and domestic affairs. . . . I at last fell asleep, but I was soon awoke in torture from a general attack made upon me by hosts of vermin of the most troublesome and disgusting genii . . .

Seventy-two years later, one Jesse Piersol (according to T. B. Searight's *The Old Pike*) wrote a friend about an overnight stop in another place. He painted a picture not so different from Fortescue Cuming's:

I have stayed overnight with William Sheets, on Nigger Mountain, when there would be 30 six-horse teams on the wagon yard, 100 Kentucky mules in an adjacent lot, 1,000 hogs in other enclosures, and as many fat cattle from Illinois in adjoining fields. The music made by this large number of hogs . . . I will not forget. . . . the wagoners would . . . unroll their beds, lay them down on the floor before the bar room fire, side by side, and sleep, with their feet near the fire, as soundly as under the paternal roof.

Soon enough, regular stage routes were in operation between the larger cities. New York to Philadelphia took two days in 1764, New York to Boston, four days. By 1806, Congress had authorized construction of the National Road and the great highway/freeway/boondoggle/plague/blessing was underway.

With gradual improvement in the road system, stage travel increased. It was not sophisticated. As with the embryonic motels, it contained its share of unexpected moments. For example:

The Neil, Moore Stage Company had a fast mail coach which left Wheeling, West Virginia daily at 6:00 A.M. and arrived in Cincinnati forty-eight hours later. For your $13 fare, you occasionally got a ride described by Philip P. Jordan's *The National Road* from the experience of passenger Adam McKinney:

When his stage left Columbus, nine passengers were crowded into the body, so McKinney elected to sit outside with the driver. After leaving Jack-town, the driver whipped up his teams. The stage tore along the road with the driver twice laying on the whip, skidded down a long hill and took the level road at a gallop. McKinney remonstrated. The driver said there was no danger. A moment later, the off-wheels ran off the road, the stage lurched over, and the teams ran off with the front wheels. McKinney, a deep gash in his thigh and cuts and bruises over his entire body, was carried into a near-by house, where he remained for three months before he could be moved.

Not even Presidents of the United States were immune. On the contrary. Ira Pomeroy did a piece for the *New Republic* in the early 1930s describing a less than benign previous century ambush of Martin Van Buren by the citizens of Plainville, Indiana who were deeply resentful of Van Buren's veto of a National Road Bill. ("They considered Van Buren a little stuffy anyway . . .")

Van Buren's driver was in on the plan:

Instead of walking his team the last half mile, he lashed them to a frenzied gallop. At the presidential stage neared a treacherous mudhole, a favorite wallow for hogs, the lad yanked hard on his left rein . . . Slowly—very slowly—the stage overturned . . . Before anyone could wade through the sucking slime to aid Van Buren, his head, topped with a badly crushed, broad-brimmed hat, popped through the door. The President gradually pulled himself out, his long black broadcloth cloak splashed with muddy water, and his tight-fitting pearl-gray trousers and fine polished boots ruined. Years later the Daughters of the American Revolution erected a large tablet [on the spot] . . .

Interurban wagon travel was not exactly mass transit, but with boats and barges it was most of the transit we had, except for horse and foot. Foot was cheap, but didn't go very far. Horses were more accessible to Americans than to citizens of any other nation. Still, a horse was expensive and useful for farming, and therefore not much to be wasted on travel of any distance when there were perfectly good waterways and wagons available.

The wagon served another, and perhaps more significant, purpose as a carrier of goods. The Conestoga freight hauler, born in the Conestoga Valley of Pennsylvania, had a model run longer than the Model T or the VW Beetle. It was in use more than a century after its invention during the time of the heaviest western migration. It could carry heavy loads (one instance documents a wagoner who carried 8,300 pounds at $4.25 per 100 from Baltimore to Mt. Vernon, Ohio. It took him a month to make the 397 miles), but it was not cheap. In addition to the wagon, a team cost about $200 and upkeep was figured at somewhat more than that annually.

After the Civil War westward migration became a flood, and one estimate has it that in 1865 the average number of teams crossing the plains each month was 5,000.

Oscar Winther talks about all this migration, so familiar to us thanks to John Wayne's Hollywood, in his book, *The Transportation Frontier,* but he underscores George Pierson's M-Factor swirl by also discussing the *return* movement: "A considerable number of would-be settlers and miners . . . went back home. One such backtracking family revealed its sentiments in these words painted on its wagon:

From Kansas and starvation
To Missouri and salvation."

Although by the 1890s the Conestogas and their cousins had long since been replaced by the railroad as the principal means of cross-country travel, you could still look out the window of a railroad coach and see them making their ten to twenty-mile-a-day journeys across the plains.

As for the stage, even after it was pushed off the transportation system by the railroad in the East, it was in wide use in the West. Passenger service began in the mid 1820s and was common by mid-century. It seemed only reasonable to westerners that if the government had provided subsidy for the development of the National Road, it should subsidize stagecoach operations as well. Government subsidy began in 1851 in the form of requiring the Postmaster General to let contracts for regular mail service—a practice of propping up transportation systems that may have seemed a canny solution in the middle of the nineteenth century, but has plagued us ever since.

By the late nineteenth century, the railroads had clearly taken over in this country for movement of people and goods. There are endless railroad histories, and some splendid biographies of their builders: Jay Gould, Jim Fisk, Daniel Drew—immense men, great villains, all with a kind of majesty even in their villainy.

Clearly the railroad tied this country together, hammering its steel into the planks of the individual states to make a traversable bridge from coast to coast. But at least as important a legacy as that remarkable bridge—looking forward to the influence on transportation systems in the United States and in particular the government and private industry's view of the automobile—was the manner in which its building was accomplished.

The railroad magnates, for all their vigor—perhaps because of it—conspired with the various governments, federal and state, to establish a precedent that *travel, access, movement* were paramount. We were a nation in the throes of a fit of manifest destiny. It all seemed to fit so perfectly together. What did it matter that individual ownership of rights of way were steamrollered? That whole states seemed to be given away to the railroads? That negligence in maintenance and operation resulted in endless fearsome accidents killing thousands of persons? That equipment was last on the list of items worth bothering with by the owners, with printing presses to counterfeit railroad stock coming first, as was literally true of the Erie, whose directors, Jay Gould and Jim Fisk, printed stock certificates in the basement of their converted opera house headquarters whenever they wanted to bolster their personal treasuries.

Oh, how the railroad robber barons (could they only have lived long enough) would have looked on Detroit and the automobile industry with the fond gaze of grandfathers, doting on the accomplishments of their mirror-image grandsons.

There was a group of contemporaries of the Railroad Kings who would not have looked on the results of their own pioneer efforts with such equanimity. The League of American Wheelmen was founded in 1880 and grew hugely with the coming of the two-wheel bicycle. The League became the leading advocate of road improvement. Road improvement, said the League, would benefit the farmer in getting his goods to the market faster and cheaper. Not much later, supporters of the automobile would say the same thing. The railroaders had already said it about their particular rights of way. Comforting, how everyone was looking after the interests of the farmer.

The Office of Road Inquiry was established in 1893, continuing the government's role not only in railroad transportation, but in *roads*. Not much later, in 1904, the United States Office of Public Roads made the first survey of road mileage in the United States and discovered that the total was just over 2 million, of which only 153,662 was improved, defined, according to Oscar Winther, as "surfaced with gravel, stone, brick, oil or other topping materials."

If the premise is sound that we are now so enmeshed in the web of our transportation system—represented principally by the automobile—that we take for granted what might be our greatest problem and seem therefore to be ignoring our greatest challenge of the next quarter century, nothing in our history serves as a better example of how insidiously the national entrapment has occurred, how casually it has crept upon us, than the development of those ancillary businesses dependent on transportation—and again principally the automobile—and nothing better serves as an example of *that* than the growth of the inn/hotel/motel/plastic castle.

Hotels early took on a significance in America they never had in Europe. Daniel J. Boorstin *(The Americans: The National Experience)* tells us how far beyond the simple providing of bed and board the hotel went in our cultural development. Hotels were proving grounds for technological innovations: plumbing facilities on the upper floors (Astor House in New York, 1836), the first public buildings heated by steam (Eastern Exchange Hotel in Boston, 1846). They had the first practical passenger elevators (Fifth Avenue Hotel in New York, 1859); they were the first buildings with complete gas lighting (American House, Boston, 1835).

And there were lots of them serving many purposes. Since small towns (or towns yet inchoate but with great expectations of becoming the new Chicagos or St. Louises) were aching to be great stars on the maps of America, hotels were often the first buildings built. Not only were they frequently built before the nineteenth-century railroads even came to town but, Boorstin says: "They were, in fact, often built for the purpose of attracting railroads, along with settlers, newspapers, merchants, customers, lawyers, doctors, salesmen and all the other paraphernalia of metropolitan greatness."

Since hotels, their towns' proud claims to social recognition, were focal points for social gatherings, they were occasionally architectural marvels or architectural grotesqueries. Boorstin again: "An English comedian staying at New York's lavish St. Nicholas—an Arabian Nights hodgepodge of window curtains costing $700 apiece, gold embroidered draperies costing $1,000, mahogany paneling, rosewood carved furniture, sofas upholstered in Flemish tapestry, figured Turkish rugs, and deep Brussels carpets—refused to leave his shoes outside his door to be shined for fear someone would gild them."

American hotels often served as places of residence, which quixotically emphasized the almost compulsive American habit of migration. What is more convenient than a hotel if you plan to stay only six months or a year?

Hotels were convention centers. They were community centers.

Above all, hotels threw travelers into a common experience that Americans took for granted—even welcomed—but which appalled Europeans. Foreign visitors complained of lack of privacy (having to dine in the building in which one slept!), which included being stuffed into communal beds from time to time. They complained of too much regimentation—breakfast was served at a precise and, to them, mysterious hour preceded by no gongs or alarms. Hotels were, if nothing else, democratic institutions. It is hard not to sympathize with the overseas visitors. But as democratic institutions early hotels were perfectly fitted to the equal, common footing, nineteenth-century, mobile American life style.

As roads and travelers and intercity routes and finally cars increased, there came a shift in the demand for lodging. Today's traveler wants to stay on the main road, and he wants something more than a communal bed in which to sleep. Boorstin, talking about the luxury motel, says, "With its stateroom-sized sleeping rooms, 'fabulous' bar and deck-sized swimming pool, it now resembles nothing so much as the luxury ocean liner, 'Getting there is half the fun.' Tourist and business travelers 'relax in luxurious surroundings.' The motel passenger, too, is now always in mid-ocean, comfortably out of touch with the landscape."

There is something further to be said about the motel that seems to bring it full circle: in the look-alike chains of Howard Johnson and Holiday Inn, Ramada and Royal, there seems to be an effort to reestablish some sense of community, of belonging to something, since each is so predictable. When one buys a franchise for a Holiday Inn, for example, one literally visits a central display of Holiday Inn rooms, Holiday Inn restaurants, Holiday Inn bars, Holiday Inn public restrooms with one's contractor and, as though pointing to a tray of pastries, says, "I'll take 200 of those, 50 of those" and so forth. There are no surprises at a Holiday Inn and, in fact, that was the theme of a recent Holiday Inn advertising campaign.

If more evidence need be adduced of the pervasiveness of travel in the American experience, to the bedrock it forms in the American economy so that by today we can proclaim from *Business Week* to the National Highway Traffic Safety Administration to *Advertising Age* that one in six (or one in seven) jobs in the United States are related somehow to transportation, look not only to the hotel and its development but to gas stations (the Lynds did in *Middletown in Transition* and were shocked). It is important to understand here that the gas station is only the shopping cart of the petroleum industry, which may claim to be part of the national solution but seems every day, more and more, to be part of the national problem.

The Automobile Manufacturers Association (now called the Motor Vehicle Manufacturers Association of the U.S.) boasted that repair shops had been around since 1899 when New York and Boston each had one but, said the AMA, what may have been the first drive-in gasoline station with an island was built in Detroit in 1910 by the Central Oil Company.

For a while thereafter finding gas was a chancy proposition. Perhaps the general store had some, perhaps the hardware store, but the motorist—considered a sportsman and therefore deserving of any problem he might encounter—was pretty much on his own.

According to a Census Bureau statistical abstract, by 1972, the year before the great shortage, there were 226,500 gas stations with sales for the year of over $33.5 billion.

The first successful oil well had been drilled in Pennsylvania in 1859 by Edwin L. Drake, a former railroad conductor whose "main qualifications for the job appeared to be the railroad pass which he still held as an ex-employee, and which would get him to Titusville free of charge" (we are told by Daniel Boorstin) and by William A. Smith, a salt borer who had some knowledge of drilling.

Clearly, the automobile and the petroleum industries grew in complementary fashion. John B. Rae is convinced that, "Without the motorcar the petroleum industry would have been in trouble, since the kerosene lamp was retreating before gas and electric illumination; but this great increase [the discovery of oil in Texas and Oklahoma] in the supply of petroleum occurred fortuitously just as the automobile began to create a seemingly limitless demand for gasoline."

What about all this? What about all the currents and countercurrents in our transportation history? Perhaps we are talking about that elusive concept, the American character. If there is such a thing, we could do much worse than to listen to historian Henry Steele Commager on the subject.

The American is individualistic, Commager says. He has always resented, still resents, and probably always will resent being told he must do something. A law is a challenge to be met head on or ambushed or defied. That lovely British tradition of graceful obedience did not cross the Atlantic to Jamestown or Plymouth Rock.

Self-reliance has always been deeply ingrained; it was necessary that the first immigrants could survive, much less succeed.

Although our frontier ancestors hesitated not in the least to make demands on the federal government when they needed money for roads or stages, they professed an absolute dread of governmental interference. "Self-reliance," wrote Professor Commager, "was elevated to a philosophical creed, and in time individuals became synonymous with Americanism."

The American was optimistic: "Collectively, he had never known defeat ... poverty, or oppression, and he thought these misfortunes peculiar to the Old World. Progress was not, to him, a philosophical idea, but a commonplace of experience; he saw it daily in the transformation of wilderness into farm land, in the growth of villages into cities, in the steady rise of community and nation to wealth and power."

Americans didn't give a damn for yesterday. If Henry Ford really did say "History is bunk," as automotive historian Professor James . Flink suggests he did, he was expressing mainstream American philosophical thought.

The turn of the century American (and until the OPEC confrontation and Vietnam, his modern counterpart) professed great faith in the free enterprise system. His forebears, shaking with anger at the government's interference in what they considered their own affairs," ... [were] accustomed to prosperity, resented anything that interfered with it, and regarded any prolonged lapse from it as an outrage against nature."

What better philosophical soil in which to plant an automobile industry? "Whatever promised to increase wealth was automatically regarded as good, and the American was tolerant, therefore, of speculation, advertising, deforestation, and the exploitation of natural resources, and bore patiently with the worst manifestations of industrialism," says Professor Commager. What more could an infant Detroit have asked?

We look for villains these days when we hear the word "consumerism" (one large circulation magazine—*New York*—even has a column called "Shopper Beware" and occasionally "Rip-offs"). The whole subscription list of *Consumer Reports* is sometimes characterized as consisting of cringing, shifty-eyed paranoids ripping their copies from the hands of mailmen to discover the product conspiracy awaiting them this month.

At the turn of the century, in the flowering of the industrial age, consumerism meant something different entirely. There seemed to be no end to the gadgets Americans were willing to buy, gadgets that soon became necessities. Early twentieth-century Americans were in love with technology. They developed an addiction for newness and, like all addictions, their habits required constantly increasing dosages. "Newness" fast became "best." Daniel Boorstin said it well, "... when novelty ceased to be astonishing and unusual and became normal and expected, the boundary between the commonplace and the surprising was blurred."

(It is looking forward a bit, but that midwife of the annual model change in the automobile industry, Alfred P. Sloan, Jr., writing in his memoirs of his career at General Motors, of which he became chairman, must have brought a smile to the faces of both Commager and Boorstin: "Growth, or striving for it, is, I believe essential to the good health of an enterprise. Deliberately to stop growing is to suffocate . . . In the automobile industry, and in a number of others, the process of growth has given us large-scale enterprise, which is now characteristic of our society. We do things in a big way in the United States. I have always believed in planning big, and I have always discovered after the fact that, if anything, we didn't plan big enough. . . . I put no ceiling on progress.")

Individualism, optimism, and materialism—fine intellectual and emotional nutrients for the arrival and planting of the automobile in the American cultural ground. But there was more.

The American wastes resources and always has and if ever there was a device calculated to ride across the countryside like a plague of mechanical ostrogoths laying waste to everything in its path, it was the automobile. Americans couldn't have cared less, had they cared at all. Wrote Commager:

> The American rarely expected to stay put and had little interest in building for the future. It was easier to skim the cream off the soil, the forests, the mines—or business investments—and go on to something new, especially when new was so often synonymous with better . . . he was reluctant to make commitments for future generations, to bind them to any place, any career, any policy, or technique which might speedily be outmoded or unprofitable . . .
>
> Dazzled by the concept of infinity, prodigal of the resources of nature and of his own resources, greedy and reckless, he did more damage in a century than nature could repair in a thousand years.

And, finally, our immediate pre-car ancestors were both covetous and suspicious of education. Everyone should go to college, but intellectuals were held in contempt. We did not like or trust experts, and we do not now like being told we may be making mistakes.

We are not so much different now from what we were then, although recent events have shaken our complacency just that little bit.

What so clearly differentiates the American from his global fellows is his mobility. Mobility for the sake of mobility seems to be more important than getting to wherever it is we think we're going.

Let us give Daniel Boorstin the last word:

> The churning, casual, vagrant, circular motion around and around was as characteristic of the American experience as the movement in a single direction. Other people had followed expeditions toward a definite place or a vivid ideal, in crusades, invasions, or migrations. But the Americans were a new kind of Bedouin. More than anything else, they valued the freedom to move, hoping in their very movement to discover what they were looking for. Americans thus valued opportunity, or the chance to seek it, more than purpose.

We were ready for the arrival of the automobile.

Part Two

"It isn't that we are such lousy
car builders, but rather that they are
such lousy car customers."
—C. F. "BOSS" KETTERING,
former General Motors Vice President

4 : *Mother City*

I

Detroit's last definable moment was in 1701, when it was founded as a French fort. It grew haphazardly until the coming of the automobile when it lost all semblance of reality, so that now when "Detroit" is mentioned it can mean: Lansing, Pontiac, Flint, Dearborn, Muncie, Milpitas, Kenosha, St. Louis, Cleveland, and a few dozen other cities.

The Detroit Yacht Club steam room.

Doug Fraser and Leonard Woodcock of the United Automobile Workers, John Riccardo of Chrysler, Henry Ford of Ford, Thomas Murphy of General Motors, Roy Chapin of American Motors.

Inner city desperation.

The Department of Transportation, the Environmental Protection Agency, the National Highway Traffic Safety Administration, the Special Subcommittee on the Federal-Aid Highway Program of the Committee on Public Works of the House of Representatives, the Bureau of the Census.

Arrogance.

CWC Castings Division of Textron, Ex-Cell-O Corporation, B. F. Goodrich Company, Hoover Ball and Bearing Co., Inland Steel, MacCleen's Valvamatic Auto Wash, Inc., Sherwin-Williams, Swan

Hose Division of Amerace Esna Corporation, Teledyne Continental Motors, Video Films, Inc., The Upholstery Leather Group, Wolf's Head Oil Refining Co., Ziebart International.

For the sake of sanity: the place American cars come from. Even then, it has undergone four incarnations.

The never-never land we call Detroit began as a coincidental collection of communities building motorized carriages whose sales success produced, in turn, a pair of industry leaders who presided over automobilia in a form of dual stewardship. The first was Henry Ford; the second William Crapo Durant, creator of General Motors.

While we now look upon Ford as the founder of his country, it was Durant who was busy setting the stage for the next incarnation by dealing with the production of automobiles less in terms of product than as a device around which to erect a crazy conglomerate of vertical and horizontal companies through railroad-legacy financial maneuverings. The result was alternating upheaval and stabilization of GM, its alliance with DuPont, Durant's departure, and the arrival of Detroit's first king, Alfred P. Sloan.

The growth of Detroit, inconsiderately interrupted by World War I, was even more inconvenienced by the advent of World War II; and yet after that global annoyance came what one automotive writer has called Detroit's Golden Years, the Imperium.

The outside world was forever interfering. Detroit could not and did not expect that the Imperial City would be brought down around itself and a curious new republic would result from a nonsensical little family dispute in the Middle East in 1973.

Four incarnations; they bear examining.

There has been a frantic pursuit to establish the birthplace of the automobile. That discovery is less important in terms of being able to understand that contemporary Detroit is really (in geographic terms for simplicity's sake) St. Louis and the GM assembly plant there, or Lordstown, Ohio or Milpitas, Calif., than being aware that *yesterday's* Detroit wasn't much different in this sense from today's. It was Springfield, Mass., where the Duryea brothers (Charles E. and J. Frank) built what is at the moment considered the first successful American car in 1893; it was

Kokomo, Indiana the next year, courtesy of Elwood P. Haynes and the Apperson brothers. The Duryeas *sold* their first car in Peoria, Illinois in 1896, and then came the flood. Cars were built in Cleveland (Winton), the Boston area (George E. Whitney and the Stanley brothers with their steamer), Bridgeport, Conn. (Locomobile), Tarrytown, N.Y. (Mobile).

By 1899 there were thirty American companies building and selling cars, according to the U.S. Census of Manufacturers. Professor James J. Flink, whose *Car Culture* is going to be viewed as a pioneer work a century hence, tells us a third of these companies, mostly building steamers and electrics, were in New England, but, "The remaining firms were equally dispersed between the Middle Atlantic states and the Middle West, which even then was the center for the manufacture of gasoline automobiles." Says Flink, "Within a decade it would become obvious to the general public that the keynote of twentieth-century American life was automobility." (Professor Flink takes the term "automobility" from John C. Burham, who coined it in a piece he did in 1961 called "The Gasoline Tax and the Automobile Revolution" for the *Mississippi Valley Historical Review*. Flink defined it as "the combined impact of the motor vehicle, the automobile industry, and the highway plus the emotional connotations of this impact for Americans." That seems broad enough.)

There are almost as many industry histories as myths that credit Henry Ford with the introduction of modern manufacturing methods, cost cutting, early technical breakthroughs, the $5 a day wage (to which many refer as the dawn of enlightenment in management/labor relations in automobile manufacturing) and the Model T, which is thought to have put America on wheels.

Much of that is true, but not all. If we take James Flink's dates: 1905, the year in which the annual New York Automobile Show "was the nation's leading industrial exhibit" and 1907, when "the automobile was commonly referred to as a necessity" and split the difference, the 1906 curved-dash Oldsmobile, which sold for $650, was in its fifth year of volume production making it this country's first big seller. The Ford Motor Company wasn't organized until 1903. Ford's Model T did not appear until 1908, but once arrived it stayed for nineteen years.

In the meantime, W. C. Durant bought Buick in 1904, built

the first high-speed engine (4,000 revolutions per minute as opposed to the standard 1,800 rpm) in the industry, built the largest automobile factory under one roof in the country, a fourteen-acre facility in Flint, Michigan; and convinced Charles Stewart Mott, who had been building axles for Buick and other companies, to move from Utica, N.Y. to Flint. He laid the foundations for the building of Buick and Chevrolet in Canada, which is to say the beginning of GM Canada, by granting R. Samuel McLaughlin the rights to use the new Buick engine in his car. By 1908, when the Model T succeeded the Model N, Buick outbuilt Ford 8,820 to 6,181. Add Cadillac's 2,380 production to Ford's, and Buick was not only the number one company in the industry, but larger than the next two combined.

Buick's venture into racing antedated Ford's and was impressive and successful. Louis Chevrolet, Wild Bob Burman, and two of the other factory drivers won half of the road races staged in this country in two seasons. Before 1908 was over, Durant had collected around his Buick factory in Flint the W. F. Stewart body plant, Imperial Wheel Works, the Flint Axle Works, the Flint Varnish Works, and the J. B. Armstrong Company which made springs for automobile suspensions. By the end of that year, Durant had created something called General Motors, had bought Oldsmobile, had entered into negotiations to buy the Champion Spark Plug company, and had merged Buick and Olds into GM, which he had formed as a New Jersey holding company.

Still, it was Henry Ford who emerged from the bewildering welter of 515 separate companies as the industry's leader; Henry Ford who built the "car for the great multitude," salivating by this time at the prospect. When Ford committed himself to selling the Model T as a static model in his new Highland Park Plant with every cost-cutting and time-saving method possible, he pointed toward a time, just eight years distant, when the car would sell at $345 for the runabout and $360 for the touring. It was what America had been waiting for.

In the first year of the new century, motor vehicle registration was estimated to be eight thousand. Ten years later it was almost half a million.

Americans had spent the previous century building the loom for a Fordian magic carpet. By the turn of the century, they were busily rearranging themselves to take advantage of the product. The last two decades of the nineteenth century saw a substantial shift in population from the country to the city. By 1890, three American cities (New York, Chicago, and Philadephia) had populations of a million or more. Thirty years earlier, there were no such megacities in America. By 1900, when there were only eight thousand cars in the nation, there were three and a half million persons living in New York, which had become the second largest city (to London) in the world.

It may seem laughable to us now, but when we started our current one hundred years there was much concern that populations could no longer be contained, that they were growing faster than they could be accommodated, that crime and corruption in the cities were raging out of control, and that the object of an urbanite's life was escape from the crowds, the noise, and the blight whenever possible.

The automobile would provide the way.

Henry Ford himself had said, "We shall solve the city problem by leaving the city."

If the alleged burdens of a turn-of-the-century New York provoke a groan of despair today, consider the irony of the argument that cities whose mobility was dependent upon horses were unhealthy places in which to live, but that motoring out of them could provide a solution, particularly since driving was a "splendid energizer of the human frame."

Flink: "In New York City alone [in 1900], horses deposited an estimated 2.5 million pounds of manure and 60,000 gallons of urine on the streets every day. Traffic was often clogged . . . by the carcasses of overworked dray horses. . . . On the average, New York City removed about 15,000 dead horses from its streets each year. A 1908 estimate that tried to take all factors into account concluded that the cost of *not banning* [author's italics] the horse from New York City was approximately $100 million a year."

That wasn't the worst of it. Medical authorities were very much aware of the connection between horse effluvia, horse pollution, horse scrappage and the day's health problems: dysentery, diarrhea, and tetanus. The February 10, 1912 issue of the *Literary Digest* quoted a London doctor in a piece entitled "The Healthfulness of Motoring" that was meant to lay the worries of

American public health officials to rest. Motoring promoted good health, he said, but ". . . to grasp the underlying causes needs a little thought . . . the circulation is stimulated by the increased pressure of the wind acting on the body, the effect being enhanced, moreover, by variations in its force." That was no bad claim, but it wasn't quite enough to make the case so far as the good doctor was concerned. "One of the most direct and noticeable results of motoring is its power of curing insomnia. . . . there are certain mild forms of heart disease which are undoubtedly ameliorated by motoring, due possibly to the enriching of the blood." Motoring also, the doctor maintained, cured baldness and dandruff. The American health establishment loved it.

If that is an extreme example of the absurd claims made for the automobile, it would be wrong to exclude a genuinely serious hope held out for it which would be repeated and repeated, rarely to our benefit and often to our detriment. The automobile was seen as the great healer of the rural-urban schism in American life. All the barriers between the isolated, burdened, ignorant farmer and the hectored, hyper, cultured city dweller would be smashed by hordes of Model T radiator shells (bumpers optional) pouring through in both directions. The result would be a happy homogeneity, the best of both worlds.

Had the early twentieth-century seers been talking about that later invention which now stares balefully at us from our living rooms with its cathode ray tube eye, they might have had a point. But at least in terms of getting goods to the market and manufactured products to the hinterlands, they were right. As a people mover the car worked, but we would have to wait for television to become a global village.

Perhaps the social and cultural schism was not healed, if heal is the right word for what you do to the ingredients of a milkshake in the blender, but a physical barrier *was* crossed. In that crossing we learned much, exacerbated many problems, created new ones, and solved one or two—primarily those involved in the movement of goods. We were also so enchanted with the idea and with the device that made it possible, we failed to see that we were encouraging the insatiable hunger of that midwestern devil we were beginning to call Detroit, while all the while it was professing to fulfill ours—a little problem that has remained as the philosophical conundrum of the marketplace ever since.

Detroit's first anointed monarch was given a course in the divine right of kings by his General Motors boss, Pierre S. du Pont, successor to W. C. Durant. But he had learned a good deal more about the automobile business by watching Durant and Henry Ford.

When Alfred P. Sloan became head of GM in 1923, the Ford Motor Company was pointed downhill, although no one knew it. Sloan himself has told us a great deal about his philosophy and his manner of implementing that philosophy in his book *My Years with General Motors*. It is regrettable that the world cannot peer over his shoulder as Alfred P. Sloan reads about the effects of his reign in Emma Rothschild's *Paradise Lost—The Decline of the Auto-Industrial Age*.

Sloan was a brilliant manager. He recognized GM's structure so that the now familiar step-up system of divisions existed within the corporation; Chevrolet to Pontiac to Oldsmobile to Buick to Cadillac. In addition, he established GM Corporate, a central planning and policy group. But his greatest moment was the annual model change.

For that, Rothschild gives him full marks, "After the 1920s investment boom [the industry] began to find increasing difficulty in improving the efficiency of Fordist technology," as well as difficulty in labor relations and in competing with newer, more sophisticated industries which "had developed technologies that allowed a much greater increase in capital and productivity," she says. The result was that in the early '20s Ford's market share was about 50 percent; that is to say the Ford Motor Company sold half the cars in the country. At the same time GM's share was only 25 percent. A decade later GM, changing models to sell more cars, had half the market and Ford was left with only a quarter.

Sloan and GM were selling; Ford was still manufacturing.

GM priced its cars at the top of each market segment. If the public perceived the market to be built in levels, like a multi-layered Baskin Robbins ice-cream cake, with cheap cars, low-priced cars, medium-priced cars, crypto-luxury cars, and Taj Mahals, GM's entries would be the biggest, gaudiest, richest, most expensive entry in each group. Henry Ford continued to build black Model Ts, cutting their price time after time and wondering why it didn't do any good.

According to Sloan, "The core of [GM's] product policy [lay] in its concept of mass-producing a full line of cars graded upward in quality and price . . ."

Rothschild is blunter and more accurate: "Sloan's idea for upgrading consumer preferences was that automobiles should change each year, and should each year become more expensive . . . Cars of the same shape and size, made from the same basic metal parts, could be sold with different equipment at different prices."

"It is perfectly possible," Sloan had written, "from the engineering and manufacturing standpoint, to make two cars at not a great difference in price and weight, but considerably different in appearance . . ."

In pages following we will discover just how refined this technique has become, so that GM will build one basic body shell and one engine and market it in four of its five divisions under four different names as four distinct cars, convinced to this day that people don't or can't tell the difference. The practice is common in Detroit, which then wonders what has happened to brand loyalty.

While Henry Ford was hewing to the Calvinist ethic of cash on the barrelhead, Sloan was pushing and promoting an idea of William C. Durant's installment-plan buying. The Guaranty Securities Company had introduced credit buying at the retail level in 1915 in Toledo and by the next year was financing the sale of twenty-one makes of cars. Durant's GM responded with the General Motors Acceptance Corporation in 1919. Henry Ford would go this far and only this far: four years after GMAC was begun, he instituted a plan through which a prospective buyer would subscribe to a weekly payment until he had saved enough to buy his car.

Perhaps that alone says enough about the difference between Ford and GM to explain the flip-flop in comparative market share.

The annual model change was certainly the single greatest impetus to the creation of an underside to the retail automobile business, the used-car market. As hard as it may be to believe, auto manufacturers and dealers at first did not like the idea of a market in secondhand cars since all they could imagine was that used cars would take away from new car sales. They came not only to accept it but to wallow in its excesses.

Daniel Boorstin commented: "Sloan's annual model, and the accompanying ladder of consumption [the buying and selling of used cars], came closer than any earlier American institution to creating a visible and universal scheme of class distinction in the democratic United States of America." Well, isn't that what kings are supposed to be about?

Emma Rothschild sees Sloan's annual model change and the upgrading of cars as having become a "world-wide model for the selling of consumer goods." Sloan showed the world, according to Rothschild, ". . . how to create and nourish demand. Refrigerators, stoves, television sets, electric typewriters are now, each year, better, fancier, and more expensive." Sloan could have a far worse epitaph than that given him in *Paradise Lost*: "[His] strategy . . . had much the same relationship to subsequent automotive history as Fordist assembly-line technology had to the development of auto engineering."

To Sloan the "dynamism" of GM was that cherished invention that is his, all his, which we now call planned obsolescence.

II

"When people are able to leave problems of bare survival behind, they are freed to aspire to fantasy symbols for gratification."

Dr. Herbert M. Greenberg wrote that in *Automotive News*'s 50th anniversary issue, its *Prologue to the Future*.* The anniversary came in 1975, but consulting psychologist Greenberg's words might have been more trenchant had they come twenty years earlier.

If ever there was an era in which Detroit could properly have been called the Imperial City—with imperial aspirations and imperial dreams—it was in post World War II. Business was cyclic; but business is *always* cyclic when you're selling automobiles. Bess and Harry, Ike and Mamie, fins and brightwork panels and three-tone paint jobs—well, why not? If the President of the United States could wear Hawaiian shirts on the lawn of the White House, couldn't our cars wear the equivalent?

Automotive News is the industry bible and one of the few automotive publications with some vestige of integrity. It also makes very clear that, existing as a trade publication to Detroit and Detroit's dealers, it serves a second master.

Fantasy symbols? Fantasy symbols? Cadillac had high and sharp tail fins. Oldsmobile's rear fenders were so loaded with pot metal that the cars looked as though they would go down by the stern at any moment.

Chevrolet extruded the Corvette with the "Blue Flame" engine.

Ford answered with the Thunderbird and, horrified to discover it had a clean, uncluttered little car on its hands, added an outside spare tire cover, portholes, and eventually turned it into a car that rivaled the *Queen Mary* in size. Chrysler had a Wurlitzer-like keyboard on which to play Snooky Lanson while shifting automatically. John Keats called them *The Insolent Chariots*:

> Ah, the Midwest! Land of simple plowmen! No doubt it was the Midwesterners' immemorial custom of attending agricultural fairs which led them all to think in terms of the biggest pumpkins, and thus to believe that if it's the biggest, it's the best, no matter whether this means digging the world's deepest sunken garden . . . or building the world's biggest, gaudiest cars . . . alas, [the automobile] was brought forth in greatest numbers in the expansive, slap-dash world of Babbitt and Elmer Gantry. Now, it has given the Midwest's culture to the nation; Detroit has shaped us in its image. Today, most Americans join in the shout, "The biggest means the best!" and the echo responds from Detroit, "More of the same"!

Emma Rothschild's echo of John Keats is very cool, very impersonal: "Modern upgrading, and 'selling more car per car,' made it possible for the auto companies to maintain the value of the auto market; in order to increase auto sales they developed, by contrast, a new style of variety marketing, the marketing of second and third cars."

Rothschild is not to be understood to be saying the consumer was an unwilling victim. In fact, if we were being exploited, we not only were unaware of the fact, we were euphoric. "More car per car" meant automatic everything: transmission, brakes, steering, seats, temperature.

All this helped Detroit to sell just over nine million vehicles in 1955, of which more than seven million were passenger cars. We would not see the likes of such a sales blitz for almost a decade.

But to sell that many cars, the industry had to use methods and devices that allowed American buyers to see its face. Pre-war Detroit may have been insular and provincial, it may have been imperious and arrogant, it may have been incestuous and uncaring, but it was only after the war that the American public began to understand the industry and its attitudes.

The Imperium showed itself for what it was beginning with the great seller's market when the land was parched for the outpouring of automobiles it had been denied during the war years. Cars were sold for the list price, which included a handsome profit of several hundred dollars. Dealers then added a "pack," which represented no value at all, but gave the seller trading room. On top of that came as much as $1,000 under the table for really desirable models. If the customer balked, he was shown the door.

The dealer, who was himself behaving like some great smirking spider to whom his victims were forced to come by their own Sloanist need, was being treated in an equally high-handed manner by the manufacturer. The builder could only convert so quickly, he distributed what cars he could manufacture to favorite dealers according to bizarre and arbitrary standards and then, when the great seller's boom began to falter at the very time his own production was burgeoning, he delivered cars whether the dealer wanted them or not. It was no idle dealer complaint that transporters, filled with unordered cars, would mysteriously appear in front of their places of business, unload, and drive off, only to be followed by another fully loaded transporter and then another. If the dealer didn't like the system, Detroit told him he could damn well get out of the business. And if he wouldn't get out of the business himself, the manufacturer would put in another dealer right next door and force him out.

Sloanist marketing reached its zenith beginning in 1955 and lasting almost twenty years thereafter. John Jerome, a former automotive writer whose stomach eventually turned to the point where he wrote a book called *The Death of the Automobile* from a hideaway in Vermont, is convinced that this postwar boom is marked most clearly by the abandoning of all pretense at making the car a utilitarian object and by the indulgence, on the part of Detroit, in grotesque, outré, and outrageous excesses.

In his view, all America wanted a Cadillac, and Detroit

therefore set out to give Cadillacs to everyone. Fords, Plymouths, Hudsons, and especially every car built by General Motors was somehow an imitation Cadillac. "The Cadillac has been called, appropriately enough, the essence of all that is avaricious and trivial in our middle-class life style. And so it is a tenet of Detroit's faith that the highest good is served when the industry makes every car an imitation Cadillac."

Even after the next sales downtrend had come and gone, Detroit was still practicing its Let's Make A Cadillac game, but it had become both more sophisticated and more desperate, since the ersatz Cadillac market had been largely saturated.

It was in the early '60s (although the genesis of the strategy had come with first division of the market into pieces very early in GM's development) that Detroit hit on what it decided was the ultimate solution. Out there in the world, concluded the marketeers, there was not only a single market, not only several markets, but an infinite number of markets.

Detroit was no longer selling cars. It was selling demand, not as it existed, but as Detroit invented and promoted it. Thus there was a market, and a market demand for station wagons for suburban housewives; utility cars for salesmen; luxury cars for managers; performance cars for the young; imitation Cadillacs for the masses. Beyond those were the sub-segments: austere station wagons for housewives who lived close to the city but not in affluent suburbs; station wagons with a little more trim for housewives who lived somewhere between the tacky suburbs and the nation's Grosse Pointes; and luxurostation wagons for the housewives who lived in Grosse Pointe. There were absolute minimum utility cars for salesmen of tenpenny nails; utility cars with two strips of chrome for salesmen of ladies ready-to-wear and for salesmen of jewelry; utility cars with as many bangles and beads on the outside as the salesmen inside were carrying in their display cases.

The real explosion of what Detroit called "market proliferation" came with pop-demography and the "identification" of endless demographic groups, each with a need for a separate car, which led to the building of such absurdities as the American Motors (formed when Nash and Hudson merged in 1955) California Marlin, representing (if it can be analyzed at all) some belief on the part of American Motors that: (1) there was a market for a certain kind of intermediate car; (2) that this intermediate car had to seem to be different from the company's regular intermediate car and therefore warranted the investment in tooling to give it a new fastback look; (3) that since it didn't really need to be very different but only seem to be different, it would have to have a new sporty name, hence "Marlin" instead of a variation of "Rambler"; (4) "California" was a magic word in Omaha and Des Moines, so the car would have to seem to be made especially for the place of everyone's dreams, the Eden to which the whole country was migrating. That in turn mandated the old Rambler with the new fastback and the new name should have some exotic identifying mark which turned out to be wood-grain decal trim glued on its side. With all this done, AMC hoped, America would think that since this car was built for the gods and goddesses of California some of the stardust would rub off if it could be owned in Kansas or Ohio; (5) finally, it would come only in certain colors to underscore all of the above.

That the Marlin bombed was no fault of Detroit's, Detroit concluded. It was the idiots who walked into the AMC showrooms and didn't understand what a terrific deal they were being offered in a brand-new, glamour car just for them at a mere few hundred dollars more than its plain Jane sister.

Two things made belief in the magic of model proliferation possible: one was purely mechanical, the other philosophical.

The British word is "rationalize." They also call it "Badge Engineering," and what they mean is simple enough. Build three basic bodies, says rationalization, and perhaps two engines, and then supply so many options and so much (slightly) different sheet metal, and so many different variations on the theme, that instead of three basic cars with two basic engine choices you have an almost infinite number.

With "youth" cars in particular, Detroit had a field day with this Mechano kit: a Mustang's option book was so long, so numbing, that not only could a buyer build it himself, but, according to one critic, there wasn't even "... a dung-regular Mustang any more." Now this was fine for the buyer who knew what the "K73 option" was and whether or not it fit with "performance group A" with the 3:11 rear axle, but what of the poor sucker who went in to buy a plain, ordinary Mustang? Sometimes he got a drag racer and sometimes he got a six-cylinder go-to-the-market car. "Build it yourself" had a lot of drawbacks.

Model proliferation ended up driving everyone crazy. Dealers hated it because they couldn't sell what they had on the floor; their inventory didn't fit the "exact need" of the buyer any longer. The buyer didn't like it much, since he may have been flattered to think of a whole industry waiting to build him a special car, but he was no engineer and he was ill prepared to decide what he needed. And Detroit ended up very ambivalent about it, since it turned around and bit back. Once people became convinced that the cars already built were really built for someone else, and they could have their very own, distinctive, personal car, they frequently became reluctant to buy anything that wasn't specially ordered for them. Jerome cites a Yale University physicist who calculated, in 1965, that Chevy offered (through minor changes in several basic bodies and engines) 46 models, 32 engines, 20 transmissions, 21 colors plus 9 two-tone combinations, and more than 400 accessories and options, so that the number of different cars a Chevrolet customer could conceivably order was greater than the atoms in the universe.

So much for the mechanical aspect of Detroit's marvelous ability to provide everything for everyone. More important was the philosophy of its doing so and the effect of its ability to so provide.

Detroit perceived it was satisfying the need of a marketplace. Never mind that the marketplace was the product of Detroit's own understanding, a creation of its marketeers as much as a clay mockup was a creation of its styling studios. Detroit insisted that it was satisfying a demand. Having done so, Detroit then decided that its technological wizardry in supplying so complicated a demand was reason for not only self-congratulation, but self-satisfaction to the point that Detroit and only Detroit had been able to decipher the white water flow of consumer needs. Thus, any questioning of the way it went about its business was not just presumptuous, it was heretical.

Two stories, one probably apocryphal and the other now the matter of much dispute, reflect the insular, self-importance of the industry in the post war years. True or not, they are recited with pride in Detroit because they reflect Detroit as Detroit likes to think of itself.

It is said that there was a gathering of industry leaders just after World War II in the Cadillac (sic) Hotel in Detroit to determine policy in terms of reconversion from war work. Henry Kaiser, who may or may not have been invited but who had been enormously successful as a shipbuilding innovator during the war and who had decided to enter automobile manufacturing, was there. At some point in the discussion, Kaiser volunteered that since the building of cars had always represented the real and symbolic bulwark of the American Industrial State, Kaiser Industries intended to become a part of the automotive establishment and he was prepared to commit to an initial investment of $20 million. There was a moment's silence, the story goes, at which point a voice from the back of the room said, "Give the man one white chip."

The second story concerns the alleged conspiracy on the part of Mack Truck, General Motors, Standard Oil of California, Phillips Petroleum, Federal Engineering, and Firestone to buy up the trolley systems in forty-five cities and replace them with bus routes owned and operated by subsidiaries of the listed companies. Those bus systems were tied by contract to buy equipment and maintenance materials from their masters and only from their masters. One theory holds this was a conscious conspiracy to eliminate mass transit from the American landscape; the other says it was merely a conspiracy to do business in an efficient if illegal manner.

The courts (district and circuit) held with the jury finding that the defendants were guilty of conspiring to monopolize "that part" of interstate commerce consisting of all busses, tires and tubes, gas, oil, and grease used by public transportation systems in forty-five cities and sixteen states. The courts of original jurisdiction and appeal did not find any conspiracy by GM, Firestone, and the rest to deprive the nation of its metropolitan rail transit systems. One of those forty-five cities was Los Angeles, which had a splendid mass transit system and now has more cars per capita than almost any other city in the world—and fewer busses.

The actions by the great companies say much about the mind set of Detroit and its willingness to pursue its interest—the making of profit—to the exclusion of public good.

III

The empire crashed in 1973. Sales would fall by almost half, hundreds of thousands of workers would be laid off. Detroit's establishment had seen none of the danger signs. While the consumer rebellion was making up in the late '60s and early '70s, while OPEC was gathering itself for an ultimatum during the Yom Kippur War, while the Congress had passed the twin Highway and Traffic Safety Acts of 1966 and established the Department of Transportation and the National Highway Traffic Safety Commission (later Administration), while environmental groups were looked upon less and less as fringe group lunatics and were being more and more felt within the electorate and the various state legislatures, while competition from other luxuries—swimming pools, boats, vacation houses—was getting more and more fierce; while all this was going on, Detroit continued to talk to itself in the steam room of the Detroit Yacht Club and on the fifth tee at Lochmoor Country Club, each company manager reassuring the other that they were doing the right thing, that they understood as no one else understood, that even if they had begun to approach the second decade of the Imperium, the end would never be in sight.

There was one warning they all heard loud and clear, and all of them either ignored it or were so infuriated by its message they dismissed it.

Brock Yates was a youngish journalist working for a magazine called *Car and Driver* which catered to what it chose, in the snobbish jargon of its trade, to call "enthusiasts." Yates, who at thirty-five looked like a world-weary narcotics agent, was well known in Detroit and, in turn, knew Detroit well. In early 1968, he approached his editor with the idea of doing a definitive piece on the collective mind of Detroit, with a working title of "General Motors and the Overdog Phenomenon." At that time, the magazine was free to do much as it chose since it had used an unorthodox style to achieve a startling growth in a short period of years and its parent company, Ziff Davis Publishing, evidently concluded this was due to its iconoclasm and left the magazine and its editorial content alone.

Yates came back with a piece eventually entitled "The Grosse Pointe Myopians," whose lead illustration was a pair of horn-rimmed glasses with the lenses shattered.

"Myopians" told Detroit it didn't understand nor did it want to understand. It told Detroit it was in trouble; that a combination of management insularity and a change in consumer attitudes was a forecast of doom. It talked about the insanity of model proliferation and quoted a Ford man as saying, "The Ford Division of Ford Motor Company has had three sales bonanzas since 1960. First came the Falcon, then the Fairlane and the Mustang. When we started, we had a 23 percent share of the market, and now, after all that hoopla, we've got 20 percent. So what the hell did we prove?" There it was for even the blind to read: a Detroit manager telling Detroit it was wallowing in some kind of insane marketing frenzy. Detroit disbelieved.

"Myopians" told Detroit its forecasts of ever-increasing acquisitiveness by Americans in terms of new cars was a lunatic confusion of data with knowledge, citing anthropologist Margaret Mead who postulated that a manager's actions are (Yates' quote) ". . . based on the fact that his independent thoughts and actions are satisfied by the sea of data in which he swims." Detroit read Yates on Mead and wondered what in hell an anthropologist had to do with selling Dodges and Fords.

"Myopians" told Detroit that its image of itself was reflected in the cars it built. And that ". . . all Detroit cars are designed and conceived on the basis of the White, Anglo-Saxon, Protestant world in which the auto executives live." Detroit didn't really understand why Yates bothered to state the obvious since (although they were, by then, a little wary of saying it) they still took as the first article of faith that what was good for General Motors was good for America.

"Myopians" told Detroit the consumer, if not already in revolt, was about to be; about to understand he had a choice in the spending of his money; about to understand there were other kinds of cars from other countries he could buy; about to understand that owning a new car every year was no longer the equivalent of a bath in the fountain of youth. It quoted C. F.

"Boss" Kettering's famous comment on the marketplace: "It isn't that we are such lousy car builders, but rather that they are such lousy car customers." Detroit nodded and murmured its reaffirmation of the Kettering wisdom.

During the same time that Brock Yates was researching and writing his "Grosse Pointe Myopians," the product planners at Chrysler Corporation were firming up recommendations for a whole line of big, new cars to be introduced in 1973 that would be enough like General Motors cars to solve one of Chrysler's nagging problems: It was always behind, and it was always too far away from GM to sell well. Those big cars, introduced at almost the moment of the arrival of the oil embargo, damn near sank Chrysler.

At Ford, a study had been initiated to forecast what the company should be contemplating in 1980 by way of product. The study was being done by one man, Irv Rubin, who had part-time assistance from a marketeer and an office. Ford got lucky with both Rubin and his forecast, but no thanks to his company's belief in him.

General Motors was still smarting from having been caught using private detectives to follow Ralph Nader, the man who blew the whistle on its small Corvair. For many reasons—now probably including corporate disenchantment with any little car—GM was leaving all plans for a small, a really small, car on the back burner.

As of the spring of 1976, Detroit managers were finally at ease with the Grosse Pointe myopians because the world has given them no choice. There are signs of a renewal, more properly resurfacing, of pre-Vietnam, pre-Depression, pre-Watergate, pre-payoff scandal arrogance with the resurgence of market strength. Worse still, most of the industry's top management to this moment doesn't know how close their *Titanic* came to the iceberg. But Detroit will never be the same again.

IV

Chrysler's executive suite sweeps the length of the sixth floor of the K. T. Keller building in its Highland Park Plant. It is in the shape of a "T," the crossmember occupied by offices of a variety of nondescript vice presidents and the sturdy, stern, longitudinal hall giving off onto the offices of the great. When Lynn Townsend was chairman of Chrysler, he had installed a complex device for entry to the entire floor. From the elevator, the visitor faced a forbidding pair of doors with a panel imbedded in the wall by their side. It was a small panel with a keyboard, and it looked much like an enlarged, ingrown mini-calculator. Only by pressing a random series of numbers in a precise sequence on the panel could the doors be made to unlock. It was the translation of the secret password to the computer age, and without the password—which meant without the requisite escort who knew the password (which might change weekly)—Lynn Townsend's world could not be entered.

The elevator, the doors, and the panel are still there, and it is still necessary to endure the ritual of the panel's mechanical challenge.

But now Chrysler people don't often bother going up that side of the building to get to the sixth floor. These days, on the *other* end of the building, access to the same long top of the "T" hall is completely, totally open. You walk through the revolving doors on the ground floor and ride six flights of escalator straight up.

There is one specific exception to the nameless, faceless vice presidents whose offices occupy space along the top of the "T": he is Richard Kimball Brown, executive vice president for North American Automotive, Chrysler's number three man behind Chairman John Riccardo and President Eugene Cafiero.

He is a tallish man, whose bulk comes not from size but from the quality of his presence. Although R. K. Brown began his career in the automobile business—"Detroit" on the West Coast—and has spent his life in it, more than anyone else at the top he is representative of the new attitude, the thoughtful, rational member of the freshly born republic. Riccardo, called the "Flamethrower" behind his back, and Cafiero are both too evocative of the old Detroit to venture ideas that might be deviationist.

R. K. Brown, who may be the only senior management man in the industry who actually lives in Detroit instead of the posh suburbs of Bloomfield Hills or Grosse Pointe, is not in the least hesitant to be outspoken about the industry's faults, present and past.

It is almost shocking to hear, in one of those enormous offices that house Detroit's aristocracy, words that unequivocally reveal an understanding of the real world. "The American people have changed a hell of a lot," Brown says. . . ."the [sales] boycott [of 1974-75] was a shock to the industry." And while that can be dismissed as the words of a practical veteran dealing in a practical matter who may well have been as imperialistic as the worst jingoist in the industry during the Golden Years, he soon dispels the suspicions.

"We are chewing up the raw materials in the world in a terrible way. We use more energy in America than anybody else does. We know that. I mean, by God, you don't need three bathrooms or five bedrooms in a house. You know, you need to ask yourself where you're going to stop. It chews up a lot of wood and ceramics and energy, making all those toilet bowls."

R. K. Brown may rail against government intervention, but that is rote; the weary litany of the lifetime churchgoer telling his beads with his mind on something far removed. "I know you have to have regulation," he says with a grimace, "but I mentally fight it. It is an abhorrent thing for me to see." They are the words of a man who has taken in a partner to keep his business alive and who regrets that he must add another name to the letterhead where his once stood alone. They are not the words of a revisionist in a jail cell.

Most important, R. K. Brown knows the industry has changed and he is at the very least resigned to it. Perhaps GM could make a $350 million Edsel-like mistake and survive, but not Ford and certainly not Chrysler, much less little AMC. He thinks of the conglomerates of the '60s, of Ling Temco and of Boise Cascade, acquiring and combining and acting out a capitalistic scenario totally devoid of any social considerations, and he shudders at the thought of the consequences should anyone do the same today. It is easy to translate this train of thought to Brown's understanding of his company's responsibility to its customers. "Any big company can go flat down [his boss, John Riccardo had earlier said the same thing, pointing to the Penn Central]. . . . on the other hand, I think everybody is so conscious of that possibility that nobody is going to make a big mistake . . . . we can't be too arrogant."

R. K. Brown knows damn well what the industry has done to alienate the public and knows even better the nature of the change that is needed. He hopes the industry is producing the cars people want. Of one thing he is absolutely certain: Brock Yates's image of a WASPish Detroit has got to go. "Certainly by our advertising—and everything else—we created that image. We used to put the car in front of the country club and use phrases about it like 'an achievement car' or a 'recognition car.' You don't do that anymore."

Of all the companies in Detroit, Chrysler was hardest hit by the upheaval that began in 1973. Of the management types in the industry, Brown is one of the likeliest to have learned from his company's trauma.

The same is not true of a square, gruff man a block away in Chrysler's Highland Park plant, the company's chief engineer, Alan Loofbourrow. Loofbourrow retires soon, and it is just as well. If he had his way, there would be a one-way line between Detroit and Washington over which the likes of Alan Loofbourrow would issue orders to the federal government and through it to the American buyer.

"They're holding our feet to the fire," is the way most Detroit executives put the federal requirements that car engines be both emissions free and economical—a mutually exclusive set of requirements in their view. The leading advocate of the "feet to the fire" interpretation is Loufbourrow; he carries it like a guidon wherever he goes. Ask Alan Loufbourrow who should design cars, who should determine their shape, their cost, and their usefulness and there isn't the slightest thought in his mind that the car's eventual owner might want to be consulted.

"That is a highly technical question." Loufbourrow has a cold, and he sniffles and snorts, pours water from a Calvin Coolidge water thermos, takes a huge gulp, and launches into what is certainly his favorite theme. "A technical, technical question. It has been technical for a long, long time. The industry has understood the technical part of an automobile, but very few people outside of the industry have." (Inevitably Boss Kettering's quote pops up on the screen of the mind.)

"In the first place, it wasn't necessary to [understand] and in the second place, what good would it do for them personally as an individual to really understand the technical [aspects] of a big business venture?"

As expected, after a good half of the contents of the thermos has been inhaled, after innumerable harumphs, Chief Engineer Loofbourrow gets around to the dreaded feds. "On this little spaceship we call earth, which is a finite amount of mass, there's only a finite amount of petroleum. Nobody knows how much that is because we haven't located it all. The advocates [the government people who want emission free engines that are also economical, the environmentalists, and the consumer advocates are all lumped into one category Loufbourrow refers to as "the advocates"] are doing their best to prevent trying to find additional oil supplies. They have been very effective in delaying the availability to the public of known oil supplies."

Loufbourrow has been in the automobile business for forty years. He says that for forty years "advocates" have been crying conservation, and yet there have always been new finds. He is confident there will be still more, but he concedes there will be an end. But when? He wants to know and know now so he can plan.

Any Loufbourrowian solution would require a kind of cooperation that seems to be confined to industry cooperating with industry and nobody else. Lord knows he doesn't have much faith in the government: "I saw something the other day I had trouble believing is correct. But it was printed; unless it's no more accurate than other printed material, it probably isn't correct. But it said 60 percent of the national budget was committed to servicing the public debt. When it gets to the point where all the tax money is . . . used to pay interest, what is the government going to operate on?"

That seems to say, although it is difficult to tell, that the press (which isn't to be believed) has given him incontrovertible evidence on which he can write off the government as an effective partner in the solution of the energy problem.

But he wants to be plainer than that: "Either we change the kind of social system we're using in this country or we find a way to make it work. Right now, most of the efforts I run across are apparently dedicated to not making it work or preventing it from working. People talk of profits as if there's something immoral about making money. This is ridiculous."

It has become very clear we cannot look to the industry to solve our problems. Detroit's attempts at perfecting clean engines through the use of stratified charge (twice-burned fuel charge) engines have been, after fifty years of trying, embarrassingly feeble. Whereupon the Japanese did in a very short time what Detroit couldn't or wouldn't do: stuffed the engine in a Honda Civic, licensed some American companies to build a similar engine, and passed emission tests by the Environmental Protection Agency with the highest marks ever given. Detroit has been no more successful with the allegedly mutually exclusive problem of making an engine emissions free *and* economical, a riddle Detroit professes is beyond solution, but that Volvo solved (*using American technology*) with a catalytic converter developed by Englehard, which builds converters for Ford and GM. In this fashion, Volvo produced a car ten times cleaner than any that had been submitted to California's Air Resources Board and got 10 percent better mileage than any previous model.

Harumph.

At Pontiac, one of the divisions of General Motors, Division General Manager and company Vice President Alex Mair at least gave lip service to the need for change in an interview with Eric Dahlquist of *Motor Trend*. He seemed to say many of the same things R. K. Brown is saying. Why did it take a multiple crisis to change the industry, Mair was asked and he answered, "In January your wife tells you that her mother and father are coming for a week's visit on July 4th, and she suggests that it would be nice to paint the kitchen.

"About April, you get around to buying the paint and brushes. And then, if you're like most people, you find yourself up all night on July 3rd painting the kitchen. That's human nature.

"These crises happen in our personal lives . . . they happen in our business lives. But you know, there's something very interesting that happens in situations like this. American ingenuity and progress always seem to come on strong in response to pressure. In a very real sense, this is our night of July 3rd."

Well, maybe. But maybe there were further reasons for Pontiac's night of July 3rd. Detroit is thought of as a one-industry town; in fact, it is a one-company town and that company is General Motors. Implicit in Alex Mair's talk about painting the kitchen for the arrival of parents-in-law is the admission that the industry needed change. Alex Mair did *not* talk about the change that Pontiac required as a result of what R. K. Brown saw as a

marketing disaster. In 1973, Pontiac Division registered just over
800,000 car sales; two years later, it managed just over 457,000. Its
rise had been almost as spectacular. In 1961, Pontiac's sales were
about 370,000; five years later they were 830,000. "Pontiac went
way up,"says Brown. "And Pontiac went right down. I have never
seen a division go down so fast." So with giant GM looking at one
of its principal profit-producing areas behaving like a leaping
tarpon on the sales charts, July 3rd could well have *been* crisis
night in the kitchen, as Alex Mair suggests, but that was likely
only because it was in the kitchen that the knives were kept. It is
clear from what GM chairman, Thomas Murphy, says that his
company knows the world has changed, and you can bet that if
the commanding general is saying it, the corps commanders are
repeating it. But they don't have to like it, and if GM's investment
of $3 billion by 1980 in tooling and plant changes to build smaller
cars is pretty solid evidence that they mean what they all say
about a new world, they're not talking about much other than
product.

Alex Mair on the 55-mile-an-hour speed limit:

> We have taken a step to modify the forward advancement of the
> country. . . . I don't think we should continue doing that. The nation
> needs a return to its feeling of leadership. Part of that is to lead in all
> things that we do. And, since the transportation system is a key to a
> nation's system, whichever nation exceeds in transporation is going to
> be a leader in other ways. and I think we Americans need to be and
> should want to be leaders . . . . We shouldn't look forward to the year
> 2000 and decide we're still going to be moving our system around at
> 55mph. That is not fast enough to retain leadership as a nation.

What difference does it make if we've managed to reduce the
death rate on the highway by 10,000 per year by instituting a
55mph speed limit? What have we lost in the dollar value of time
wasted lingering along the road—*malingering* along the road when
we should rush, rush, rush to leadership?

Leadership of what? What "forward advancement of the
country" is Alex Mair talking about that we have so impeded? The
forward advancement of Pontiac Division's new marketing approach which emphasized "performance," the sale of its wildly

decaled Firebird TransAm sports coupes and its Sunbirds, tricked out to look like spaceship race cars, perhaps?

R. K. Brown, John Riccardo, Alan Loofbourrow, Alex Mair are all middle-aged (or older) men who have passed through a recent period of great revolution. Their reactions tell us much, but if it is Detroit's future we wish to examine, it is probably more productive to talk to younger Detroit, to 1985 Detroit.

Although it is becoming rare that engineers rise to dizzying heights in the Detroit pyramid, at lower grade levels they sense the industry's pulse as well as anyone. They deal in hardware instead of sales hokum; if there is a real world anywhere inside the industry, it is theirs.

Andy Gilberg is a Grade 7 engineer for Ford; his friend Larry Parker is a Grade 9. Grade 7s don't make decisions; Grade 9s do.

In the rigidly stratified system, each is accorded perquisites according to his grade: The price category car each is permitted to lease at the special employee rate, the size of his office, the color of his carpet, whether he is deserving of a window or must stare at a blank wall. Parker is not yet thirty; he may well find himself a division general manager and vice president before he is given his gold watch. Gilberg is older and, until recently, he has deliberately refused to rise above the grade he now holds since he would then have become a part of "management," his time taken up with policy instead of routine. He is not sure he has made the right decision. Parker is wiry, dark, and intense, with a strong lower middle class New Jersey accent.

Gilberg might easily be the model for a Walt Disney movie about an absentminded engineer. Give him a problem about suspension systems, ask him what might happen if an air bag deploys prematurely and the driver loses control of his car, and Gilberg will launch on a lucid, felicitous, engaging description, all so logical, all the technical problems and intricacies so easily and carefully put into precise lay terms, that it would seem here is the rarest of men, a technologue who is more human than android, more at home with language than with mathematical symbols. But depart from his specialties, and suddenly Gilberg is an alien in a hostile world. He can't quite find the right word for "fork"; he literally misplaces the front of his house and, walking from his car to the house's side or back instead, bruises his forehead by bumping into walls. Gilberg is cripplingly deficient in those simple skills that even a six-year-old has learned. His mind is elsewhere.

Both Gilberg and Parker race automobiles. A seemingly terrifying thought in Gilberg's case, except that racing, to him, is a kind of engineering, so we are safe. Gilberg's car is a single-seater, open-wheeled car with a top speed of perhaps 140mph. He is a competent amateur racer, placing generally in the middle of a forty or larger car field with less than the best equipment. Parker is not so ambitious. His competition is confined to smaller, less demanding events, and his car is a modified street sports car.

It is clear from their racing that both Gilberg and Parker are taken with cars as machines, as leisure devices, as expressions of their competitive urges; as symbols of something far more than mere profit-producing modules. This catholic view of the automobile suggests that if Gilberg or Parker or older Gilbergs or Parkers were running the automobile industry, their focus would be on something beyond the bottom line. Such men might be receptive to alternative transportation devices (indeed, Parker worked with the Department of Transportation as a liaison from the Ford Motor Company when D.O.T. presented an exposition of such alternatives), but if not that, they would certainly understand that people use cars and think of cars in very definite and specific ways. From there, it is not a long intellectual journey to the conviction that the people who do the buying are the people for whom cars should be designed.

Would a Gilberg or a Parker, age forty or forty-five in 1985 and sitting in high councils, suggest that perhaps Ford Motor Company did not know best after all, that the industry might build cars that would genuinely suit the needs of the car-buying public? Would Larry Parker, vice president, perhaps even president of Ford, pick up his phone one day, ask for a conference call with Ralph Nader, the Secretary of Transportation, the executive director of the Sierra Club, the National Automobile Dealer's Association and utter the word "detente"?

Gilberg's living room in his tract house in Ypsilanti overflows with warmth and optimism about the future of the industry. The Ford Motor Company is infiltrated, both Parker and Gilberg agree, with people who *like* cars, people who are willing to see cars as they are and as they should be. One in ten Ford management-level employees is enthusiastic about the auto-mobile, they guess, but they are willing to be realistic about it as well. Ten percent is not a bad cadre for a fifth column. Almost immediately, prospects for a rational future begin to plummet.

Gilberg thinks that when "people escalate" within the company, their enthusiasm and their open-mindness tend to disappear. "More of their time is spoken for in job responsibility," is the way he puts it.

Parker begins to express some bitterness. He is a nuts and bolts engineer whose responsibility (shared with some few others) is to see that the cars designed by Ford can be serviced after they are designed and built and bought. He sees prejudice at his level in favor of engineers who are involved in something called "product planning," a loose, ill-defined activity that requires its practitioners to put a package together that embraces the will of the stylist, the nuts and bolts engineer, the sales people, and the accountants. They are master compromisers and Parker, who does not like them, nonetheless sees their place as important. "You know [Ford] thinks there are a lot of guys out there with calibrated butts who can tune a suspension [but] there are very few guys who can make smart decisions about what products we should make. I'm not sure I totally agree with that, but that's the way it is. So upper management has a lot of product planners and very few hardware types."

Parker is bright and young and far enough along in the company already so that he may well realize an ambition. "I think I can be an exception to the system." He went to school in the '60s and that taught him it was possible to be a revolutionary. It is dislocating to sit listening to entrenched, industry-employed, Detroit-indoctrinated men talk about making top level decisions that take the *car* into consideration as being "revolutionary processes." Is this the renaissance manager in embryo?

For a while it seems there is more than just willingness to view Detroit's products as cars that can be changed, modified, built to suit needs; or built in fewer numbers; or built to conserve energy or raw materials. Parker approves of governmental intervention in the building of cars. "I think the government has heightened [management's] social consciousness or accelerated its social consciousness." But he also thinks that social consciousness was there before the government got in the business of making cars sane devices.

"The auto industry is probably [best] equipped to tell the government what the intent of the law ought to be."

We might have needed a law to prod the industry along, to force it to build safer cars, but the law is best understood by the industry, best interpreted by the industry, best regulated by the industry. Echoes of Alan Loofbourrow.

But how about the dreamer, Gilberg? "You know, cars interact with people so you've got to consider that when you design them. People may be dumb, the population as an average may be dumb, so the car has to be designed [that way].

"In fact, it might be a form of negligent behavior to sell good cars to the general public. Look, suppose you gave everybody a car that feels like a Corvette and little old ladies think that they can punch the throttle and zap around six cars in traffic and start doing it? They don't have the reflexes to control a car that has that kind of capability.

"Then you have a terrible situation out in the real world . . . with people who have high performance cars and low performance reflexes."

But that's an extreme. What's wrong with a plain good car that doesn't behave like a rocket, but brakes properly and handles properly and accelerates properly, a car Gilberg and Parker themselves would be pleased to drive? "We've never designed a car to be exactly the way it should be in every respect for the average man," Gilberg admits.

That seems so atavistically arrogant, so defiant of *any* kind of reason, even Detroit reason, that Parker rushes into the breach. "It's the art of compromise. The automotive industry has a very elaborate system of determining or quantifying what all the compromising is . . ."

"Yes," Gilberg picks up, "the things that determine what make the car competitive in the marketplace. Not the things that make it necessarily safe in the hands of the average flake on the highways. *That has never been a consideration in the design of cars . . .* (author's italics)."

To which Parker adds, "[Top management] has an objective, and the objective isn't one of being responsible to the society to the degree that you're not a successful business. The objective is to remain in business.

"... the job I have is selling something that isn't very quantifiable, serviceability.

"To the extent that I can show what the competition does or what the adverse effect is going to be on warranty [costs], I can win a battle ... but if you can't show [that what you're advocating] will really sell more cars, you've lost the battle."

Grade 9 engineers and Grade 9 civil engineers and delicatessen owners fighting City Hall and Air Force majors lose a lot of battles. But what if those majors become five-star generals, those delicatessen owners the mayors of their towns, the civil servants presidents, or the Grade 9 engineers company vice presidents?

Hypothetical question to Larry Parker: "What would you do with the problem of car serviceability if you were in a position to make some ultimate decisions?"

"I might be willing to fight a battle for a car where you have to take apart the front end to service the engine. But everything is a compromise; [up there] the compromises would be different."

We are hearing Larry Parker and Andy Gilberg, the class of 1985, tell us that to change Detroit is going to take a long time. "It's not Utopia," they both say, but they're content to work within the system and to support the positions of the industry. It is hard to believe, should either become one of the great leaders of Detroit, that his views would be any more considerate of his constituents—the people who must buy his products—than are the views of the men who run Detroit today.

V

"Paternalism" says the gray-haired man in the office with a view of the Detroit River. He says it with a most curious combination of resignation, humor, tolerance, and scorn in his voice.

"They [Detroit's managers] just knew better than the public"; and then this man, who seems so weary, so burdened by a lifelong battle, so small as he sits behind his desk, arises to what seems an astonishing height, standing straight before the long table in an office not so large as the chairman of Chrysler's, but major management large, and with an almost predatory smile finishes his sentence, ". . . except that the American public is now teaching them a lesson. That they have minds of their own."

He is Douglas Fraser, vice president of the United Auto Workers, and but for the swing of one vote and his own willingness to defer to the union's board, its president and successor to Walter Reuther. Instead, Leonard Woodcock is president of the UAW. There is a consensus that on Woodcock's retirement, Fraser will succeed him.° With the UAW divided into departments corresponding to the major manufacturing entities, Fraser is UAW's man for Chrysler Corporation affairs.

He remembers it all, from his own start on the line through the battles to establish the union, not only within the union membership but the bitter, bloody beachhead that had to be established with the corporations. He remembers each strike, each war; for wars are what they were. And he speaks of the union's victories with his hands cupped in front of him, as if holding every bitterly won trophy.

They have drifted together, these labor and management antagonists. They are closer in view now, much as wartime nations which have fought centuries to a standoff reach an unconscious commonality with each peaceful interruption. Like those nations, Detroit and the UAW know these peaceful years are exceptions, as each side, gasping for breath, husbands its resources to renew the fight.

Meanwhile, on both sides, the leaders grow in understanding of their immense responsibilities and, as they do, come to feel a near respect for their antagonists.

How many enemy generals could sympathize with the structural weaknesses of their opponents? "I think that a lot of people don't realize how large Chrysler Corporation is. I keep telling myself, I suppose because it gives one self-comfort, 'Well, if it really comes to it, would the government stand idly by and let it happen, see Chrysler fail? Would we have a repeat of Lockheed? A repeat of Penn Central?

"But I am not too sure of this [the Gerald Ford] government. This government's so committed to the free enterprise system, without exception, and I disagree with them in terms of their economic philosophy. But at least they *have* a philosophy, even if

---

°As of January 1977, this was all but a formality.

that philosophy is somewhere to the right of Herbert Hoover. . . .

"This administration might just let them die."

But that mood lasts only a moment until a blast of the fire of those early union–management wars is rekindled. "There is only one way to discipline the auto industry. To do exactly what the American people are doing. To revolt."

Fraser dismisses any hint that the sudden move to small cars and the sudden move *from* small cars—recessions and boom in the last few years—constitute just another cycle in the cyclic world of automobile sales. Two things are happening, Fraser says. The first is a recognition by everyone—the builders and the buyers—that there is a limit to fuel. And the second is that the car no longer represents what it once did. Gone are both the searchlights which used to illuminate new car showrooms at introduction time and the concept of the car as status. Fraser is also sure that the suffocating paternalism of old-time Detroit is slowly disappearing.

In fairness to management, he thinks people drive large cars because they *want* to buy large cars and that "Detroit/Madison Avenue snow jobs" are not entirely responsible for the dinosaurs that clog the highways. Still, Fraser is not willing to let Detroit completely off the dinosaur hook. "[Detroit] still assumes it knows what the American consumer is thinking. I don't think it does know. I think it has made enough mistakes to make that point." Detroit, thinks Fraser, should be willing to listen rather than to tell.

And yet he hedges even on that. "Telling" instead of listening is the way it used to be, he says, but he is not sure it is absolutely that way anymore.

"In fairness, I think the attitudes that predominated have dulled.

"[Those attitudes] were that the only reason [for existence] was to produce more, to make more profit, to provide greater dividends to the stockholders. That was their mission and that was their sole task.

"Some people say that in this area the 1967 riots changed attitudes in the auto industry; that since then there has been a greater degree of social consciousness. Whether or not that is a fair assessment in the sense of being a motivating factor is arguable.

"I think Henry Ford II can make a pretty good argument that

he had a sense of social conscience before that time and I would agree with that assessment."

Fraser would say the same of Roy Chapin of American Motors, but, ". . . the other two [the retired Townsend of Chrysler and Richard Gerstenberg of GM] would have more difficulty making the case."

Since that time Fraser sees a change for the better in Detroit so that now he is willing to say of his old and his new enemies, "In terms of their attitude toward their responsibility to the communities in which the plants are located ... there has been a considerable improvement . . ."

But paternalism and the inertia of the bureaucracy cuts both ways. The UAW is a big, big union. It is certainly paternalistic and even Doug Fraser concedes it is bureaucratic. It is the nature of an institution, he says—federal, corporate, or union—to be reluctant to change its ways; its manners, and its habits. It is a great weakness, and he deplores it at the same time he celebrates what his union has done for its members.

Fraser wants it known that, contrary to much that has been said and much that has been written, the presumption that every man who works on an assembly line has somehow lost his dignity and his individuality is not correct at all.

"Let me say that working in an auto plant [and Doug Fraser, who started in one would know] is tough work. That is true of most jobs, the overwhelming number of jobs. There is no featherbedding in the auto industry.

"Most cars come at you sixty an hour, and you are doing a repetitive job. You are putting on sixty left front wheels an hour—maybe the lefts, fronts, and rears on one side. It's a monotonous and repetitive job [and that makes it very hard] for a worker to get a sense that he is making a contribution.

"It is difficult, I suppose, to get from that kind of operation a sense of satisfaction and achievement, which I think is very important in individual work."*

---

*It is important to understand that only about 25 per cent of blue collar category auto workers actually are on assembly lines. ". . . the image of assembly line work as symbolic of the total character of auto industry factory life is misleading. . . ." says B.J. Widick in *Auto Work and its Discontents*. Widick, now a Columbia University professor, speaks first hand. He spent 15 years as an auto worker at Chrysler.

Rick King would do something more than just agree with that.

King worked in a Ford plant in California, in a sanding booth at the Milpitas assembly works. Now a filmmaker, he wrote about the UAW and one of Doug Fraser's "repetitive jobs" in the *Washington Monthly* in 1976.

He was told, he wrote, that if he didn't have any guts he'd quit the first day. He almost did. He was told that he'd come to hate the job so much that he'd "... hate Ford, this plant, your foreman." He did. King's job was to hold an air sander in one hand and sandpaper in the other, removing metal burrs or blobs of paint from one side of each car as it passed in front of him. Three men besides King worked in the booth. "The four of us adjust," he wrote. "The work is always physically exhausting, like playing a game of football or soccer. But the real punishment is the inevitability of the line. I want to take a walk, go to the bathroom, have a Mr. Goodbar. It doesn't matter. There's always another car."

The noise, the repetitiveness, the sense of being no more an individual than a component in the car in front of you is overwhelming on an assembly line. Sabotage is the most frequent recourse.

Wrote King, "Sabotage against the cars themselves is common. As a matter of course, we used to force the trunks closed in a way that ensured the cars couldn't be painted properly ... Every day, mirrors are smashed and quarter panels are ripped. The art lies in sabotaging in a way that is not immediately discovered."

And later, he defines the chilling dynamic of work in the auto industry.

"What makes the assembly line work efficient is fear, not engineering ... Once inside the factory, the fear system is immediately apparent. Every problem becomes a crisis because it threatens to disrupt the smooth flow of the line."

But isn't this what the United Auto Workers exists to ameliorate? Sure, as Fraser says, the jobs are tough. "No featherbedding," he says. But if the UAW wars have not at least compensated in money, or in dignity, or in benefit of some kind for this desperately oppressive work, why have they been fought?

This is King's answer: "Of course, all locals are different. Local 560 can be characterized by my own representative, who spent ten minutes one day delineating the problems of the auto industry to me. The root of the problem, he explained, is that workers are lazy. . . .

"A few years ago, someone was killed in Body Section. A piece of machinery fell on him. The story is that the chairman of the Health and Safety Committee presented his regular report at the next meeting a few weeks later. He didn't mention the dead man. When asked why not, he pointed out that the man hadn't filed a grievance. Consequently, he couldn't investigate the problem."

Emma Rothschild's exhaustive analysis of the 1972 strike at the General Motors Chevrolet Vega assembly plant at Lordstown, Ohio, gives emphasis to what King wrote. "Worker grievances at Lordstown concerned not only the speeding up and intensification of jobs, but also the disciplinary character of plant management: workers must ask, and wait, to leave their jobs for one or two minutes; must ask, and wait for permission to get married on a Saturday; must show a doctor's note if they stay home when they get sick; or a note from the funeral director when they go to their father's burial; or a garage bill if they arrive at work late because their car broke down."

In some muddled effort at understanding what had happened in a plant GM had boasted would be the most efficient in the world, one company labor relations executive said (quoted in Rothschild), "Changes in the social environment are affecting our business in the area of motivation and behavior of employees," and Rothschild goes on to cite GM's attribution of a higher percentage of educated and minority groups in the labor force as being contributory to the strike.

It is likely Doug Fraser would agree; it is certain he would fiercely condemn General Motors Assembly Division, which took over the running of Lordstown, for its nineteenth-century repressive attitude. But Fraser has seen it all before, and it is not the educated to whom Fraser feels attached.

He looks upon those hundreds of thousands of UAW employees, who were not only laid off but ran out of their supplementary unemployment benefits, the SUBs that the UAW fought the industry so hard to get, as his constituents. And in the ugly days of the 1974–75 depression, he saw them literally starving.

Yes, he concedes the mindless, dehumanizing aspects of

working on the line. "The worker's mind is elsewhere; he occupies himself with other thoughts. I know I did. I never concentrated on what I was doing. I learned the job and my mind was a hundred miles away.

"I think that's the way you beat the system.

"On the assembly line you are a captive except for the relief periods. . . . But then, in the auto industry there are also the skill trades ... where you use your initiative. A dye maker, an electrician is a tremendously talented individual.

"And, you know, the auto worker gains a sort of economic security that other people in our society don't. A very high percentage own their own homes."

It is no bad accomplishment, Fraser is saying, and he documents it carefully. "GM released a figure [in the fall of 1976] that labor cost is now $10 an hour. Included in that is what we call statutory benefits: the cost of unemployment compensation, social security, and so forth.

"If you carve that out, that would probably be about 60 cents an hour, so you are talking about $9.40 an hour. Over $1,000 (total per year) of that is premiums for the health plan and it is a very, very good one in the auto industry.

"We are one of the few groups in our society that benefited during the last couple of years of horrendous inflation; the absolute purchasing power of the auto worker has increased."

If Fraser were to confront King he would make a convincing argument: In the early days of the industry, workers came from Europe, ". . . so that no matter how difficult it was here, it was relative clover. And that is one reason the kids in there today have a higher education." Now aspirations are higher. Rightly so, thinks Fraser, but there is an unfortunate side effect. A bright worker graduated from high school and with ambitions to go to college thinks, "I really shouldn't be here. I should really have gone to college."

"It seems to me," continues Fraser, "that this has an effect on their attitude and they are saying to themselves, 'I am really better than this.' "

As for King's life of despair: "I suppose," Fraser says, "it depends on an individual's alternatives. Maybe this is an unfair way to use figures, but in the depths of our layoffs there were

200,000 to 230,000 people unemployed. When call-backs began, nearly everyone showed up. Nearly everybody responded to a call, which is highly unusual.

"Now you could argue that this is not because their jobs are so satisfying, that it was really because they had no alternatives. But I think there's a middle ground."

Fraser was saying there was little job satisfaction in King's understanding of the word. But there were jobs and they were jobs people could live with and live by.

Finally, Fraser would answer King and Rothschild on the subject of the UAW's service to its members by citing its history as a pioneer warrior on the broad front in matters affecting all labor: pension programs, supplementary unemployment benefit programs, health programs. He is proud of that. "We have been innovators. We took on fights other unions didn't. We attacked on a philosophical front, in a principled fight."

Doug Fraser, Leonard Woodcock, and Detroit are poised for perhaps the final long battle: ultimately it could be the battle that will change Detroit more than Fordism, Sloanism, the Golden Years of Empire, or the shock of the consumerquake.

The union is closing in on worker participation in management of the automobile industry. It will be as bitter a fight as either side has experienced; Doug Fraser will probably not live to see it won or lost. He thinks it will be won, and the odds are on his side.

It is that fight—the joining of the assembly line worker, the craftsman, the foreman, in decision-making processes—that holds whatever promise there is for the incorporation of the automobile industry into mainstream America.

For Detroit has come to pander to this country's worst instincts in the name of pursuing national goals and mobility and individual freedom. It has built a country within a country in which even its young rebels are cajoled, enticed, and smothered.

It has fought control by government, by the marketplace, by social pressures in as fierce and chauvinistic a fashion as the worst remnant of the most repressive empire.

Detroit made addicts of us all, and having given us a drug to satisfy our habit, it has encouraged us to increase the dosage a millionfold. Our addiction is wildly out of control, and we have the great midwestern pusher to thank. If now the drug factory is threatened, if now it has begun to realize the awful consequences of its acts, there still remain tens of millions of addicts in the nation both crying for a cure and fleeing it.

There remain, too, the thousands of mini-factories called dealerships. The word is appropriate. Detroit's dealers hustle customers daily in every crossroads in the land. Detroit chooses to see these multimillion annual transactions as one great happening in what it calls the marketplace.

5 : *The Marketplace: Field of Combat*

There, on the big, *big* screen in the showroom of the MGM Grand Hotel in Las Vegas is Mt. Everest. In Vegas, Mt. Everest, even projected on a screen, is bigger than the Himalayan Mt. Everest.

A jagged, superimposed road runs up the mountain's side, along which, at spaced intervals, are flags with numbers on them: 15,000; 28,000; 40,000, and so on. The road stops before it gets to the top of the mountain. Where it ends, there is another, and last, flag. It reads: 87,000.

Standing on the stage is a man with a vision. At least that is what he is booming into the microphone to the packed house. "I have a vision!" he shouts, pointing dramatically to the mountain on the screen behind him. "We will reach the top of the 100,000 mountain!"

The man with the vision is the national sales manager for Fiat of America. In his audience there are more than 4,000 Fiat dealers, their wives, mistresses, hangers-on, and families. Ever so subtly, Fiat is telling those people, whom they had flown in from all over the United States and Canada, that it would be nice to sell 100,000 cars by the end of the calendar year.

Six months later, in Scottsdale, Arizona at the Mountain

Shadows Inn ($55 a day for a single room), the managing director of Rolls-Royce Motors is talking to *his* dealers, flown in from the United States and Canada. He, too, has a vision. It would be nice, he says, gazing at the ice-carved statue of the Rolls-Royce hood ornament that decorates the hors d'oeuvre table, if his dealers thought kindly of the company's new offering, the $90,000 Camargue. He would try, he tells them at dinner, to see that at least forty become available for sale in the United States during the coming year.

Whatever the car, however high or low its price, the annual sales blitz begins with men from the factories telling their dealers they have visions. Before the cars can be sold, the dealers have to be.

At the end of 1976, almost 1.5 percent of the dealers in the United States having gone out of business in the previous year, there were 24,453 of them left. Calculating very roughly that 80 percent of all households in the United States have one or more cars—about 48 percent have one car, about 27 percent have two cars and about 5 percent have three or more cars—and the nation has a passenger vehicle population of 109 million, the result is almost 25,000 dealers arrayed against a number of persons who equal the population of perhaps three Canadas. A mismatch? Not exactly, for the car dealer in America is as close as we come, these civilized days, to being a professional gunfighter. This view—not entirely overstated—holds the automobile dealer to be the anointed ruling elite of the marketplace. It is he, not the customer, who walks the showroom floor with spurs jangling.

Visible in Muncie, in Detroit, in Los Angeles, in every city and crossroads town in the nation, the dealer is the storm center of the conflict between the buyer and the manufacturer. He performs the act of selling, but it is hard to categorize him in any absolute terms as the seller. Yet, despite being the recipient of more Better Business Bureau complaints than almost any other businessman in every community in the nation, the dealer is as much a victim as he is a predator.*

We will discover that the dealer's return on investment is

---

*Again in 1976, the national Better Business Bureaus crowned the automobile the country's number one consumer complaint champion—more Americans complained about the car than any other single device they owned.

surprisingly low, almost as low as his social position in his community.

In return, he is the target of vilification by consumer groups who see him as responsible for the shoddy practices of the industry. To some extent they are right.

He is the object of obscene courtship by the financial agencies with which he does business. They vie for the commercial paper he churns as a result of his installment-plan selling and offer him as much a piece of the interest percentage action as the usury laws will allow, minus their own cut taken off the top. This, in bankers' parlance, is called the "contingent reserve," but it is so profitable to the dealer that he makes as much as the equivalent of a full gross profit on a fourth car for every three cars he sells and "puts through the bank." The buyer does not know this, and neither the dealer nor the bank tell him.

"More New-Car Loans Set Five-Year Terms in Move to Spur Sales," was the headline in the lead feature on the front page of the *Wall Street Journal* early in January of 1976; "Next: FHA Auto Mortgage?"

"Remember when a few hundred dollars down and $100 or so a month would put you behind the wheel of one of Detroit's finest?

"Well, the good old days are back. Sort of.

"... But there's one catch: Those low payments are made possible only by stretching out the length of the loan, from a couple of years in the good old days, to four—and sometimes even five—years now. And that catch is stirring quite a bit of controversy—controversy about whether stretched-out loans are costing auto buyers too much money, whether they step up auto sales now at the cost of future sales, and whether they will induce lenders to make risky loans."

If the *Journal* is right, the buyer is paying almost as much as half the cost of the car in order to finance it, is staying off the market for an ungodly amount of time depriving the dealer of repeat business he must have to survive, and the repossession rate is likely to rise. Who wants to pay $100 a month on a four-year-old car that has been made obsolete by continued "planned obsolescence," has traveled 80,000 miles and shows it, and is costing almost as much each month to maintain as it does to pay for? By submitting to the lure of "$100 down, five years to pay," the customer has been given reason to hate the dealer, the car he owns, *and* the lending institution. The certainty is that he will not be back on that dealer's showroom floor.

Banks are critical to a dealer's business, but they are out for number one. In the case of financial institutions, number one does not sell cars, it sells money.

The dealer is regulated by federal, state, and municipal laws and codes, albeit only recently, which act as constraints not only on sharp business practice but also on perfectly innocent functions he must perform in the normal course of his activities. In many states there is a variety package of consumer protection legislation aimed directly at the automobile business and, more specifically, at the automobile *dealer*. There are laws that control the servicing of cars (California's are the model), and there are laws through the departments of motor vehicles that regulate the manner in which cars can be sold. Many states have truth-in-lending laws that are faithful but stricter copies of the federal laws. For these blessings, the dealer has his past behavior—and perhaps his present behavior as well—to thank. Not many dealers see it that way.

The dealer is the focus of the fury of a large percentage of his customers. Some are angry about the terms imposed when they bought their cars, but most are furious at the shabby service they are provided. It is not only the consumer who is ripped off in the dealer's service department. It can be the dealer himself, or it can be the manufacturer as in one instance which resulted in the murder of a factory service man found floating in the Charles River. (That extraordinary case involving a Lowell, Massachusetts Chevrolet dealer, we will come to later.)

He is publicly caressed on television and in the newspapers by his manufacturer's advertising agency, whose sparkling young copywriters and graphic designers tell his angry clientele what marvelous cars he has to sell and what an upright man he is. When Chevrolet Division spent $95 million two years ago on print, radio, and television, their intent was to lure the customer into showrooms of their retail representatives, not to make the American watching, listening, and reading public all warm inside about Chevrolet Division. That advertising, like all advertising, was expensive hyperbole. It raised unrealistic expectations. It offered—came close to *guaranteeing*—something that could never be produced. Yet when it worked, it worked on the basis of fifty years of consumer conditioning to accept promise of perfection that could not be fulfilled. "When you get a lousy room at a Holiday Inn, you don't complain to the headquarters of the company in Memphis," says the publisher of *Automotive News*, "you call the desk and raise hell. That is what the franchise business is all about." That is what franchised automobile sales is about as well, but you have a hard time telling from auto ads.

The dealer is clamped in a viselike grip by his manufacturer. "Hungry Giant: GM Provokes Battle in Industry As It Bids To Raise Market Share," read the headline in the *Wall Street Journal*, January 7, 1976. "We want all the business we can get," the *Journal* quoted GM chairman Thomas Murphy. "Cars are sold one at a time, and we plan to try for every sale." About three paragraphs down in the story, the *Journal* quoted a competitor: "If they (GM) wanted to wipe everyone out by 1980, the only one that could stop them is the government."

To sell those cars—not only GM's but everyone else's—the dealer resorts too often to methods that establish an adversary relationship between himself and his buyer; more accurately, methods which exacerbate an adversary relationship that already exists.

He discounts or he deceives; frequently both. Whatever he does, he has made an enemy or reinforced animosity. He has become an active partner in the marketplace's distrust of the automobile business. Give the dealer a great deal of responsibility for that distrust, but remember that his actions are only part of the cause.

As has been implied or explicit thus far, the dealer must also face his own past. Automobile dealers have behaved so badly in the last two decades that a burden as heavy as that imposed by the manufacturer, the banks, and the governments combined bears down upon him. It is the infrequent customer who walks into a dealership these days with any expectation that he will be fairly treated. His experience—and the experiences of everyone he knows—tell him otherwise. That all of these people may have been right in the past but that they may no longer be right is little consolation to the dealer today. He is faced with an enemy combatant, not a customer.

Who else has the customer to choose as his target?

II

The car selling establishment and the industry grew in tandem, symbiotic but not necessarily Siamesed.

During Detroit's Romulus and Remus era (the Henry Ford, William Durant stewardship), builders of cars—and remember there were five hundred or more in addition to Buick and Ford—financed the buying of the components from pre-delivery collection of money from the dealer.

Most of these companies building motorized carriages were tottering little enterprises. Capital outlay for, say, one hundred axles was beyond the limits of their treasuries. Out would go a salesman from one of the companies to visit bicycle dealers, carriage dealers, hardware store owners in cities and villages in the neighboring states. They would sell a car, or two, perhaps even more, and collect in advance. Then with the money paid by the bicycle dealers, they would scurry back to the factory and buy the parts with which to build the cars they had just sold.

The great master of this was, naturally, Durant. "Naturally," because salesmanship was Durant's long suit and tortuous financial transaction was his longer one.

In many senses, the dealer financed Detroit. First, he put up the money to buy the car. And because dealer money was used to build not just cars but to build the entire retail side of the automobile business, the automobile manufacturer—unlike the builder of other consumables—had created, all unaware, a franchise system that relieved him almost entirely of any costs involved in retail sales.

The car dealers were themselves modest entrepreneurs. In San Francisco, for example, Billy Hughson was a bicycle dealer who was prosperous but who did not preside over an enormous establishment. When Henry Ford went to him with an offer of an interest in his company in exchange for $5,000 in real money, Hughson had to go to his bank for a loan.

But the San Francisco bankers turned Billy Hughson down

when told to what use he expected to put the money; the very idea of an automobile was anathema to their conservative hearts. Because of Hughson's business reputation, however, they told him they'd lend money on his integrity, with the condition that it be used only to buy merchandise. Billy Hughson became a Ford dealer; in time, one of the biggest Ford dealers in the nation. But the opportunity to be a partner, and a large one, in the Ford Motor Company was denied him by his bank. Hughson died a rich man. He could have died a multi-millionaire.

Charles S. Howard was another San Francisco bicycle dealer, but either his bank was more generous or his purse was. When Buick asked him to become a dealer, he contracted to buy a large percentage of the company's production. Howard, who obviously had the means to be an investor in the company if Durant had allowed, chose instead a contract that would guarantee him a territory and a third of Buick's production. It is difficult to say what might have happened had Howard become a GM stockholder, given the company's tortuous financial twists and turns over the next years. But he ended as the West Coast distributor for Buick, and his wealth enabled the Howard family to become great California landowners.

GM would have its trouble with the banks soon enough. Durant would feel their brunt, but at least they were impartial in their hostility to the automobile.

It was the banks and the bankers who forced the manufacturers to seek money for the very building of their cars from new dealers. It was the banks and the bankers who made life equally difficult for dealers who wanted to buy cars. Nor did they relent much until after World War II. In the middle 1930s, one dealer went to his bank with plans for a magnificent dealership palace in the middle of automobile row in a growing city. After much agonizing and temporizing, the bank granted the loan but only on the condition that the plans be modified so that if the automobile did not continue to be a salable commodity, the building could be converted into a hotel at very small cost.

If dealers began as entrepreneur colonies, they became allies to monarchical Detroit. Many were not dealers at all, but distributors. In the eleven western states, for example, Don Lee distributed Cadillac; Earle C. Anthony, Packard; Charles S.

Howard, Buick; and James Waters not only distributed DeSoto, but had a thriving business that converted them to taxicabs and whose sales arm reached as far east as Delmonico's and the Waldorf on Park Avenue and as far south as Claudette Colbert and Fred Astaire. Waters even had his own ships in which to deliver the cabs. Waters, the ship magnate, drowned in a swimming pool at a party.

Both the industry—which is to say the manufacturers—and the dealers and distributors were in the midst of adolescence, and growing at a prodigious rate. Already, many were proving incapable of meeting the world on its demanding terms and were either consolidating or turning to other, less ulcer-inducing tasks than the building and selling of cars. Much of this industrial and commercial Darwinism was more than the consequence of mere growth; the automobile business was already experiencing demand cycles that would characterize it seemingly forever. A lot of the cyclic behavior, of course, simply couldn't be helped, no matter how enterprising the dealers, no matter how canny the builders. There was a post World War I recession, a boom and then a world-wide collapse.

The history of the dealer/distributor relationship with Detroit during these years, as well as during the years of recovery, was a history of supplying an honest demand and while doing so alternately trying to stay alive, scurrying with great sacks of money to the local vaults, and starving. As Detroit lived, so did the dealers, but distributors were already beginning to feel industry intrusion into what they rightfully considered their own province. Eventually, independent distributors were eliminated and the task of getting the car to the dealer was taken over by the factory.

In retrospect, this probably was a proper factory function all along, but recall that the dealer/distributor had financed the manufacturer in his early years. Now to see great chunks of territory—and with it great sources of profit—being preempted by newly expanded, consolidated, and healthy factories must have been galling to those individual businessmen who had created automobile retailing.

It was after World War II that alienation began. And it began with the dealers. With the exception of a few '42s, there had been no new cars available for four years. There was a car thirst across the land that is hard to imagine more than thirty years later. A new car of *any* kind in 1946 distinguished its owner as a man of influence (how else could he get one?), wealth, and power. It must have given much the same cachet as eating steak daily during the German occupation in France, with only the slight stigma of collaboration attached.

For four long war years, the dealers who managed to stay in business had existed on used cars and the few new cars they had left in their inventories. Now, beginning with a trickle of warmed over '41s and '42s, the new postwar cars began to arrive in their showrooms. The American public was waiting with the same pale, sweaty foreheads and shaking hands that characterize an overdue heroin addict looking for a hit. Almost from the moment the second mushroom cloud dissipated over Nagasaki, the lines started to form at the dealerships.

The temptation was too great. There were very few dealers who simply took names and delivered cars at a reasonable price when they became available. With demand so large and supply so short, the dealer invented a thieves' delight of fictitious charges in order to double, treble, quadruple his profit. The first was the simple, straightforward, all-American bribe. If you wanted a car, but there were one hundred names on a list ahead of you (and this would be at some rural dealer whose *year's* allocation might be thirty cars), you could be accommodated. That is if you would accommodate the dealer with $500 or $1,000 in cash in addition to the price of the car. As if by magic, your name would move to the head of the list. The bidding became lively. The resentment against the dealer grew even livelier. Some customers became downright hostile at being solicited for a bribe. But most paid it; the lure of a new car was too strong.

As the industry recovered, car sales almost quadrupled from '46 to '50. That year, the industry sold over 6 million cars.

But then another downdraft hit. Sales dropped from 6.3 million in 1950 to barely over 5 million the next year and a million less than that the year following. During the next two years, the industry stabilized at about 5 million units, but it was gathering for the great car war of 1955, at which time the Imperium began its glorious history and the dealer, as an independent businessman, lost his last claim to acceptability in his community.

It was not entirely his fault, if you are willing to accept the premise that a businessman has a right to act in whatever outrageous fashion he chooses to keep his business alive. For these were the years, the John Jerome Golden Years, in which Detroit produced so many cars that they were unloading them at dealers' doors by the megatruckload whether the dealers had ordered them or not.

By this time, the distribution was wholly in the hands of the manufacturer, who had broken the sales territories into zones. Each zone, covering in some cases part of a state, in some a whole state, in others several, had sales and service chiefs. In the car plague that Detroit unleashed in '55, the zone sales representative was Typhoid Mary. He was given impossible quotas to fill and, in turn, imposed them on the dealers in his zone. A solid one-hundred-car-a-year dealer would be given a quota double that, and no choice in the matter. If he balked, his deal would be taken away from him or another "point" (the industry term for a new location), would be put in next door to him.

The dealer's answer was The System.

The System began in the Southeast among Ford dealers. A management firm called Hull Dobbs was brought in to advise dealers on sales methods that would give them devices for stuffing cars into the pockets of every citizen in range.

Hull Dobbs (and its imitators) began with the premise that people had to be given an extraordinary reason to buy cars. The reason would be a manufactured one—a staggering discount in most cases, or a premium of a free television set or a mink stole. That would be enough to lure otherwise cautious customers to the showroom. It would also be enough, if properly practiced, to bring in an entirely new kind of customer: the man who could never before afford a new car. This was straightforward, if sharp, even corner-cutting, in its business ethic. But it did not stop there. For The System depended on two devices.

The first was the presumption that the customer, given reason, would exhibit an extension of the dealer's own money attitudes, which is to say his true larcenous nature would surface. Thus, huge sums were allocated to advertising on the local level to promote loss leaders or impossibly generous terms of sale. "Mooch" advertising would offer a $2,500 car "this weekend only" for

$1,495. The car never existed, of course. More properly the *car* existed, but the dealer (or in dealer parlance, "the house") would never sell it at that price. Or the same $2,500 car could be bought for nothing down and $50 a month—another impossibility. Or the customer would be offered, on television and in print advertising, "$1,000 more than your car is worth"—another impossibility.

That was the first premise of The System: Car buyers were larcenous at heart and therefore if they were offered something to steal, they would come in and steal it.

The second premise was far more sophisticated. It was embraced in the nature of The System itself, a highly developed method of selling a car *under any conditions* once the "irresistible" advertising had brought the customer to the door. It said *anybody* could be sold a car.

Waiting at the curb was the "liner." The liner's first job was to write a sales order, no matter how absurd, no matter how impossible of fulfillment by the dealer, no matter how bizarre. Thus, if a customer, lured by the $1,495 car advertisement, appeared at the dealership with a used car worth $100 waiting to buy the $1,495 car (which was really selling for $2,500, remember) for $1,000 and, if, in addition, he wanted $900 for his own trade-in, it was the liner's absolute responsibility to have the man sign a sales order on those terms. In the meantime, he summoned the used car "appraiser."

The appraiser, who may or may not have driven the trade-in to determine its actual worth, was charged with making sure the car the customer drove to the dealership disappeared. He might park it ten blocks away; he might hide it upstairs in a multistory dealership; he might simply throw the keys on the roof of the building; he might actually wholesale it to a used car dealer; but *under no circumstance* was he to give the customer, brought in at such cost and in so canny a manner, an escape route.

Meanwhile, the liner, sales order in one hand and customer in the other, took both to the "assistant sales manager" who was more than likely a salesman with no agency authority. The manager invited the buyer to sit in a "closing office" that was bugged. The System had a name for the "assistant sales manager"; he was called the "T.O." man, or turn-over man. When the deal was made, and it *would* be made, the T.O. man got the lion's share of the commission, for it was his job to "bust" the customer off the deal, that absurd, impossible deal the liner had written on the sales order blank and which had given the customer reason to go to the closing office in the first place.

Now, these were the days of the "price pack," another invention that is variously credited to the manufacturer through his zone sales representative or marketing vice president, a few enterprising dealers, or The System. It was a simple substitute for the post-war bribe, but very much disguised. There was no federal price-sticker law, and the manufacturer, dealing with an independent businessman, could only suggest a retail price for his product. (This last is still true.) So the dealer, instead of the relatively honest solicitation of a bribe, simply wedged a fictitious amount of money in the car's price—perhaps $500, perhaps as much as $1,500.

Notice then what the T.O. man had to work with in busting the customer off the liner's deal—the written conditions of the sales agreement:

1. A customer already in the dealership; better still, already hopeful of driving out in a new car; and that customer's signature on a piece of paper.

2. A price pack which amounted to a non-existent amount of money he could give away as either discount or overtrade. Thus if he absolutely *had* to, he could sell that $2,500 car for $1,495 if he had put in a $1,000 pack, and still make his original profit. Or, if he absolutely *had* to, he could offer the customer $900 for his $100 car and give away only $800 of the non-existent $1,000 price pack, thereby making not just the normal profit on the $2,500 car, but $200 additional. Of course, this was all done on the basis that the $1,495 TV special had been sold. It hadn't, of course, since it had never existed. So deals were always predicated on cars that cost much more.

3. In addition to the price pack, the dealer had his "Okie Charmer," the combination admiring and deprecatory name he used for his calculator—usually, in those days, a Friden. The Charmer was a marvelous machine for it mesmerized the customer. The T.O. man operated on the principle that all three elements in the sale of a car— the amount given for the trade, the cost of the new car, and the

amount of the payments—could be gimmicked in one way or another so that the customer would be dazzled into confusion. By using the Charmer at lightning speed and calculating the deal in reverse order from the manner in which the customer understood it, one of the three elements (or if he was lucky, two) would become so confusing to the buyer that the T.O. man could further manipulate the price without being caught.

4. With the office bugged, he could walk out the door, suggesting the customer talk the new deal over with his wife or family, and go next door to listen to their objections. He was then in a position to return and overcome them.

5. If the customer was genuinely incapable of paying for the car, the T.O. man would take him to the next door office of the "stick man," the finance expert, who would figure a way to get the money somehow. Perhaps it would be through a finance company with the family furniture as collateral (hence the term "stick man"), or perhaps the down payment would be borrowed from a finance company (called "the happy man" because he made so many people happy by providing money, or "the mouse man" for "Mickey Mouse deal") and the loan on the car itself from a bank.

6. If during any of this maneuvering the customer objected, there weren't many places he could go without the car he had driven to the dealership. It was gone, and the dealer would use almost any excuse to see that the customer didn't get it back.

7. The T.O. man's imagination and the lack of any regulation of business practice short of the state criminal code.

The industry went over seven million for the first time in its life, an accomplishment it was not to achieve again until 1963. Much of the credit was due to the T.O. man's seventh weapon, his imagination. Here are just two horror stories of The System in the Golden Years that illuminate the extent of such imagination.

A man who had recently arrived in a large West Coast city was lured into a "big three" dealership by deceptive advertising. He had no job, no credit history, no bank account. The liner nonetheless wrote a deal for a new car and turned him over to the "assistant sales manager." It was a Saturday and the banks were closed. There was no argument over the price of the car; in fact the man was willing to pay the price plus the pack. He had never before thought of himself as able to buy a new car but now, with the car visible on the showroom floor and the sales manager assuring him "something could be worked out," the man not only didn't question the price but was in that advanced state of buyer intoxication car salesmen call being "etherized." Never mind that he was a flake, never mind that he was a *leaky* flake. ("Leak" and "leaky" come from the vision of the ink used to fill out a credit application leaking right through the paper and leaving it blank because the person applying for credit is such a bad risk.) The sales manager proposed that the buyer fill out and sign a blank check for the down payment. But I don't have a checking account, said the man. Never mind that, answered the sales manager, we'll take care of all that on Monday. So the buyer, stars in his eyes, filled out a check, writing in the name of a local bank which he had never seen. The sales manager gave him a blank conditional sales contract or chattel mortgage to sign, filled out a temporary paper license plate and registration form for the car on the floor, pasted the paper plate to the bumper and waved goodbye as the stunned customer drove off with a car he never thought he could own, didn't deserve to own, couldn't afford to own but, in fact, found himself owning.

Or so it seemed until he called the sales manager on Monday, asking how matters would be arranged so his blank check on his non-existent bank account, "would be taken care of."

"Taken care of?" asked the sales manager.

"Well, yes," said the man. "You know, the check on the account you told me to write. The account I don't have. What are we going to do about it?"

"What account you don't have?" asked the sales manager.

"You *know*, the one you told me to say I had, the phony one I used to make up the down payment."

"You mean to tell me you *don't* have an account at that bank?" the sales manager asked with mock horror in his voice.

"What'd'ya mean, *don't?* Of course I don't," said the man. "You were the one who suggested I write that damn check in the first place."

"I don't know anything about asking, or telling, or anything else concerning your financial condition. All I know is that I have a check here written by you on a recognized bank and it has your signature on it. Now writing bad checks in this state is a felony. If that's what you've done, you'd better get this thing straightened out yourself or get your ass in here right away and let us try to keep you out of jail." At that point the man was ready to do anything. His car and his life were in ruins and by the time the dealership had finished with him, he was virtually an indentured servant. The sales manager had "rolled a car on a stiff."

The second story is even more curious. A regular Army colonel was negotiating for the buying of a car, but was offering $50 below what the dealership was willing to take. There were two similar cars on the floor, except one had power steering, one did not. The colonel wanted power steering.

So the sales manager said, "Listen, we won't tell the general manager about this, but I'll tell you what. We've got a night service shift, and I know the service manager real well. You give me $50, take the car without the power steering and tonight you come back and I'll get the service manager to slip in the power steering at no charge, O.K.?"

So far as the colonel was concerned that seemed to solve his problem. He was paying what he wanted to pay, he was getting a car with power steering. So right then and there he took the car without power steering only to discover to his humiliation and fury when he came back after dark that the dealership had no night service shift, much less a night service manager, and power steering is not an aftermarket, add-on item. The colonel was too embarrassed to complain.

The System spread widely. There were almost always two or three system houses in every medium-to-large city. Advertising on television, particularly in Los Angeles, was filled with earnest men perched on stepladders, or caressing their police dogs, or slapping the hoods of cars with sincerity, *begging* to give cars away, if only the listening public out there would give them the chance.

Primitive versions of The System were practiced by used car dealers. In fact, they had been treating customers with disdain for years. Now they could treat them with systematic disdain.

What The System ultimately established was the supremacy of the house. With all that slick processing, all that shell-game maneuvering, all those Okie Charmers, all the huckledebuck, razzledazzle going on, the buyer soon gave up. Even the toughest, most knowledgeable customer was taken by the Systems houses. In fact, it was the prayer of the practitioners of The System art that they would be lucky enough to get a buyer who thought he knew what he was doing. One such salesman, paid on commission only, had a car absolutely sold at a price acceptable to the dealer and to the customer. But not to him. The deal did not meet his professional standards. He wanted $25 more, and he spent five hours getting it. That did not seem productive, since during that five hours he might have sold two more cars and made a great deal more money than his percentage of $25, so why did he do it?

"The sonofabitch *owed* it to me," he answered. "When he walked in here he owed it to me."

To the consumer, The System legacy remains: It is the house that holds the upper hand. In no other selling organization is that the case. A consumer would no more think of being intimidated in his department store than he would be at the local Safeway. But that is not true of an auto dealership.

These days The System, where it exists, is much modified. It should not exist at all, of course, and many states have outlawed its practices. But there are still closing rooms with Okie Charmers and wiretaps. And there are still liners and T.O. men.

It is not right, then, to put the whole blame of alienation of the car buying public on the manufacturer. But it is also less and less just to blame the dealer network for past sins. With the coming of the Republic in Detroit, a concomitant change has embraced the retail establishment.

Since The System is now the exception and not the rule, the seller must now sell on the car's merits or his own charm or the need of the consumer, or not at all. The federal government's intervention (which we will examine in Part III) has drastically slowed Detroit's model proliferation. The industry is now spending too much time and money trying to satisfy the safety and environmental demands of the feds to engage in an orgy of frill and fancy, so the buyer's choice is made easier. The government has also required the dealer to sell in a more straightforward way by passing truth-in-lending laws, which means there is little trickery and foot-faking when it comes to how much a car is going to cost.

All of this is much to the buyer's advantage.

But it is also to the dealer's advantage. Since an automobile is necessary to people's lives and must now be sold in a reasonably honorable fashion, the dealer can now move back into the business community as a decent, upright member. There is legislation brewing that will promote straighforward relationships between dealer and banker. Perhaps some day he will have the same kind of relationships with his supplier, the manufacturer.

To both parties in the car-selling/buying transaction, some measure of trust has returned. But not all. Too many dealers still insist that it is the dealer who should be in a position to dictate the terms of a transaction to the buyer. This is the auto retailer's equivalent of the auto builder's arrogance—a legacy of the Imperium.

So long as that exists, cars can't be bought and owned with a sense of having participated in a normal, everyday business dealing, nor can they be owned as comfortable possessions bought at the right price from a top-of-the-deck dealer.

We are on the path to coming to terms with the buying of a car.

Dealers are on the path to understanding that cars must be sold directly, honestly, and without depriving the buyer of his dignity or his confidence in himself or the product.

Perhaps the most important impetus in this direction comes from that great alliance of 21,000 or so new car dealers called the National Automobile Dealer's association, the NADA.

Keith Crain, the bright young publisher of *Automotive News*, puts it this way, "The NADA is an enormously powerful organization. If you take all the brick and mortar, all the inventory, all the capital investment of just the GM dealer members, you have an equivalent sum to the company itself."

You also have an organization with a great deal of clout. Perhaps it was shrewd, albeit necessary, for the early manufacturers to abandon the retail side of the business; in fact to create a separate entity or series of entities to stand in their place in the market. During the early years, the Sloan years and the Golden Years, there was a sufficient commonality that, with the exception of local squabbles, the automobile industry could fairly have been said to include the retail establishment.

But when the industry began to view dealerships as chattels

and dealers as serfs, forcefeeding cars and sending out zone sales reps with big sticks, they gave the dealers more than ample reason to band together in opposition.

Thus, in November 1975, after a warranty scandal in a dealership in Lowell, Mass. and the suggestion of others of the same kind in two eastern Chevrolet zones, GM imposed harsh terms on all dealers who wished to renew their franchises. In effect, GM demanded something more than just an advisory voice in what were, after all, independent businesses. The NADA reacted with haste and effectiveness. Diplomatically but forcefully, it convinced GM to back off from a number of the particularly troublesome requirements the company had insisted upon, and in February of the following year, GM sent out a letter amending the November ultimatum. The dealers had forced GM to back down.

That was not the first NADA fight with the industry, nor will it be the last. Its importance lies in the magnitude of the victory and in what that victory represents. No longer could one speak of The Industry and mean manufacturers and dealers together. They might be in the same business, but they were not necessarily on the same side anymore.

It would be naive to expect that the dealer body stands pristine in its motives and altruistic as an advocate of the consumer against the extreme positions of Detroit.

Nonetheless, the potential is there. There is a great and powerful group that is integral in the car building/selling chain that, given reason, could champion the buyer and not the builder so long as benefit to the buyer were also benefit to the dealer. The dealer must understand where his interest lies. He must decide where his survival lies. At that moment, the moment of realization by the dealer of the nature of his constituency, we can look forward to sanity in the marketplace. Sanity in the marketplace is a long step toward taking a sane look at the car.

III

Mt. Kisco, New York, is in Westchester County, about which it was once said that an upwardly clawing New York City dweller could have no greater ambition than to own the biggest house on the highest hill in Westchester. Mt. Kisco is a pleasant little town, green inside and out. It is on the Harlem Division of the Penn Central, and therefore comfortably distant from the Hudson River (and the Hudson Division) with its depressed, mini-inner city communities.

The town itself is small. It is a service and shopping node for the half-to two-acre contractor neo-colonials ($80,000 and up) that surround it. It has a new shopping mall, where staffers from *The Reader's Digest's* baronial castle in Pleasantville spend an occasional lunch hour, and it has new car dealerships representing almost all makes. The handsomest of the lot is the four-year-old Chevrolet dealership: T. A. Byrne Chevrolet.

T. A. Byrne is Timmy Byrne, thirty-four years old, slim, dressed as though he belonged in a partner's office of the prestigious Wall Street law firm of Cravath, Swaine, and Moore. He is a liberal arts graduate of Georgetown University who majored in history.

His father and his uncles were partners in a Chevy deal in nearby (but city-sized) White Plains. Tim Byrne must have gotten on very well with his father; he must have admired him. Despite being encouraged to do almost anything else in the world but sell cars, Tim Byrne went to work for Byrne Chevrolet in White Plains. With the death of Byrne, Senior, life began to get difficult at Byrne Chevrolet. Tim Byrne continued to work there, but it was obvious that he was chafing under the administration of his uncles.

In 1973, just before the oil embargo hit, Tim Byrne managed to open his own store in Mt. Kisco. He is the new generation automobile dealer, but he knows the business the way a Las Vegas pit boss knows his tables. Like the pit boss he knows the angles and the odds.

Timmy Byrne has a capital investment of $1.5 million in his Chevy store and another $1 million in merchandise. In 1976, an improving year but not a very good one, he did about $6 million worth of business. He grossed about 1 percent of that and he confesses, as he sits in an office that looks indeed as though it belonged to a partner at Cravath, Swaine, that he makes a "comfortable living." At this moment, Byrne Chevrolet has an inventory of $135,000 in parts, $144,000 in trucks, $500,000 in cars, $62,000 in demonstrators, and $60,000 in used cars.

T. A. Byrne's customers may not be typical of customers of a Chevrolet dealership in a small town in the Midwest or the South; their median income is probably greater; many of them commute to New York City to their jobs and carry New York City skepticism around like cufflinks or earrings, but they are not far away from what the insulated marketeers within the Chevrolet Division imagine mom, apple pie, and Chevrolet customers to be wherever they might be found. So we cannot presume a skew in Byrne Chevrolet's clientele.

That is what Division thinks, and if they are right, there is a real revolution about to take place in the selling of cars. (We will look at Byrne's views of his customers in a moment, but there is time for a pause to understand T. A. Byrne Chevrolet's relationship with the factory and the degree to which the factory is able to make judgments about T. A. Byrne Chevrolet's customers.)

Chevrolet Division looks upon its Mt. Kisco store as just another franchise. Timmy Byrne defends the franchise system on a broader base than Keith Crain, the publisher of *Automotive News*, who is content to rest his arguments on the vague virtues of small business. He thinks it's "the most expeditious way the manufacturer could possibly find to merchandise and service his products. I am saying that it is cheaper and easier for the manufacturer to have the dealer sell and service his cars."

On balance, Byrne likes that; not only does he think it serves the manufacturer, he thinks it serves the dealer equally well. "Given an active dealer—an *interested* dealer, a *concerned* dealer— at the risk of sounding like Chevrolet's advertising agency, I maintain the franchise system must make a difference in the marketplace.

"The manufacturer and the buyer have no immediate relationship. When someone in Mt. Kisco buys an automobile the transaction takes place between T. A. Byrne Chevrolet and the customer. Chevy built the car, but we took the money. We are the people the buyer sees. If he has complaints, he can't get Pete Estes [GM president] on the telephone, but he can call me."

Byrne would far rather trust himself to deal with the buyer than he would trust the Division. Byrne's livelihood, the success of his multimillion dollar business, and his self-esteem are on the line. He wants no one responsible for those critical affairs in his life but himself. But he concedes that as the middle man between Chevrolet Division and the buyer of Chevrolet Division's cars, he faces any number of problems.

Completed cars leaving any one of Chevrolet's assembly plants pass through a complicated bucket brigade within the company's distribution network. The Division has ten regional offices and, within those, forty-eight zones, each with a zone office. And each zone office has its zone service and sales chief.

"The zone office is the point of contact between the manufacturer and the dealer, its sales rep determines what products you receive and in what numbers. The zone office determines further what parts you will get and in what numbers. The office, and the people who work out of the office, have a great deal of influence."

Just how much influence Timmy Byrne won't say. But there are strong clues. If the service manager in the Massachusetts dealership was able to kite $600,000 worth of false warranty claims (which is to say defraud Chevrolet of $600,000 by counterfeiting claims on non-existent cars or charging work off to brand-new cars still on the showroom floor), it is almost certain he did it with the knowledge, if not the connivance, of the zone rep.

But that is service department fraud. Widespread as it is (as we're about to find out), it is not the only embezzlement that takes place within a dealership with the knowledge, if not the insistence, of the zone representative. "Favoritism and kickbacks are ways of life in new-car business, where field men hold heavy hammer over selling dealers in key distribution sectors. To wine and dine factory guys is every dealer's modus operandi—that is if he wants extra consideration on popular models and less 'thoughtfulness' on dogs [difficult-to-sell cars]," said the industry newsletter *Motor News Analysis* after the Massachusetts scandal broke. That scandal resulted in a dramatic housecleaning by Chevrolet in the zone offices affected. Zone employees were called into motel conference rooms and divided into seemingly arbitrary groups. In the first room, Chevrolet Division officials asked for credit cards, keys to company cars and, from a map on the wall, determined the cost of a taxi ride to the discharged employee's house, and paid the fare on the spot in cash accompanied with a pink slip. In the other room, the Chevrolet people did the same thing, and then told the employees to wait for the people from the District Attorney's office.

"Thus, extensive publicity about Chevrolet's Boston, New York, and Detroit mass firings . . . developed nothing new in what automakers and their dealers have experienced for many years. Warranty reimbursement padding? Gift certificates, turkeys, and booze? Freebies at massage parlors and expense-paid trips to Nassau? *So what else is new?*", asked *Motor News Analysis.*

"What else is new" came from another member of the Chevrolet group in the affected area only after she had extracted a promise that her name would not be used because, ". . . after that man was killed, I am actually terrified of being hurt if I say anything."

Some zone sales reps don't allocate cars, she said; they sell them. On the surface that seems only reasonable, but they don't sell them on behalf of Chevrolet Division; they sell them to line their own pockets.

"Take a dealer in a place where there's lots of snow in the winter. He has a lot of demand for the Blazer [Chevrolet's four-wheel-drive vehicle] and there are only so many to go around. So if a dealer wants one, the zone guy tells him 'it's going to cost you $500' and what he means is that it's going to cost $500 over and above the price Chevrolet charges the dealer with the money going straight into the pocket of the zone rep."

Corvettes, in notoriously short supply, can bring up to $1,000 in under-the-table bribes to the rep from the dealer. In hard times, the dealer doesn't have much choice if he wants salable cars.

"I think what happened," she said, "is that after this thing with the warranties, Chevrolet unzipped the whole thing. They took a look inside all the zones in the country and couldn't believe what they saw. So they just zipped it right up again and nobody's heard much since."

That is not exactly true. The November franchise agreement about which the NADA complained so bitterly came at a propitious moment for Chevrolet. The five-year franchise agreements were expiring and, given the Massachusetts experience, GM came down hard.

The *Wall Street Journal* outlined the new provisions of the agreements along with dealer understandings of what some meant in its issue of October 30, 1975.

"The company [GM] ... is requiring all dealers to sign [the new agreement] by Saturday if they want to stay in business." Among its provisions, according to the *Journal*:

> NADA analysis of the requirements concluded that a dealer could be put out of business for false warranty claims (as he could have under the old agreement) but "severely limit(ed) his defenses by making him liable for false statements submitted to GM by his employees regardless of whether the dealer knew about them or not."
>
> ... That restitution had no effect on GM's right to terminate.
>
> ... That GM could "yank a franchise" without discussing the dispute with the dealer prior to doing so.
>
> ... That dealers would be required to keep two years' worth of records to be used as GM saw fit which, the *Journal* quoted one New York dealer as interpreting to mean, the company arrogated to itself, "... wider power to investigate its dealers, or to help others investigate them."
>
> ... That dealers would be required to tell customers in writing when parts other than those made by the company were used in repair of the car. "Some dealers see this provision as a GM effort to end dealers' use of cheaper, private-label items bought from parts cooperatives. A Minnesota Chevy dealer charges: 'They're trying to protect their parts business and this looks like a license for them to overprice without competition,' " said the *Journal*.
>
> ... That further NADA legal interpretations saw GM as trying to "... force dealers to participate in advertising and promotion programs, including rebates; to set up car rental or leasing operations—even to move to a new location."

Some of these dealer contentions were doubtless true as evidenced by GM's retreat from its hard line ninety days later. Some of the provisions in the original GM contract were clearly in the customer's interest, or could have been if used to curtail or stop, for example, the use of sleazy ripoffs of parts by unscrupulous dealers. Forcing some dealers to open books to investigative agencies of the various states can hardly be thought of as an invidious gesture by GM toward the buyer or even the honest dealer. But the point is that the company was using muscle, and a lot of it, in sometimes arbitrary pursuits.

Industry muscle, says Byrne, still is used so that cars not ordered can be shipped, as they used to be in the golden days. A dealer not selling his quota (which may be totally unreasonable) might be told his nearest competitor is selling right up to expectations, and until he, the underachiever, begins to sell as many cars as the factory thinks he should, he isn't going to get salable merchandise. Another dealer might be put in next door and that dealer might belong to the factory and therefore be getting his cars much cheaper than the independent.

The establishment of so-called factory stores is done in Chevrolet through a GM division called Motor Holdings (at Chrysler through the Dealer Development, or DD program), and often it is a perfectly straightforward proposition. Motor Holdings finances a bright, budding entrepreneur in a new point or at an old dealership which is being sold because an area warrants additional coverage (Broward County in Florida, Nassau on New York's Long Island); market surveys show an area with a greater potential for sales than now being made ("an area not performing to the Division's satisfaction," is the way Byrne puts it); as a favor to a top executive's son; out of malice toward a nearby dealer. Those reasons and more.

So long as the new factory-backed dealer performs he will be left alone. But woe to the dealer who does not meet his quota. "Now under the Motor Holdings program the manufacturer becomes also the financial arm of this new dealer," Timmy Byrne explains. "It is the financial supporter of the dealership. If the dealer is not doing his job, the factory will be with him all the time. Major decisions will be made by the factory. The factory will examine the dealer's books every week. The factory will decide on used car buying and selling policies. The factory will dictate what new cars to order and how many. The factory will accompany the dealer to the men's room. In other words, the independent dealer will be independent no longer."

That is the nature and the strength of the factory's clout within a dealership.

What of the customer's clout?

According to Byrne:

We made the customer price conscious. He didn't want it. He didn't force us into it. We—meaning the dealerships, the dealers, the sellers—made the customer the skeptic he is today.

We had more cars than we had customers and the twin results were the discount and the price buyer.

Now, I am asked from time to time to speak to a Rotary Club about how to buy a car. I tell people not to have too many preconceptions. I ask them to go into dealerships with an open mind. That's a lot to ask, and I know it. Customers have been preconditioned to think of the dealer as a bandit. We are high pressure people. We are crooks. Not only that, we make so doggone much money on each car we sell that to walk in and buy a car without preparing yourself in advance is to ask to be robbed. Well, I don't blame them for thinking those things. I'd be scared to death to walk into this place. (He waves an arm around his spacious, airy showroom.)

But cheating the customer? There's going to be less and less of it simply because the dealer can't afford to do it anymore.

Rolling back speedometers . . . ?

Bugging closing offices? A dealer's got to be insane to do that today. The local paper gets something like that and it's Watergate local. . . .

Switching cars? Two blue station wagons, one at $3,000 and another at $5,000; you sell what the guy thinks is the $5,000 car and give the customer the $3,000 one. Crazy . . .

Driving the trade away? The man wants to go home, he has no car, "Sorry, sir, we misunderstood and sold your car. But if you *want* a car, we've got one for you". . .

The highball? [Offering more than you can possibly give for a trade knowing the buyer is going to shop elsewhere—a surefire device for bringing him back] . . .

The low ball? [Quoting an absurdly low price on a new car for the same purpose—bringing the customer back] . . .

The bait and switch? [Advertising the non-existent impossibly low-priced car and then switching the customer into a realistically priced one, or unrealistically priced one if you're an artist] . . .

The customer is not going to stand for those things today. He's going to call his lawyer. And he's right. Sure, those things are done today. They're done in larger metropolitan areas, although I don't like to generalize that much. They're done by old-line dealers. They're forced by manufacturers who would *like* perhaps to sell cars honestly but have huge inventories. But the new buyer is becoming sophisticated. He is better educated. He is more familiar with the product.

I am pleased about that (says Timmy Byrne brushing a speck off his vest), but I am in a minority. It's a growing minority and it's going to change to become the majority. It has to. The old-line dealer is going to change not because he wants to but because the marketplace is changing. It is now beginning to be filled with people who know something about buying.

The greatest single deterrent to abuse in this business is the informed customer.

Perhaps Tim Byrne doesn't realize how small his minority is. The fact is customers may not be encouraged to shop for the car or for the money with which to buy it. There are a variety of sources from which to borrow money. Many members of credit unions, which traditionally charge interest on the decreasing balance as a loan is paid off, sign contracts with the financing arm of the manufacturer or a bank, which charges throughout the life of that contract on the total amount owed when the contract was put in force. The difference between paying 12 percent interest with ten installments left to go on a forty-eight-month loan on the original $7,000 and the far lesser amount left after having paid thirty-eight installments, is considerable.

The customer is not encouraged to shop for repair prices, and it is virtually certain he doesn't know that the nice, fresh-faced lad in the white coat with the words "Assistant Service Manager" on it who is writing his repair order is in fact what's called a "Service Writer" and is paid a commission for every job and every part he sells.

There is a small town across the country from Mt. Kisco where Steve Johnson° works. It is a bedroom community of San Francisco, and Johnson is a service manager of a Chrysler-Plymouth dealer there. The scenery may be different, the railroad may be the Southern Pacific and not the Penn Central, but the

°That is not his real name.

people are much alike. The dealership in which Johnson works is surrounded by people who would have much in common with the burghers of Mt. Kisco. Their houses might be flatter, but they cost as much or more; the men might not wear ties at the country club, but the women's jewelry sparkles in the summer sunlight just as dazzlingly.

Timmy Byrne, 2,800 miles and three months away, had said, "When I came into the business, I was told the back end [the service and parts departments] was the price you had to pay for your franchise. That's changed. The front end [sales showroom] cannot carry its share of the load as it used to, so a dealer must make his money in his shop if he is to make money in his dealership."

Steve Johnson has to laugh. "Do you know what the most profitable part of a dealership is? I mean *the* department that makes the biggest margin on what it does or sells?" The used car department, perhaps? "Bah, the *parts* department. Fifteen goddamn percent, that's what it makes. Fifteen percent!"

Johnson should know whereof he speaks. He began in the back end in a state-approved apprenticeship program in San Francisco, which led to his journeyman's card as a mechanic. He went on to become a service writer, took time off to buy and operate his own independent repair shop, and returned to a large dealership as its service manager. He moved in that capacity to several dealerships in Northern California, but between each move he experimented with other aspects of the business: he owned a foreign car aftermarket parts store; he sold hand tools to mechanics in dealerships across a particularly lucrative territory (no low-paying enterprise when you consider that a good journeyman owns between $2,000 and $5,000 worth of tools). Several of his service manager posts were in foreign car agencies before he went back into the domestics.

The back end of a dealership makes money, but Steve Johnson isn't entirely sure he's comfortable with the manner in which it contributes its share to the overall monthly profit and loss statement of the dealership.

He's on salary plus commission. His service writers are on salary, much smaller both in total and in proportion to the commission *they* make. His shop is unionized.

Foremost among the less legitimate ways in which the department over which Johnson presides adds black ink to the dealership's bottom line is overselling services and parts.

There is a repair shop law in California—one of the few states that have one—that pretty much prevents the outrageous ripoffs that go on in the mysterious caves of the automotive alchemists. In California, which used to be thieves' heaven for mechanics, there is now strict control by the Bureau of Auto Repair, a state agency. The bureau does not bother Johnson or Johnson's cohorts very much, since overselling is the easiest, most profitable method of making money in the back end anyway. Best of all, it is absolutely legal.

Overselling is dependent on the American's unwillingness to understand his car. This multimillion-dollar racket, for that is what it is, would be snuffed out as though a hurricane had hit a match flame if car owners bothered to do just one thing: read their manuals. But they don't, so Johnson's dealership can count every month on a big contribution to profit from the sale of unnecessary services and unneeded parts.

The easiest items to oversell are parts and jobs that have to do with the car's safety. This, according to Steve Johnson, is a typical scene: "Some guy—actually it's better if it's a woman—brings in a car and says she's got a problem because the thing pulls to the right when it stops. So you write 'check brakes.' Right away that leaves it way open to almost anything.

"So you pull a wheel and decide maybe it needs linings, maybe not; say it's got 70 percent left, which is really ample. But this is a brake job, which is a safety thing. So you get the lady on the phone.

" 'Well, you know,' you say, 'we've taken your car apart. You were complaining about your car pulling to one side and your brakes are really down to where they have to be completely redone.'

"Now you pause for a second to let that sink in and then go on, 'We wouldn't just replace the linings because the drums are a bit scored. And I'm afraid this is going to be a pretty lengthy job. The wheel cylinders are leaking, and your master is starting to seep.'

"This is the way we do the selling because you know, by now, the lady is pretty scared. So we give her another reason. 'If we did half a job and just put the lining in and fluid started to leak on the linings, then you'd have to come back in and we'd have to put brand-new linings right on again. You know, you'd be paying double for the same job that should be done correctly right now.

" 'Of course, you want to be safe, right?' "

But what happens when it's not a woman, a "helpless woman," but a man—strong, knowledgeable, sure of himself? Everybody's the same. There is no such thing as a service customer who knows what's going on. Man, woman, or child, they're all helpless, and they all get the benefit of the same charade.

"Nobody ever objects," says Johnson. "What they almost always say without even thinking is, 'Do you really think I need it, you know, to make the car safe? Well, then, you'd better do it.' Nine out of ten times you'll get that. The tenth will cry and moan, but they'll end up authorizing it."

Johnson takes particular pride in the next oversell gambit. Even though there seems to be advantage for the customer in it, as Johnson speaks he's like a con man, proud of what might be the most legitimate device in the world so long as it's done to *seem* like a badger game. Perhaps it's pride in craftsmanship. "The guy comes in for a lube, oil and filter. You always give your lube man a check list. 'Look at this,' you tell him. 'Check that. Look at the U-joints, check the brake pads while it's in the air and make a report.'

"Plus you train your mechanics the same way. 'If it needs replacement, write it down, or if it's important, tell me right away, and I'll call the customer.' Otherwise, if it's nothing that important, I'll make a note of it and tell them when they come to pick up the car: 'This and such needs to be done in another 2,000 miles; brake pads should be replaced in 5,000 miles,' I'll say. Then you get half those people to come back."

Johnson never worries now about how the customer is going to pay, even when he presents an outrageous bill. It used to be that some would refuse and there'd be a terrible scene. These days everybody has some kind of credit card. There's a Master's thesis waiting to be written on how many unnecessary auto repairs are done each year courtesy of the inventive, greedy mind of the bankers who invented BankAmericard and Master Charge.

The big back-end ripoff is in parts; otherwise how could the

General Motors accounting statement almost all car dealers use to discover where they stand each month show that the parts department outperforms service and new and used car sales? A normal markup for parts is 40 percent. A really good parts man will find a source for parts that serve the same purpose and are probably just as good as the "authorized factory parts" the ubiquitous signs over parts counters always advertise. But these alternative parts cost perhaps half what the factory charges. The dealership's service department bills those parts at the full retail factory prices, so the markup suddenly skyrockets to 90 percent.

There are outright thefts, pocket-pickings, that take place in many dealerships, independent repair shops, and gas stations, but they are almost impossible to pull off in states like California with its strict repair laws. At one time or another Steve Johnson has done or seen them all. For example:

Nothing is done to the car at all except to present a fictitious repair bill.

The car is washed but otherwise untouched and then presented with a flourish, along with the bill and the modest statement that washing is a common practice at this conscientious dealership.

If the complaint is that the car is pulling to the left, air is put in the left tire or taken out of the right. A large bill results.

A car brought in for a tune-up or a "terrible miss" in fact has one plug wire loose. It is reattached, a thirty-second job. The customer is charged for new plugs, new points, new condenser, adjustment of carburetor, and three hours labor.

A major illness is treated with a Band-Aid—at major illness prices.

Used parts are put in instead of new ones.

Rebuilt parts are put in instead of new ones.

These specifics Johnson counts out with weariness. He is a blunt, brusk, fast-moving man whose speech is rapid-fire and whose impatience is bristling from every feature of his face. To Steve Johnson, the problem in all this is not the abuse but the attitude of the American car owner. "Americans would rather drive their cars until they stop than get them fixed ahead of time."

To a man who has devoted his professional life to fixing cars, this is brutality. He particularly cannot understand it in California with its Bureau of Auto Repair. "You've got a better chance of getting your car fixed right in this state than any other place I ever heard of. I think that [the] law has really helped. It has helped the legitimate garage operator and it's helped the dealer. Mostly, though, it's helped the consumer. No doubt about that.

"But he doesn't care anyway."

IV

The character of the marketplace is seen most clearly in the buyer/dealer/builder relationship throughout which certain immutable principles and unshakable prejudices run.

(A caveat: there are endless relationships that extend beyond these. The buyer and his insurance company is one such. The dealer and his banker another. The industry and the aftermarket—the goods and services, batteries and diagnostic centers that function as extra-industry substitutes—is a third. They are not less important than the buyer/dealer/builder chain, but that is the one that is most visible; moreover it is the complementary side to an examination of Detroit, and therefore it becomes the lens used here to peer into the marketplace in the hope of seeing clearly how it works.)

The buyer/dealer/builder death clutch (for that is often what it is) is an adversary relationship, as we have discovered. Industry attitudes toward the customer are condescending: "People are . . . discovering that consumerism is more of a special interest group crusade than a sensible means of improving and protecting their interests—and the regulations which go with it are extremely costly and end up tagged onto the price of everything they buy," according to the Firestone Tire and Rubber Company house organ of September 1975. People in California are not discovering that when they bring their cars in to be fixed, at least not according to Steve Johnson. People in Mt. Kisco are not discovering that when they walk in to buy a car and fill out a conditional sales contract which the law now mandates may not be offered until all the terms are spelled out.

Dealer/industry attitudes are expressed in equally suspicious, acrimonious terms, "New Jersey's GM dealers have formed a General Motors Action Committee. . . . The group's immediate purposes are to inquire whether GM: 1. Has appointed so many dealers within the metropolitan areas of New Jersey as to foster unjust and inequitable conditions in the marketplace; 2. Is systematically conducting a program of unjust and inequitable warranty policy ... ; 3. In its 1975 dealer sales and service agreement ... is acting consistently with just and equitable principles and sound business practices." *Automotive News* of March 29, 1976 is saying that if Firestone wants to be critical of consumerism, so be it; but consumerism isn't the only chafing area in the marketplace. The dealers are angry at the builder in response to the builders' harsh demands on the dealers.

But paramount in the adversary system is the burden of guilt. It is on the dealer when the manufacturer speaks. It is on the consumer when the dealer speaks, the best example of which is the presumption (despite the T. A. Byrne Chevrolets that are coming more and more to represent the baseline auto dealer) that the customer always faces when he walks in to buy a car. *He* is larcenous. (Even Timmy Byrne will say he thinks buyers have larceny in their hearts; he will say that it is the dealer who planted it there, but it is there nonetheless.) He is the corrupter of what otherwise would be a forthright system of doing business. Therefore, in order to protect its interest, the automobile business, from industry to distributor to dealer, must retain the upper hand.

The adversary system is practiced by courtesy of the franchise system. Without it all this intimidation would have to seek other, more tortuous channels.

Franchising gives the individual manufacturer a death grip on its dealers. A point can be taken away. Another added just down the block. The franchise—in which there is frequently only one manufacturer's line of cars to see and, when there are others, they are noncompetitive cars—deprives the customer of an easy opportunity to comparison shop. The franchise limits the dealer's cost of inventory to one group of cars using one brand of parts.

There will always be efforts in the marketplace, as there are efforts in the industry, to evade consumer laws in pursuit of retaining the upper hand. Thus, leasing, which now accounts for upward of 25 percent of all car sales, is viewed by many as a simple way around the banning of "balloon payments." It used to be that cars could be advertised as costing "$100 down, $25 a month for twenty-four months." Well, true, but at the end of those twenty-four months the balance of the cost of the car plus the cost of borrowing the money to buy the car came due in one enormous payment, perhaps as large as $5,000. That was called a "balloon" and it was frequently overlooked by the buyer (who was given a blank contract, remember) and never advertised.

When this was outlawed in many states, dealers looked around and found the lease lying dusty in their attics. The lease offers much the same advantages to the seller that the old $100, $25 a month dodge did. Most leases require no down payment (that is what appeals to the lessee) but at their expiration, the difference between what has been paid on the car, less interest and other charges, and what the car is actually *worth* comes due. What is this but a new form of balloon payment? A new form of "$100 (or no money) down"? Most accountants will say the lease offers no tax advantages at all to individuals; yet in the public mind, the delusion remains that there must be *some* tax loophole through which to slip by leasing instead of buying.

The lease/balloon is yet another device used by the seller to somehow flatten the crazy curves in the sales graph.

For we, in our arbitrary way, have determined that the automobile business will always be subject to the cyclic nature of our demand. "Car purchase decisions can be made and implemented very quickly," writes R. P. Smith in "Consumer Demand for Cars in the U.S.A.," a University of Cambridge doctoral dissertation in economics, "and are largely determined by the state of consumer confidence at any moment.

"In consequence there does not exist a stable short-run demand for car purchase, for it depends on the consumer's timing of acquisition and replacement, which can be varied in response to the state of confidence or expectations. These expectations are not based on a stable extrapolation of past income, but on a subjective evaluation of the 'state of the news'; hence they are subject to all kinds of *social and psychological influences*. The state of confidence is also very volatile and subject to sudden and violent changes."

"Subjective evaluation" is the controlling phrase. What are a single small businessman, 20,000 and more small businessmen, one giant industry to do if their livelihood depends on "subjective evaluations"? Manipulate the market is their answer, and they try like hell.° Despite their best efforts, the industry press showed they were having marginal success in 1974.

June 16, 1975, *U.S. News* & *World Report*: "Detroit Concedes: Little Cars Are Here To Stay. Small cars, at an accelerating rate, are taking over America's highways and now the auto industry says the trend is irreversible."

July 5, 1975, *Autoweek*: "The Big 3 All Aim for New Mini-Car Market. (By Bob Irvin) Detroit—After much research on domestic subcompact cars, Chrysler Corp. is now leaning toward building an American version of its new front wheel drive Simca model—to be introduced in 1978-79.... It would ... follow a pattern being established by General Motors, which will introduce as a 1976 model a Chevrolet now being built in Europe, Asia, and South America.... Ford is thought to be considering a similar approach with its new minicar...."

July 19, 1975, *Autoweek*: "Auto Sales Slump Fails to Affect Luxury Car Sales. Detroit—The auto sales slump hasn't had much impact on luxury car sales. 'Our luxury car sales are fabulous,' said Lincoln-Mercury Division General Manager William Benton ..."

September 22, 1975, *Automotive News*: "Early-September Sales Are Highest Since 1971. (By Paul Lienert) An above-average September opener is the latest sign that the damper may be lifted soon on the depressed new-car market in this country."

October 12, 1975, *The New York Times* Special Fall Automobile Section: "Detroit Acts to Restore Lost Appeal. (By Agis Salpukas) 'Never ... never,' said Matthew S. McLaughlin, vice president of marketing at the Ford Motor Company, shaking his head. He had just been asked whether he had ever seen so many sudden shifts in the auto industry in so short a time."

October 27, 1975, *Business Week*: "Quite a Difference from Last Year. Just about this time a year ago, new car sales collapsed and pitched the domestic auto industry into its worst performance in

°As hard as they try, one of the distinguishing characteristics of the retail market remains disinterest. It is a common and frustrating experience for buyers to walk into a dealership and stand around waiting for someone to answer their questions; sometimes even to take their checks. Although there almost seems to be, there is nothing deliberate about this. The dealer is not suicidal. He is not even uncaring, particularly when it comes to his pocketbook. It's just that some are not very good businessmen.

fourteen years. Now, for the first time since the Arab oil embargo, sales are turning up solidly, if not spectacularly."

February 11, 1976, *The Wall Street Journal*: "Thinking Bigger: Detroit, After Making Smaller Autos, Finds Customers Shun Them ... (By D. W. Austin and W. M. Bulkeley) Las Vegas—The gasoline crunch of two years ago taught the nation's auto makers a hard and costly lesson: No matter how much they wanted to believe otherwise, the days of the big, gasoline-guzzling car were clearly numbered. So with that dictum firmly in mind, Detroit quickly set out to offer America more cars that would conserve fuel—in other words, smaller cars. There's only one problem. Right now, anyway, America seems to be thinking bigger again ..."

February 20, 1976, *The Christian Science Monitor*, Automotive/ Car Care Section: "Scaled-down Detroit Tries to Satisfy Fickle U.S. Consumers. (By Charles E. Dole) Has Detroit again been caught flat-footed by another shift in consumer demand? The massive downward move toward small cars has slowed. As a result, the domestic industry now is doing a fast shuffle to boost the output of bigger cars while cutting back on the production of small cars ..."

April 12, 1976, *Automotive News*: "Sales Surge Cuts Supply of Cars to 53 Days April 1. (By Joseph J. Bohn) New-car inventories were extremely low for an April 1 period. Most of the shortage is traceable to General Motors, many of whose dealers are undoubtedly singing the blues as they try to satisfy surging customer demand with order pads and near-empty backlots. ... A supply of 53 days would be considered low at any time, but it is especially low for this time of year and for the kind of "up" market which has developed ..."

If there are some things they *can't* control, a sure-fire principle on which the marketplace manipulators depend is that the consumer will be kept ignorant. The marketplace, and the industry as well, will always benefit from an almost complete failure by the American consumer press to supply information about automobiles: How to tell the good from the bad; prices high or prices low; warranty thorough or warranty sham; cars that have fulfilled owner expectations or cars that have been model-run disappointments. Despite the seemingly endless citations above, the hardcore *public* automotive press is limited to one weekly offering consumer information—*Autoweek*—although it is primarily concerned with auto racing and rallying and its information is clearly tilted or, frequently, bent. There is an excellent trade weekly—*Automotive News*—and a number of trade newsletters, by far the best of which is *Ward's Automotive Reports*. The business press, particularly *Business Week* and the *Wall Street Journal*, is the only widely disseminated, reliable national source for information on cars, on the marketplace, and the state of the industry.

Coverage by television is poor except for situations filled with disaster that provide "good visuals," such as the masses and masses of cars sitting out unsold and covered with snow at the Michigan State Fairgrounds during the sales disasters of '74–'75.

As for the daily newspaper, it is a disgrace that an industry so large and so influential in all our lives is either ignored or covered by advertising salesmen. There is a handful of real newsmen on the beat. Of them, Bob Irvin of the *Detroit News* is by far the best. He is professional, dogged, skeptical and filled with the requisite integrity.

Most of the rest of the not-very-many people assigned to write about automobiles in the daily press wear two hats. Hugh Randolph of the *Oakland Tribune* is an example of one such news/ adperson. Early on, when he came to the paper as a young and forthright man, he was given the auto beat. He inherited a job that included jollying up car advertisers and then writing about their products. He did his best to keep the jobs separate, but that is something a non-schizoid cannot do. Hugh Randolph continues to try: he has a page a week to fill and he tries to fill it with driving impressions and hard news that cover aspects of the marketplace a customer needs to know in order to buy a car. But hard as he tries, and as much respected for that effort as he is by his peers, when you call Hugh Randolph at the *Oakland Tribune* you get the advertising department secretary.

Dan Boone is another story entirely. The auto editor of the *Los Angeles Herald Examiner*, Boone is a cheerful, earnest man who makes every trip to see every new car and report on it. But from his desk at the *Herald Examiner* he calls or sometimes goes down to the Volkswagen dealership in which he has an interest. You can feel sympathy for Randolph, you can feel only contempt for Boone, particularly since, in the words of one of his colleagues, "He's never written anything bad about *any* car."

Women's magazines frequently have regular columnists writing about cars. Unfortunately, although they write about good, solid subjects like "How to Prepare Your Car for the Coming Winter" or "What To Do in Order to Have a Fun Weekend Camping," they almost all seem to write down to their audience. There is no reason why *Cosmo, The Ladies' Home Journal,* or *Better Homes and Gardens* should not have a hard-hitting column by an expert on consumer matters. They don't, though there is at least one first-rate journalist, Denise McCluggage, who tries.

The men's magazines aren't any better. *Playboy* is ejaculatory or precocious on the automobile; *Esquire* literally doesn't understand how to handle it. For an April 1976 auto section, the magazine called in, as editorial advisor, a staffer from a car enthusiast magazine.

The motives of the enthusiast magazines—*Road & Track* (owned by CBS), *Car and Driver, Motor Trend,* and *Road Test,* to take only the top ones—are at least right out there for you to see. They talk to subscribers or newsstand buyers who are fetishists and they are supported not only by their readers, but by their advertisers, the car manufacturers. Anyone expecting objectivity from a car magazine is incredibly naive.

Objectivity is what you get in *Consumer Reports*. It happens to be *wrong* objectivity, but at least it's objective objectivity. Judging a car the way *Consumer Reports* judges it is a lot like tasting eleven brands of vanilla ice cream and deciding which has the highest satisfaction quotient—something *Consumer Reports* also does, by the way. Their test procedures are the same as the test procedures of the "buff books," *Road & Track* and the rest. The magazine uses the same "test track," a road racing course in Lime Rock, Connecticut. Testers don helmets, stuff themselves into the car to be tested, and go wailing around the many-turned little track to determine "handling." It is no more reasonable a procedure for *Consumer Reports* than it is for *Road & Track*. The testers are automotive engineers, but so are the testers on the buff books. You will get a tight review of some measurable aspects of a car in *Consumer Reports*, which is good; you will get a list of things wrong with the car when it was bought from the dealer (the buff books "borrow" cars), which is good; you will get a "frequency of repair" record, which is good; but you will not get a real sense of what the car is, because after all, in its carefully weighed judgments, *Consumer Reports* refuses to place a car in context and make absolute judgments. For example: "The Datsun 280Z is the best combination of performance, reliability, and comfort you can find in the sports car market—a far more sensibly priced package than the Porsche 924," is the kind of sentence you will never read in *Consumer Reports.*

Magazines put out by the manufacturers, such as VW's *Small World*, Ford's *Ford Times*, or Chrysler Corp.'s *Dodge Adventurer* are disguised advertising. When Chrysler Corp. introduced its 1976 Aspen and Volare (Dodge and Plymouth versions of the same car) *Dodge Adventurer* featured an Aspen on the cover, a two-page interview with Robert B. McCurry, Jr., Chrysler's Group vice president for U.S. automotive sales, entitled "Why Aspen?", and thirteen pages of "editorial" copy on the car.

The wire services—and in particular the broadcast wire—are almost useless. This is the text of an AP story sent out April 8, 1976 and flagged to the attention of News Program Directors (Bureaus): "A recent wire survey of the use being made of the various scripts moved on the broadcast wire showed almost no one used the one-time-a-week script, 'On the Road.' The performance committee of the Associated Press Broadcasters, which conducted the survey, has recommended, therefore, that the scripts be discontinued. The last edition of this script will move on Saturday, June 16, 1976."

These failures by newspapers, magazines, radio, and television seem to mean that their editors don't think the American public wants to know anything about the automobile. Perhaps they're right. But if so, it is a telling comment on your willingness to let yourself be manipulated by the marketeers. Whether you have stopped to think about it or not, most of the information you have about your car comes from the enormous advertising budgets of the industry and the various dealer councils.

In May 1975, *Madison Avenue, The Advertising Magazine* devoted a special issue to automobile advertising, interviewing ad managers and division managers and featuring an "automotive roundtable discussion."

John Morrissey, general marketing manager of Ford Division, was quoted as saying: "The basic Granada message hit money, space, and economy directly and boldly. It was the same kind of factual reasons-why-to-buy which characterized all our 1975 advertising." Presumably, one of the "factual" reasons was the mileage figure put out by the Environmental Protection Agency, a figure arrived at in the laboratory, not on the road, and the object of scorn by every knowledgeable automotive person in the world—rightfully, because it ignores such vital factors as varying temperatures and headwinds.

Chrysler was in the middle of the great Joe Garagiola rebate program—balloons and carnivals—and R. K. Brown, speaking for the company, was corporately self-congratulatory because Chrysler started the whole thing—soon to be followed by the rest of the industry—and that it ". . . was front page."

Gail Smith, GM's general director of advertising and merchandising, was in a reproachful mood toward the public in *Madison Avenue's* special issue: "As advertisers, we are all on center stage in the arena of public review. We're lifted up, tossed about, thrown down and seldom given the credit for our creative role." That is to say, the creative role of "fulfilling the needs of a broad spectrum of publics . . ." Which might be interpreted as meaning fulfilling a broad spectrum of GM Division sales quotas.

AMC was pushing its buyer protection plan, which covered everything on the car and was written in plain language—a real step forward for the industry. It was a victim, however, as AMC often is because the protection plan—a real, honest-to-God warranty—was not given editorial space, since the *industry* is not given editorial space and most of the information came from AMC advertising. It was effective advertising, but there were certainly doubters, as well there should have been considering the company had to resort to paid time to put forth knowledge the consumer had a right to know from an objective source. But in its advertising for the Pacer, the new "wide, small" car, AMC was not so straightforward. "How do you merchandise the virtues of wide and small in the same product message?" asked Bill McNealy, AMC group vice president for North American marketing, rhetorically. They, the company and its ad agency, had some trouble with that one, ". . . Which [was] understandable when you are working with an exciting, totally new product concept." Well, the Pacer was pretty far from a "totally new product concept." It *looked* different, but it was a big car squeezed together to form a kind of terrarium-like object with a short wheelbase. Still, nobody ever said that paid advertising messages had to be critical of the product they were trying to persuade the public to buy.

VW has always had good advertising, so its director of advertising, John Slaven, didn't have to be defensive. In fact, he went very much on the offense in *Madison Avenue.* "The 'problem' [that Detroit advertisers were trying to combat at the time of the sales slump] is the new consumer of today and the industry's inability to see him." Slaven summed up VW's view of the problem: ". . . the automobile market over the next five years is going to be a difficult challenge for all of us. You must have the right products, you must be priced competitively, and you must talk to the consumer through advertising that is directed to the consumer, not advertising that satisfies committees, pacifies the board of directors, or praises your management."

It would be nice if this could happen, considering the enormous reliance the American public puts on advertising for information about automobiles. Unfortunately, VW does not always practice what Slaven preaches. A recent ad campaign cited a *Road & Track* article naming the VW Rabbit the "Best Sedan in the World Under $3,500," as a result of a test. VW advertising changed "sedan" to "car" and furthermore it did *not* say that *Road & Track* had suffered many problems with the car in its extended test, most of them *after* according it the "Best . . . Under $3,500" honor. Included in those problems was a broken crankshaft, which is about as serious a mechanical failure as you can have. So people reading VW advertising in search of a small, economical car were trusting: 1. a magazine that catered to its advertisers, one of the largest of which was VW, and 2. a test which ended in a catastrophic failure that was never mentioned.

It is not uncommon, this incestuous relationship between the buff books and their advertisers. Annually, *Motor Trend* gives a "Car of the Year" award. It does not seem to be a coincidence that the company manufacturing that car is a heavy *Motor Trend* advertiser, nor that it mentions *Motor Trend* prominently in its own advertising.

The final immutable principle that rules the marketplace and that can be seen shining through the great plate glass windows of dealerships all over the country, is that there is no retail input into the products sold to the public. Not even the dealers have a discernible voice in the product. So insulated is Detroit that when Chevrolet introduced the Monza, a small car, one of its top engineers said, "This is our first responsible car." That was not why Chevrolet built the car, of course. But it was a nice coincidental point to make. The Chevrolet engineer was immediately asked how in God's name he could say such a thing in public, and why Chevy had not been responsible before, and he answered, "We never had to be."

Chevrolet again used coincidental responsibility (coincidental to marketing appeal) when it advertised its little VW-size Chevette with the theme "It's About Time." At a GM board meeting, one director naively asked if that theme wasn't tantamount to admitting Chevrolet had been building and selling the wrong cars until the "It's about time" Chevette came along. There was an embarrassed silence. Chevy tried a third time in introducing its new "small" standard size car for 1977. "Now That's More Like It" was the campaign theme, hoping to suggest it was responding to public demand rather than—as was the case—building a car that conformed to federal requirements for safety and federal requirements in fuel economy. Making a sales virtue of necessity, it's called.

Gil Carmichael is a VW/Mercedes-Benz/Chrysler–Plymouth dealer in Meridian, Mississippi. Like other dealers in the United States he takes what the manufacturers want to build, and they don't ask him his opinion of their cars. But that doesn't mean Gil Carmichael doesn't have opinions. He does, and they are good ones. Gil Carmichael is an advocate of what he calls the "Ethical Car." It is a small car, seating four adults, with a top speed not much over the speed limit, costing somewhere around $3,000 and getting about forty miles per gallon. Carmichael wants that car because his customers want that car, or so he believes. He also believes that such a car would mean preservation of the automobile in an energy-short world, and Gil Carmichael is in the car-selling business and wants to have cars to sell. Right now he's got the VW Rabbit and that's about all in the way of an "ethical car."

Said Carmichael to the International Congress on Auto Safety in San Francisco, July 13, 1975: "Prior to October 1973 we were . . . in larger cars, at high speeds, going down bigger and better new Interstate highways. Now we are looking for . . . a new type of auto society we hadn't thought about. Smaller cars, existing roads, slower speeds."

Given the principles and the prejudices of the marketplace, how are we to conclude whether Carmichael is right or wrong? People are buying bigger cars for the moment, but how are we to know what that means?

We know only that the consumer, the American car-loving, car-consuming buyer:

Doesn't know how to buy a car.

Doesn't know how to maintain a car.

Doesn't know one warranty from another.

Doesn't know the intricacies of the car money market.

Doesn't know how to get his car fixed, or where.

With a marketplace whose distinguishing characteristic is an almost complete absence of understanding by the buyer, whose needs—other than the seller's—are being met?

Part Three

"If we could convince people that
seat belts give them sex appeal or tell
women that shoulder straps would increase
their cleavage, we might get somewhere."
—PROFESSOR SUSAN BAKER, past
president, American Association
for Automotive Medicine.

6: *Bureaucrats and White Chargers*

I

If the drug industry was shocked by the intrusion of the federal government with the establishment of the Federal Drug Administration (1930–31); the railroads with the Interstate Commerce Commission (1887); the radio and infant television businesses by the Federal Communications Commission (1934), the automobile industry reassured itself it had no such worries.

First off, thought Detroit, it was far too big and far too important to be regulated from outside. Second, it assured itself, it had always regulated itself scrupulously. Third—and this was Detroit's ace in the hole—the federal government had been its *partner* since 1916, when the Federal Aid Road Act had been passed.

So it must not have been a pleasant day in the multihundred-thousand-dollar mansions of Bloomfield Hills and Grosse Pointe when the Senate subcommittee invitations arrived in the mid-1960s.

The first reaction was incredulity. The Automobile Manufacturer's Association office in Washington, whose phones were surely ringing off the hook, was in equal shock. Unmindful of how arrogant it must have appeared to Senator Abraham Ribicoff's Subcommittee on Executive Reorganization, the AMA's man in

Washington reacted to the subcommittee's invitations with horror. Appalled at their failure to understand protocol, he told them, "*Those* people don't testify. You just tell us what you want to know and we'll produce the appropriate expert."

"Those people" were the presidents and chairmen of Detroit's giant manufacturers. "Those people" had long been accustomed to near obeisance by Washington. "Those people" paid good money to lobbyists who held the government's hand, no doubt occasionally crossing its palm with silver. "Those people" were absolutely confident some mistake had been made. They were right; a mistake had been made. But it was "those people" who had made it.

As with the great consumer revolt, it was not as though there had been no storm warnings. It's just that Detroit had been looking the other way. There were at least five hurricane pennants flying before the subcommittee decided to act.

Public disaffection with the automobile was growing. Once, in the grand, crisp nights of the Sloanist Septembers when new cars were introduced, windows at dealerships were soaped over for weeks prior to the unveiling, teaser ads ran in newspapers, and on the night of the debut great spotlights would cleave the air while crowds poured into showrooms. No more. Spotlight companies across the nation were converting to the making of decorative firelies for Boy Scout jamborees. Love affairs rarely survive the brutality and infidelity to which the public had been subjected by the auto industry for a decade. People would still buy cars. They would buy them in record numbers. But not because we were a nation etherized any longer. We needed each other—Americans and our cars—but we could do nicely without the hypocritical courtship that went along with their addition to our families. It had finally become clear, even to us, that it was not a marriage proposal that was being offered by Detroit.

Then there was that failure of courtship itself. To a disenchanted public, Detroit attitudes were becoming visible for the first time. Heretofore, we had watched the cars in their annual metamorphoses, enchanted with the fins turning into wings and dazzled by chrome, but now we were looking increasingly at the car as an appliance, and we concentrated our gaze instead on the companies that made the cars and on the people who ran the companies. The view did not reassure. Real saturation points were being reached with the car. It was hard not to be angry at car makers when weekday afternoons and evenings—and a good part of the weekend—could be written off in advance to a romantic, steaming adventure stuck in traffic on parkways, Interstates, and freeways across the country. For those who had the time to contemplate in their cars, or to read the newspapers on the way to work the following morning on the train, or to wonder simply what in hell had happened to the svelte creature he used to go riding with alone on country lanes, the answer seemed to lie more and more with Detroit and its view of the world. It was becoming pretty clear that Detroit had Washington cowering.

For example, the Federal Trade Commission was certainly aware, as even the most naive of used car buyers were aware, that odometers were being turned back. But the FTC turned its blind eye.

For another example, Chevrolet Division was, as it is now, as large as the rest of GM put together and GM made the market. "Break up GM" was hardly a popular slogan. There were barely whispers of antitrust actions. Where was the Department of Justice?

Content, in 1965, that it could rip off a fifth of every five-dollar bill spent in retail establishments in the United States and call it theirs, Detroit didn't give a damn what anybody thought. There comes a time when the bad guys take to wearing white hats and walking the streets just as though they belonged, knocking over saloons and holding up the stagecoach in broad daylight, daring anybody to do something about it.

In its high-handed sales methods, its arbitrary exercise of power of life and death over supposedly independent dealers, its monopolization of the market, its ignoring solid worth in pursuit of more car per car and therefore more profits, Detroit was pushing the clock to high noon.

So the American buyer, loved no longer and loving no longer, was taking a long, long look at those who had wooed him for so many years. That is to say, those who were left were. Fewer and fewer were, and a lot of them were in the hospital.

America, in the middle '60s, was indulging in an orgy of 16 million accidents a year. Death by car was the single greatest cause of violent demise in the nation. By all causes—from cancer to crime to warfare—the automobile was the fourth deadliest killer in the United States. Of all persons hospitalized, a third of them had the car to thank.

Detroit pointed to the safety establishment, crying it was not the industry's fault, it was the "nut behind the wheel," and what were the safety people doing about him? They were kowtowing to their masters in Detroit. "Most accidents are in the class of driver fault; driver fault is in the class of violated traffic laws; therefore, observance of traffic laws by drivers would eliminate most accidents." That was the private (for there was no *public*) safety establishment's syllogism.

The National Safety Council—then as now intoning holiday weekend traffic fatalities without mentioning that they are almost exactly the national average for any weekend in the year—funded unspecified "traffic safety services." Local safety groups, supported by local businesses, were accredited by the Council. In addition, there was the ineffectual pawing of outfits like the Auto Industries Highway Committee, the American Association of Motor Vehicle Administrators, the American Bar Association, the International Association of Chiefs of Police, the National Commission on Safety Education of the National Educational Association and the National Committee on Uniform Laws and Ordinances.

The groups in all spent about $9 million a year.

Most of it came through the auto industry and its friend and partner, the insurance industry. Neither asked for much and both got what they asked for. The Auto Safety Foundation, that group founded by auto executives through which the industry made its token contribution, echoed the National Safety Council syllogism, "Being inanimate, no car, truck or bus can by itself cause an accident any more than a street or highway can do so. A driver is needed to put the car into motion—after which it becomes an extension of his will."

The echo of "Guns don't kill people, people kill people," is impossible not to hear. The trouble is, "Guns don't kill people ..." makes a better argument, if only because the gun is a discretionary possession. Nobody *has* to use one. Cars are not discretionary. Since we need cars, since cars are indispensable, public policy should impose absolute liability upon them as products. Indeed, many courts have sustained that view. Therefore, it is not the "nut behind the wheel" who is at fault if the car causes an accident because of mechanical failure. Extending the argument only a little, the *driver* should be protected against the *car*. Courts have held that, too, and it is that contention which forms the basis of the new safety establishment argument.

So add to disenchantment with the car and to industry unawareness of the disenchantment, a pile of 50,000 or so dead bodies and a nation's hospitals filled with highway accident victims.

Mix in a little muscle flexing by the government, which by then was on its way to employing *more* people than the auto (and related) industries—one in five compared to one in six. And finally add the increasing value of activities that seemed more productive to the national good than an unceasing churning out of varicolored cars; activities like aerospace and communications, which seemed, and were, bright new technologies which gave us the same sense of pride as a people that the now dreary and familiar auto industry once did. And, in the case of communications, provided us with shiny, fresh gadgets to buy as well.

Then strike a spark.

The spark's name was Ralph Nader, whose book *Unsafe At Any Speed* blew the doors off Detroit so far as the public was concerned. So far as the industry was concerned, however, it was merely a Roman candle signaling the end of a Krakatoan eruption. The man who *really* made the earth shake and the columns crumble in the imperial city was an unknown named Jerry Sonosky.

II

It is summer 1974, and Mercedes-Benz of North America is solving a vexing problem at an improbably posh ski resort near Stowe, Vermont. Mercedes-Benz is not saying it has this vexing problem. It is certainly not saying the conference it is holding near Stowe is meant to solve that problem. On the contrary, it is saying exactly the opposite.

"We are here to talk about safety," says the company's public relations director. "We are not here to talk about Mercedes-Benz.

This, I hope, is the last time I am going to use the name of the company I work for. If I slip during the next few days, it's only because it's hard to forget the name imprinted on my paycheck."

There is no question but that he means what he is saying. He has brought in as many representatives of the women's magazines as have accepted invitations (not many), some hard-core motoring press, and a few people from mass circulation Sunday supplements.

Mercedes-Benz's problem is that the company has built the safest passenger car on the market and can't say anything about it. If they advertise what knowledgeable engineers and observers know—that every mechanical characteristic of the new, big sedan as well as its revolutionary interior packaging to protect the occupant in case of collision combine to put it miles ahead of anything else available—and if somebody is injured or killed in a Mercedes, the company is open to product liability suits. Such advertisements, in fact, would be engraved invitations to product liability suits. So Mercedes cannot say publicly that it has the safest car in the world.

But Mercedes *can talk* about safety. In fact, it is the very exquisiteness of the fit between Mercedes's need to mention it has the safest car on the world market, and the greater need to inform Americans that it's about time safety again became the subject of public concern, that relieves Mercedes of the shadow of promoting a selfish interest. "First of all, safety is beginning to disappear back into the woodwork," says the M-B man. "Second, people never knew what in hell it was to begin with."

To this conference near Stowe, Mercedes has brought not just the press, but three enormously knowledgeable people to talk for the record. Phil Hill, America's only world race driving champion (now retired) is here. From Germany, proper and precise, is Peter Von Manteuffel, a vehicle safety expert from Daimler-Benz, the parent company. And there, slouching in a chair with his back to the wall, is a member of the prestigious Washington law firm which represents Mercedes-Benz of North America: Jerry Sonosky, Esq., partner in Hogan and Hartson.

Sonosky is a tough, quick, and intimidating man. He was Senator Abraham Ribicoff's 32-year-old chief counsel when the invitations to appear were sent to "those people" in Grosse Pointe and Bloomfield Hills. He would deny it, but if anyone can be said to have written the traffic and safety legislation that has changed American driving habits and American cars, it is Jerry Sonosky.

Sonosky was a New Frontiersman. Nothing seemed strange to him in assaulting imperial Detroit. But it did and does seem odd to him that the machinations of the committee (hiding Ralph Nader in a conference room); the bitter exchange in the committee room between GM president, GM chairman, and a senator on national television; the discovery that Nader was being followed; and the extraordinary capitulation of an industry which had thought itself invulnerable—that all these things should remain the stuff of newspaper, magazine, or book writing.

He expressed this surprise to William Jeanes, who returned from the conference at Stowe to do a piece for *Car and Driver* (it belonged in the *Atlantic* or *Harper's*) that was a thriller; particularly for conspiracy addicts. It is also most likely the definitive piece on how and why it came about that the industry is regulated by the federal government. It aroused almost no comment from the readers of *Car and Driver*. Except among his colleagues, it brought Jeanes no acclaim. Jerry Sonosky remained an unknown outside of the circles of those few Washington/Detroit watchers who had been aware of his role all the time.

Three happenings conspired to bring about the Ribicoff committee's attention to the industry. Ribicoff, who as governor of Connecticut had instituted an inspired campaign to sweep red-light-running criminals and lane-changing felons from his state's highways, had drawn up a list of problems he might investigate as chairman of the Subcommittee on Executive Reorganization of the Senate Committee on Government Operations. On the list was the dreaded automobile. First of the three congenial coincidences was that *The New York Times* carried comment on a book written by Dr. William Haddon, Jr. proposing, among other things, that it was a *second* collision that was responsible for many injuries in auto accidents: the collision between the car and the object within it. Second, a chance meeting with a man who was aware that the committee of which Sonosky was chief counsel had auto safety on the list, recommended as a committee consultant a friend who happened to know a few automotive facts. The friend's name was Nader, and he was doing research for a book about the automobile. Finally, a random reshuffle in government within the Department of Health, Education and Welfare that was moving the Accident Prevention Bureau downward in the hierarchy from a "division" to a "branch" turned up Big Casino. The Ribicoff committee needed something that had to do with executive reorganization to give it authority to poke a finger into Detroit's underbelly, and that innocent and absurd coincidence of moving the APD from one category to another within HEW was the excuse.

The Ribicoffers poured in. It would have been just another congressional investigation into just another ho-hum matter (in fact the early hearings were exactly that) if Senator Ribicoff and Jerry Sonosky had not decided that in a further session they would call on the heads of the industry. That prompted the TV networks to take interest. But likely even that wouldn't have been enough to accomplish the *really* important goal of getting the White House involved, for both the Senator and Sonosky knew that President Lyndon Johnson's interest would have to be focused on cars and safety if they were to go up against Detroit successfully. They fretted about how to do that. They needn't have. Detroit, in the persons of the chairman and the president of GM, came to their rescue.

With TV lights ablaze and the GM royalty onstage, questioning was proceeding at a predictably slow pace when Senator Robert Kennedy happened to drop by the committee room as a result of a chance reminder during a recess for a roll call. Kennedy was a member of the committee, but had been off on a more important matter. He listened for a moment to the exchange, and then, for some reason his interest was captured so he asked a few questions of his own. The ensuing dialogue might not go down as the turning point in the nation's history, but it very likely will go down as the turning point in the history of Detroit and the automobile.

GM President James Roche had revealed that the company had spent a little over $1 million on safety the previous year. Senator Kennedy's interest was further piqued.

> *Senator Kennedy*: What was the profit of General Motors last year?

Mr. Roche: I don't think that has anything to do . . .

Kennedy: I would like to have that answer if I may. I think I am entitled to know that figure. I think it has been published. You spend a million and a quarter dollars, as I understand it, on this aspect of safety. I would like to know what the profit is.

(GM Chairman) Frederick Donner: The one aspect we are talking about is safety.

Kennedy: What was the profit of General Motors last year?

Donner: I will have to ask one of my associates.

Kennedy: Could you, please?

Roche: $1,700,000,000.

Kennedy: What?

Donner: About a billion and a half, I think.

Kennedy: About a billion and a half.

Donner: Yes.

Kennedy: Or $1.7 billion. You made $1.7 billion last year?

Donner: That is correct.

Kennedy: And you spent one million on this?

Donner: In this particular facet we are talking about . . .

Kennedy: If you just gave 1 percent of your profits, that is $17 million.

This exchange took place in July. In November, *Unsafe At Any Speed* was published by a little house (Grossman Publishers) in New York. Since it seemed to be an attack on the Corvair—GM's compact of the moment—it had a specific and avid audience. When word began to spread of its deadly indictment of the auto industry, sales of the book took off.

With the exception of some questionable conclusions about the technical failures of the rear-engined Corvair, *Unsafe . . .* was a devastating criticism of the entire automobile safety establishment, from industry disinterest, to private unconcern, to a discussion of the danger of automotive emissions. It was the *Silent Spring* of the automobile industry.

Whereupon GM gave Jerry Sonosky and Senator Ribicoff another helping hand. The hearings had captured attention all right, but not enough. It did not bring Lyndon Johnson quite to the point of slamming his fist down on the desk and swearing to go after Detroit. GM did that.

One night, as Sonosky was working late in his office in the New Senate Office building, a security guard knocked deferentially on his door. Sonosky told him to come in and the guard, not at all sure he was doing the right thing, told Sonosky that he had noticed someone had been following the by-now out-of-the-closet consultant to the committee, Ralph Nader. Sonosky offered the security guard a drink, thanked him, picked up the phone and called Senator Ribicoff.

All along, the problem had been generating enough momentum from whatever source to get a bill written. Sonosky figured he'd found it. "Senator," he said on the phone that night, "I think we've got a bill."

When it was discovered that GM had hired private detectives to follow Nader, President Johnson came down hard. He wanted a bill. There is dispute over who is responsible for the wording. Today, Sonosky gives the executive branch credit. It is hard to understand why he should be politic at this late date, but almost certainly the words came from Sonosky. Whichever, the bill was referred to the Senate Commerce Committee for hearings.

At this point, the industry tried a last defense. Having publicly apologized to Ralph Nader (and later having to settle out of court with him for $450,000), GM joined its sister companies in insisting any safety problems could be solved best without government intervention. Detroit would voluntarily clean up the "Nation's Number One Health Problem," as Dr. William Haddon called it. Sonosky and Ribicoff were aghast. Just before a lunch break, Sonosky asked an industry representative if this was indeed what Detroit proposed. Yes, he was told, and after lunch the position was reaffirmed.

In desperation, Sonosky used a threat he thought would never stick. He told the man the Ribicoff committee was prepared to reconvene and to demand the recall records of all cars built between 1960 and 1966. Jeanes quotes Sonosky as saying that upon hearing that the industry man "... turned *white*."

Sonosky, chuckling happily in Stowe on this summer's day, sees it now as pure bluff. "There was no way we could have compelled them to produce those records," he says. "I really can't tell you if they knew that or if they were just shaken. But they produced them."

The records showed that ". . . almost one in five autos built in the preceding five years had been defective . . ." wrote Jeanes.

Ribicoff and Sonosky got their bill: The National Traffic and Motor Safety Act of 1966.

III

"The principle," Ralph Nader wrote, "is that the rule of law should extend to the safety of any product that carries such high risks to the lives of users and bystanders." The manner in which the rule of law was applied was a bureaucracy, spelled out by the National Traffic and Motor Safety Act, that applies safety standards to almost everything in sight, many of them to the automobile.

The second war with the industry (the first having been passage of any law at all) was whether in fact these standards would or could be applied. The first battle of that war revolved around two slippery words, "performance" and "design." Detroit saw the definition of those words as critical in any delaying action. Washington—specifically Jerry Sonosky—saw the definitions as critical in winning or losing the war. "Performance" meant standards that would lay down boundaries, period. Thus, if a braking standard were written, it must say brakes must perform to given limits. But there could be no "design" standards, because design standards would say not only what the limits, the boundaries, might be but they would go further and say what the design of the brakes must be to conform to those standards. That Detroit would not stand for.

Sonosky says his committee conceded they would ask only for performance standards, but that from day one the intent was to have design standards. "Of course that was the goal," he admitted in the Stowe conference. Ultimately, design standards would be the only way to insure that Detroit built cars that were safe, he said.

As of this writing there are federal standards or regulations covering sixty-three aspects of industry-built vehicles from glazing materials to child seating systems.

These do not include automotive emissions (an entirely separate subject, fought on a different battlefield by other kinds of armies) or the provisions of the Energy Policy and Conservation

Act of 1975, which has a massive effect on what cars look like, how big they can be, and how they perform.

Says one prominent automotive engineer/journalist: "I really can't say if cars are designed in Detroit or in Washington anymore. I don't *think* they're designed in Washington, but I'm not willing to commit to that."

Says Detroit with one voice, "They're holding our feet to the fire."

Ten years after the fact, *Automotive News* could say in its "Prologue to the Future," ". . . it would be a mistake to assume that the auto industry wants—or would get—freedom from all regulation . . ." The Detroit industry weekly could even go so far as to concede the original necessity, which must give Jerry Sonosky, if he reads *Automotive News* any longer (Ralph Nader is still a subscriber), considerable satisfaction. ". . . years of advertising," wrote Helen Kahn, *AN's* Washington bureau chief, "had conditioned consumers toward an escape and a dream vehicle, going faster and faster, multicolored and gleaming with chrome, with all the glamorous options and one-upmanship on frivolity and Detroit had helped to trap itself into regulation."

Few quarrel with the fact that the regulations imposed by the agency created within the new Department of Transportation (an agency originally called the National Highway Traffic Safety Agency and later upgraded to an Administration) are good for both the consumer and the industry. They have not been extreme. On balance, there has been a minimum of dramatic errors.

It is difficult to imagine or to remember the days that every car on the market had differing positions for the gear selector indicator on its automatic transmission quadrant. "D" for drive would be all the way to the right on some cars, all the way to the left on others. Reverse was equally quixotically placed. The result was that a person used to driving, say, a Dodge, would get into a Chevrolet, put the car in what he thought was "D" for drive, and launch straight backward. One of the first standards rationalized gear-indicator positions on cars throughout the industry. Other standards were equally beneficial and equally innocuous. A great many of them, such as standard 214 on side door strength, standard 203 dealing with "impact protection for driver from steering control system," and standard 204, "steering control rearward displacement," were not only long overdue, not only addressed to the second collision problem, but turned out to be of great advertising advantage to the auto companies.

In 1976, Ford Motor Company showed a series of television commercials of its little Pinto marked up with white stripes (like a Department of Agriculture consumer chart on cuts of beef drawn on a steer hindquarter) pointing out all the safety features of the car. It was an effective commercial, but it didn't bother to say that the safety devices so dramatically charted on the Pinto weren't Ford's idea, nor had they been Ford's choice; they were there because the federal government said they had to be there.

There were two standards—one having to do with seat belts and the other with bumpers ("restraint systems" and "exterior protection")—that have been disastrous. There is another on occupant crash protection that could be the biggest calamity of them all.

Automobile racers and airplane pilots have long since understood that you should not have projecting objects in your immediate surrounding area, nor should you lunge forward in response to the kinetic energy generated by your vehicle's crashing into something hard. They have been wearing so-called "four-point" seat belts for years. A four-point seat belt is a shoulder harness. In race cars and in aircraft, such belts are not lovely and they are not particularly comfortable. (Race car drivers have now gone to the six-point harness. It includes not only a lap belt and two shoulder straps, but a pair of crotch straps to prevent sliding down on impact, a phenomenon known as "submarining.")

Unfortunately, aesthetic appeal and comfort were two of the principal criteria for consumer use of belts. If seat belts were to be worn, they would be worn only if they weren't an inconvenience. If they were ugly, they would be kept out of sight. The first belts were both ugly and uncomfortable. Predictably, they were not worn.

The government replied by requiring that a buzzer be installed to sound a jail cell rasp if the engine was turned on and the belt not fastened. Buyers disconnected the buzzers.

The next step was the infamous interlock, a complicated system that prevented the engine from being started at all until the belts—and by now a single cross strap as well—were fastened.

It was an expensive system, and the cost was being passed along to the car buyer. Belts had become neither more graceful nor more comfortable in the interim. While the dealer was prohibited from tampering with the interlock at risk of a large fine, a huge aftermarket service business sprang up overnight to disconnect the system, since there was no provision in the law that the *owner* of the car could not do as he pleased. Still, there were enough people in the world who did not have the wit or the resistance to get the interlock disconnected to make the hue and cry deafening.

Well, it should have been. A belt, particularly a three-point belt, is a good thing. It keeps you in your car (and the numbers are very clear that say it is in the car that your best chances of survival come in any kind of crash), and it keeps you from hitting the inside of your car. But when it is accompanied by the song of a chainsaw, when it is so difficult to put on that you must try three or four times to disengage it from its scabbard before it will slide out so it can be connected, when it is so uncomfortable as it lies across the chest that you feel your collar-bones and ribs are in traction, when it is so constricting that both men and women, entering their cars on a hot summer's day in crisp clean clothes emerge looking as though they had spent a month slithering on their stomachs along the floor of an empty freight car—when a seat belt confers all these blessings, it is only because we are an orderly people that we hue and cry instead of storming the Washington monument.

The infamous interlock had another disadvantage. It was not so sophisticated that it could distinguish a congressional user from a common-man user. As a result, that infuriating buzz and all the attendant annoyances of the required belt fell upon the ears and chests of Congresspersons as well as everyone else. The surprise was that it took the Congress so long—almost a year—to struggle in wrath with the interlock before commanding the National Traffic Safety Administration to get rid of the damn thing.

Getting rid of the damn thing was relatively easy. Finding some sort of substitute is not easy at all, and is leading us toward a choice of a device which will be an expensive imposition on the consumer with no concomitant guarantee of improved safety. Or a second civil war.

Back to that problem in a moment.

In the meantime, aside from little mistakes like funding the building of cars that were very close to tanks (so called Experimental Safety Vehicles that "killed" their dummy occupants when they hit objects at relatively slow speeds—exactly the thing they were designed to overcome), the federal government and the industry were gradually arriving at an accommodation on the subject of safety features that had to be built into cars. Many automotive people found themselves accepted within the bureaucracy and they were able to modify the views of the early revolutionaries, probably for the good of the consumer, the government, and Detroit.

In its willingness to listen to any safety advocate with credentials, legitimate or forged, the government lent an ear to the Insurance Institute for Highway Safety. The IIHS had *always* had an axe to grind and it was always an actuarial axe. The IIHS, you will recall, was a joint funding agency with the Automobile Safety Foundation in the ugly days of "voluntary" cooperation with the ineffectual private safety establishment; the insurance company cartel in unholy alliance with the automobile builder's cartel to keep safety on the back burner.

Now, the first of the administrators of the National Highway Traffic Safety Administration, the author William Haddon, Jr., M.D., was on the insurance company payrolls as the executive director of the IIHS.

In a widely publicized series of photos and film strips, carried in every newspaper in the land and by almost every TV station, the IIHS showed what happened when two cars met head-on. They hurt each other. For some reason this startled the National Highway Traffic Safety Administration. Dr. Haddon was able to convince the standard writers at NHTSA that bumpers built to resist damage caused even at low speeds would protect specific "safety-related items"—in particular lights, brakes, and steering. The result was a standard that mandated absolute resistance to damage in a five-mile-an-hour crash. ("Impact" is the jargon.) There is not much argument that headlights would be broken in such a crash. But there continues to be lively debate about the vulnerability of other and more important elements of the car Dr. Haddon claimed needed the shield of a staunch bumper.

Haddon, in the meantime, was coming under heavy attack for his advocacy of the bumpers. It was said, not entirely without justification, that the bumper standard was written for the benefit of the insurance industry. It cut down on minor claims, but when the five mph barrier was breached, the financial damage done was greater than before, a disproportionate share of which was being borne by the car owner as it always is in an automobile accident. Thus, it was claimed, the insurance cartel had written a standard purely for its own benefit under the screen of safety. It did not help that the standard phased in the new bumpers, requiring that they become stronger and stronger over a period of years but *not* requiring until the whole program was well along that they be compatible heights. There resulted for several years the ludicrous sight of great protecto-bumpers jutting from the fronts of automobiles that simply didn't match the height of the great protecto-bumpers jutting from the fronts of other automobiles. During those years, what NHTSA and Dr. William Haddon, Jr. had wrought was a battering ram standard.

Further, the bumpers were ugly. They were heavy, and since they were placed on either end of the car as is the habit of bumpers, they greatly affected the manner in which the car behaved to its detriment. (Weight placed at a swinging object's extremities tends to exaggerate its arc.) The bumpers were expensive and their cost, plus profit, was passed along to the consumer.

As this was written, the hot debate within the entire safety establishment is about something that at least, unlike bumpers, clearly is a safety matter. It is a climax to the original seat belt argument and a final confrontation between the proponents of "performance" standards and advocates of "design."

It is the great air bag controversy. In dispute is the method of dealing with the second collision.

Air bags ("air cushion restraint systems" or ACRSs) are balloons which are kept packaged in the center section of the steering wheel and in a position on the passenger side that corresponds to it. They crouch there, surrounded by sensors linked to other sensors in the front of the car, waiting for a collision. The moment the car hits an object with sufficient force, the air bag is commanded by its sensor system to deploy. Out it blooms in a microsecond, cushioning the driver and the passenger as they are in the beginning stage of the process of colliding with the inside of their own cars. The bags deflate very quickly, but not until they have absorbed the force of the forward-catapulting driver and passenger. Air bags, if they can be made to work with a high degree of reliability, will probably be effective. The trouble is, nobody seems to know for sure. In 1975, at the Fourth International Congress on Automotive Safety, Russell A. Smith and Charles A. Moffatt, through the Office of Statistics and Analysis of the National Highway Traffic Safety Administration, delivered a twenty-four page summary of accident experience in air bag equipped cars.

When they were finished, a lot of people had a lot of information and no conclusions. Having already equipped 1,000 Chevrolets with air bags, GM cranked up to produce 100,000 cars a year with ACRSs for sale to the public in 1974. Prior to that, Ford and the Eaton Corporation (which makes air bags) collaborated to put 800 cars on the road in both government and private fleets. Volvo had 75 air-bagged sedans on the highway.

The first problem NHTSA ran into in its efforts to discover whether the air bag works or not was that nobody wanted them. The public exercised its option not to buy the GM full-sized cars— Buick, Cadillac, and Oldsmobile—in which they were offered. So NHTSA, hoping that a 100,000-car-a-year capacity would produce potential sales of 150,000 cars over the twenty-month period in which they were available, watched in dismay as only 9,000 persons elected to protect themselves by the deployment of inside balloons in case of an accident. This did not do NHTSA's data base a great deal of good.

There was a second problem involving a failure to report accidents in which the bags *did not* deploy. Given both these difficulties, Smith and Moffat decided, "The most significant problem is that the small number of accidents involving air bag-equipped cars excludes entirely the possibility that the injury reduction exhibited by the field data is statistically significant." That is, maybe air bags work and maybe they don't. We can't say. However, we *can* say this: Air bags will cost either $125 (the government's figure) or $250–$300 (the industry's figure) and they can be used only once. They work only in collisions in which the front of a car hits something. They do not deploy (except by accident) in side impacts, rollovers, or rear smashups. There is one problem which we are not sure we have solved: A dummy replica of a small child placed in front of an air bag that deployed suddenly was "killed." Finally, to be effective, air bags aren't enough by themselves; driver and passenger must both wear three-point seat restraints.

Notice then: the federal government wrote a standard about occupant protection in case of a crash that almost dictates the use of air bags. It would take a very stretched imagination to consider it a "performance" standard. But to the government's astonishment their own fact-collectors couldn't prove anything about the worth of air bags, while the real world was going about meeting the standard with seat belts. You would expect this might discourage the continued pursuit by the air baggists of their crusade. You would be wrong. One California Office of Traffic Safety official, awaiting a ruling from Washington on the air bag, felt it was likely the Secretary of Transportation ". . . was leaning in the direction of making them mandatory."

When the long-awaited edict from departing Transportation Secretary William Coleman did come, it must have disappointed the man from California. Coleman, carefully straddling a fence, recommended that the industry equip a large fleet and make air bags an attractive option by pricing them well under the industry estimate of their cost. Coleman's recommendation was more than a hint. He made it clear that if General Motors and Ford in particular (to whom he allocated a minimum number of cars that should be built with air bags) weren't inclined to participate in the program willingly, they would be dragged into it by the feds. The companies (and Daimler-Benz as well) were predictably happy to cooperate. Thus, by the end of the decade, there should be a half-million car fleet out in the world guarding their driver's lives with air cushion restraint systems. At the very least, they should provide the much-needed data base.

In this case, the air cushion restraint is a design standard. A strong case can be made for Detroit's exception to its imposition. For the goals of the design standard are being reached *without* the air bag. In Australia, Sweden, France and some fifteen other countries, mandatory seat belt use laws have reduced death and injury dramatically. By now, most cars on the American highway have seat belts. They must be used in addition to air bags for the great pillows to be effective. They are far cheaper than the proposed ACRSs. It is difficult to understand why a performance standard—in this case preventing the second collision or reducing its fearful toll—shouldn't be a perfectly satisfactory societal solution. Proponents of air bags are not at all pleased that they have not been made mandatory. Opponents are disgruntled by the heavy-handed action of the DOT in virtually coercing the industry. Meanwhile, many safety experts are exasperated that we are not doing what we could do right away: require American drivers to wear their belts. Nobody is happy.

Some of the least happy people are the heads of the state Offices of Traffic Safety. In creating the National Highway Traffic Safety Agency, the 1966 law also created microcosm agencies in each state. They would have nothing to do with safety standards; their province was in the "national traffic" part of the National Traffic and Motor Safety Act.

These are the Offices of Traffic Safety. Each state has one, headed nominally by the state's governor, but directed by an agency chief. They are funded by the national administration according to population and total road mileage in a 75 percent to 25 percent ratio. They carry on a variety of programs, many of them excellent, such as selective traffic enforcement at places in their states where accidents are particularly common. They fund accident investigation. The OTS give money for ambulances to rural communities too poor to afford up-to-date ones.

But they are also charged with carrying out the policies of NHTSA. Should a future Secretary of Transportation, acting on a recommendation from the administrator of NHTSA, decide on mandatory use of seat belt legislation instead of mandatory equipping of cars with air bags, it will be up to the states and each Office of Traffic Safety to try to persuade the legislatures that this is what must happen.

It is important that they be persuasive. When big daddy NHTSA tells the states it wants something done (at the moment a program of periodic motor vehicle inspections), the states either do it or the subsidy tap is abruptly closed at the Washington end. Thus, NHTSA wanted all states to require motorcyclists to wear helmets—a highly sensible position but one taken by several sovereign members of the union to be an undue invasion of their rights. California, for one, refused to enforce the Washington edict. California, with about $50 million in federal funds on the line, was in peril of losing it all until the feds backed down, probably because they realized the issue had ten out of hand.°

The motor vehicle inspection problem is clearer and a more accurate portent of what can be looked for increasingly on the part of the states. The OTS budgets are limited. The job of implementing effective traffic safety is expensive and large. Early estimates by the federal government indicated somewhere between 4 and 6 percent of auto accidents could be traced to mechanical failure, essentially failures of maintenance. A later Illinois study dropped that further to about 2 percent maximum. An even later and far vaguer federal estimate then proposed that as many as 12 percent of highway accidents could be assigned to mechanical troubles. The difference in the earlier 6 percent and the later 12 percent was attributed to some kind of magical domino effect.

This is important because of a shibboleth that goes by the title "cost/benefit ratio" (or in engineerese, cost effectiveness). The OTSs everywhere, as well as the National Highway Traffic Safety Administration, genuflect in the presence of cost/benefit ratios.

"Should we put seat belts in school buses and save little persons' lives?" the question might be asked.

"What's the cost/benefit ratio?" is sure to be the answer.

So, considering that to implement a periodic motor vehicle inspection program in a sparsely populated state like Nevada would cost about eight times the entire federal subsidy for the Nevada Office of Traffic Safety in exchange for a return of a maximum of 12 percent accident reduction, such a program is not considered particularly cost effective by the state agency chief. The only option he has is to delay, particularly since he gets money from no source other than the federal government and to

°Federal law has undergone substantial changes recently in the manner in which funds can be cut off. No longer may the Secretary of Transportation withhold a state's highway construction funds—except with regard to highway beautification or in the case of defiance of the national maximum speed limit. In addition, the secretary can now take into consideration the gravity of the offense in deciding how much he'll withhold—he isn't *required* to withhold the entire amount.

institute this new *mandatory* program is going to put his office out of business and him out of a job.

Thus, we have a large federal administration which funds large and small state agencies that are charged with traffic safety, including the implementation of federal plans that are often either unrealistic or impossible or violations of what the states perceive to be their rights. If the state agencies do not carry out the orders of their master, they will cease to exist. If they are wiped off the map, away goes the intent of the law that created the Washington safety establishment. Past NHTSA Administrator, Dr. James Gregory, once said that the problem lay in the fact that state legislators were too close to their constituents. Too liable to be influenced. "I'm not saying it's *bad*," said Dr. Gregory, "I'm saying it's a fact of life."

There is also virtual indifference to at least one of the three problems Ralph Nader originally proposed as forming the safety triangle of driver, highway, and car. The National Highway Traffic Safety Administration deals with the car. The Federal Highway Agency and the OTSs deal with the highway and control of it. Who deals with the driver—apart from the policeman pulling him to the side of the road and writing him a ticket—an ugly echo of those absurd old days of the nut behind the wheel?

No one. Probably because Americans do not admit the problem.

IV

An optional course at the Bondurant School of High Performance Driving is a three-day series of lessons, costing $420, which teaches chauffeurs of American corporate executives assigned to South American countries how to evade pursuit. It is referred to by the less reverent students in Bondurant's other classes as "The Tupomaro Escape School." As bizarre as this sounds, it is a sensible course being taught at one of perhaps six public driving schools of any worth at all in the United States. After all, *everybody* knows how to drive. Right? Not exactly.

Bob Bondurant is an ex-Grand Prix driver, a racer who competed for the world championship. That is the very top of the ladder in motor racing, and in order to be given an opportunity to join the twenty-five or so drivers from every motoring country in the world who are able to start in a Grand Prix, you must have proven first that you are one of the two or three best drivers in your own land. Bondurant might have been a contender had his head not been turned by an offer to be technical advisor and teacher to the stars for the film *Grand Prix.* Thereafter, driving in a race of lesser caliber in the United States, he had a very bad smash and was laid up for a year.

It was the end of his racing career but not the end of his driving career. While he was in the hospital, it occurred to Bondurant, a methodical, thinking man, that his experience in teaching such movie stars as James Garner how to handle a race car might have more practical application. He had ample time to contemplate what that further application might be, and he concluded there should be people just beginning a racing career who would want to be taught the same things James Garner had to learn. When he left the hospital, he left racing and began the Bob Bondurant School of High Performance Driving.

Bondurant, whose real cleverness was in the area of handling a car, but who was no bad hand at self promotion, had by coincidence or intent been brought to an understanding of a problem not many others had even considered. Perhaps one of the reasons for nuttiness behind the wheel was the lack of instruction in rational behavior.

Bondurant began his school advertising in racing publications and drew a growing student body from prospective racers—Walter Mittys and potential A. J. Foyts alike. Whereupon a curious development took place. Police departments, whose members had to engage in high-speed chases day in and day out, began to come to him asking that he teach the techniques of performance driving to their force members.

Eventually, some officers in the California Highway Patrol were showing up at the Ontario Motor Speedway offices of the Bondurant School. And soon enough, Bondurant, who is as fond of money as the next man, concluded there was an opportunity to add yet another course for the driver who simply wanted to understand how to drive properly, albeit fast, but who had no intention of ever racing.

The next step was the introduction of the Tupomaro Escape School.

Somewhere in between Bondurant conducted an interesting experiment. He decided to teach his own son, who was just under fifteen, the basics of driving. Immediately thereafter he was persuaded to teach another non-driver, even younger, the same things.° Bondurant's son had some experience behind the wheel of a car. The other boy had never sat in the driver's seat before he arrived at Ontario Speedway.

Both boys first had to learn what every other new driver has to learn: how to steer a car and how to stop one. Since the school cars were race-prepared sedans, sports, and open-wheel racers, they also had to learn how to use a gearbox, with and without clutch. They spent the first two days of the five-day course in ground school, being shown, through the use of models, what happens to a car as a result of forces put on it in all circumstances and *how to apply those forces to advantage.* They then went out in sedans around a small oval for a full day, around and around, learning to double clutch, coordinate shifting, braking, and steering; learning to notice landmarks around that oval that would signal the points at which to begin each maneuver.

The following morning they went on a skid pad and through an accident simulator. A skid pad is a large area of paved ground made as slippery as possible by sloshing oil, water, and soap on it. Students being taught recovery techniques on a skid pad are sent out in cars with bald tires and a system for locking up individual brakes, or brakes on front or rear only by the accompanying instructor. They are then shown how to drive through impossibly slippery conditions. The instructor locks the brakes and forces a spin. The students are taught how to correct, or more properly how to ride with the spin, and recover from it. They are taught how to induce a spin—first a 45- to 90-degree slide, then a 180-degree spin, controlling the car as it goes backwards; then a full

---

° The second boy was the author's son. After returning from the Bondurant School, the boy was able to drive in a highly skilled fashion, having come to an understanding of applied vehicle dynamics. That is to say he could deliberately provoke and recover from a 360-degree spin as naturally as the average driver can parallel park. That was the trouble. When he went for his driver's test, he displayed brilliant technique (properly subdued) in handling a car. But everyone had forgotten he would be required to show he could park, a maneuver not taught in the highly sophisticated Bondurant curriculum. The boy failed his driver's test, despite holding the 14-and-under lap record at Ontario Motor Speedway.

360. Very soon, the panic and the accompanying paralysis that come with finding yourself in a spinning car disappear.

Indications are very strong that it is this paralysis, occurring at the extreme moments in a car's behavior, that prevents most drivers who have never experienced such behavior by their cars before from applying reasonable actions to recover and avoid accidents. They have never been taught what to do. Therefore when a car begins to embark on a series of extreme adventures, not only is the driver caught utterly by surprise and frightened into a deep freeze, but even if he were clear minded and cool enough to do something, he wouldn't know what to do. For slides and skids and spins, the skid pad teaches him to overcome the fear. (In fact, there comes a moment when the spinning of a car under complete control is like mastering a difficult ice skating maneuver: it is a source of pride and therefore something to be done deliberately, under the proper circumstances, of course.) It also teaches him how to correct the car's aberrant behavior as easily as most drivers are taught to brake for a stoplight.

Braking—more properly, *not* braking—is exactly the point of the Accident Simulator.

The simulator consists of a strip of pavement that opens into a three-lane estuary. The original strip is marked by pylons, and the opening width of the estuary is also marked by pylons into three tight lanes. Above them is an elevated series of lights, one for each lane. There is an electric eye at the side of the single lane which, when broken by the passage of a car, triggers the lights on top of the three estuary lanes into random sequences. Thus, a driver might find himself entering the single lane with the overhead lights all green. His car, breaking the beam as it exits the funneling lane, could trigger a sequence of two reds and one green, three greens, three reds, two greens and a red, or any permutation thereof. But he never knows in which of the three lanes ahead, *immediately* ahead of him, the green will appear.

He begins by entering the single lane at about 30mph and discovers that he has only a split second to decide which lane is green. His reaction is to stop. He cannot. A car will not stop from 30mph in so short a distance. He knocks down pylons right and left. He tries to stop again, and perhaps a third time. Each time he discovers it will not work.

Sooner or later, the driver concludes the only solution is to make for the green-light lane. Now it is merely a question of refining the technique by making his maneuver quick and clean and by entering the funnel faster and faster. He has learned that when the road is blocked ahead, or when a child darts out in front of him, braking is the worst thing he can do. The solution, *the only solution*, is evasive maneuvering. American drivers do not know this. How could they? At the moment of their first experiencing the phenomenon, it is already too late to deal with it.

The final day for both boys was taken up with subtleties of high speed driving in sports cars, but neither was put in the open-wheel, single-seater racers. There is a point to driving experience, and that was lacking with both of them. Judgment, in some sense, does come with time.

One thing they were taught on that final day was "trailing brake." Trailing brake—important on the highway only in extreme situations—relies on the phenomenon of weight transfer (technically, apparent weight transfer).

We are all familiar with the feeling of being pushed back into our seats when we accelerate and being pulled forward when we brake. This is the effect of weight transfer. Under braking, the front wheels carry the burden of the load. The front wheels also steer. As you enter a turn quickly, you are anxious that the steering be dead accurate. Trailing brake says that by applying differing degrees of pressure to the brake pedal, you put varying loads on the front wheels and give them greater or lesser traction ("bite") as a result. Thus, if you wish to turn in tighter, you brake harder; if you wish to widen your turn, you back off the brake. These are subtle pressures. Throughout the Bondurant course, smoothness and subtlety are emphasized. But it is astonishing to ride a car through a turn *steering with the brakes*.

None of this is arcane. All of it is learnable by fourteen-year-olds who have never driven a car in their lives. Bondurant proved that. There are two kinds of knowledge imparted, equally important. The first is that a car is a machine that will behave predictably under given circumstances and there are ways in which it can be controlled. The second is a different order of learning: that mastery of real driving techniques requires concentration of incredible intensity, but leaves as its trace not only an understanding of the concentration needed to drive but a willingness to give what is necessary, because once driving is a skill genuinely mastered, doing it well becomes a source of pride.

The public knows nothing of all this. Americans, Americans tell other Americans, are the best drivers in the world. In fact, they are among the worst. One reason is that the driver educators who *do* know about these techniques haven't the facilities, or the freedom, to teach them.

The government's position is equally discouraging: First, the nut behind the wheel is an incurable psychotic so why try to change him; second, even if every driver in the nation understood and mastered emergency driving techniques, driving is "attitudinal" and therefore the driver education problem has nothing to do with driver education as a process which describes and teaches the mechanics of how to handle a car. Instead, it is a course in metaphysics and behaviorism at the high school level.

The public has decided it knows how to drive. Indeed it does, so long as the driving is done on Interstate highways and so long as it is done under near-ideal conditions. Not one in 10,000 drivers—and that is being charitable—has ever learned what to do in an emergency to save his life or the lives of others.

He could be taught. Except that the teachers won't teach him what he needs to know. They don't want to. Or they don't care. Or they haven't taken the trouble to learn how to drive themselves. High school driver education programs are a disgrace. They are frequently taught by the least qualified teachers in the school, people who are incapable of teaching anything else. Curricula are divided into six hours of driving (shared with as many as three other students) and thirty hours of classroom work. When Bob Bondurant arrived at a driver educator's seminar in Oakland a few years back, set up a skid pad outside the motel in which the conference was being held, and offered to demonstrate his methods of teaching as well as those techniques that could be learned, he was virtually ignored. School districts do not want to know about skid pads although high school parking lots are almost all large enough to accommodate a skid pad in a corner somewhere, and the cost of conversion would involve only removing such obstacles as light poles and buying some used oil. High school students are sent out into the world as drivers. They are not drivers at all. They are victims.

State driver testing standards are appallingly low. No mention is ever made of evasive maneuver. No test is given for it. It is doubtful if, among the thousands of state driving examiners in this country, twenty have ever hear of a *real* (as opposed to a classroom) accident simulator. An accident simulator is a relatively inexpensive device—perhaps $1,000—and could be installed on the grounds of every Department of Motor Vehicles in the land with the money coming from an increase in driver licensing fees.

Both state and federal governments have concluded that teaching people how to drive—even if it were possible, which in their view it is not—would be so lengthy and painful a process there is not much point in trying. The cost/benefit ratio is too low. You can change the car relatively easily and in a reasonably short time. You can learn to build safer highways. But the driver? Ticket the son of a bitch; that's the only kind of lesson he's likely to understand.

Even enlightened bureaucracies, like California's traffic safety establishment, are not inclined to tackle the problem of teaching drivers how to drive. According to Tom Lankard, special assistant to the secretary of California's Business and Transportation Agency, state studies have shown that the problem of driver inadequacy is one of driver attitude. That is to say, drivers don't care how they drive. They pay no attention to their driving. Since that is true, what difference could it possibly make that they might be taught to drive really well? They *still* wouldn't be paying attention to what they were doing.

This is specious. When a person learns to do something well, really well, he does it with pride and attention whether it be cooking, skiing, or driving. If there is an "attitudinal" problem, and California is right on that one, it can be solved only by bringing the careless, inattentive driver inside the driving process. You do not change attitudes with a club. You do not solve attitudinal problems on the public road by increasing ticket quotas for the highway patrol. You solve attitudinal problems by changing attitudes, and you do *that,* in the case of drivers, by giving them a reason to pay attention to what they are doing. You teach them how to drive well, and with that comes pride in driving, and with pride comes attention.

Driver education failures are appalling. But state and federal governments can solve them. It is far more difficult to solve the problem of the drug abuser who accounts for more than half of the accidents on the road. Mercedes-Benz of North America has offered to fund a curriculum for driver education (although in three years no one has taken the company up on its offer), but not all the money in the world could help the drugged driver problem. There have been a million studies, as many pilot programs, and twice the number of conferences at every level by every sort of administrator, educator, doctor, highway engineer, journalist and bureaucrat.

The principal offender is the drinker. He rules the road. Legislation doesn't work. Sweden has very strict drunk driving laws, so strict that conviction can result in a year's jail sentence. Turkey's laws are even stricter, although it is not true that conviction brings with it the severing of the hands. Sweden and Turkey continue at their pre-Draconian highway kill rates.

Education doesn't work. We've tried every kind of program, and we haven't made a dent in the drunk-driver-as-menace statistic.

Not even sophisticated electronic devices work, although they offer promise. Honda developed a console for the steering wheel that had a keyboard which the driver had to play in a pre-set fashion before the engine would start. Presumably, if the driver were drunk, he would have to call a cab and pick up his car the next day. The keyboard defeat system was never marketed.

In this country the reason for the failure of an effective drunk driving program is obvious: Almost everyone drinks. Judges drink, legislators drink, and worst of all, voters drink. There simply isn't a prayer of getting any tough drunk driving penalty passed in any legislature in the nation. If by some miracle one were passed, there are very few judges who would enforce it. If it were enforced, it probably wouldn't help. The grim fact is nobody has a solution. Most of us insist on drinking, and therefore we will continue to kill each other.

No comparable difficulty exists in dealing with the driver who smokes marijuana. Dr. Satanand Sharma at UCLA has done much work in this area and has discovered that the drug's effects are different from those of alcohol, but not much less affecting. Marijuana's only advantage, in the eyes of the enforcer as weil as the smoker, is that a drugged driver can overcome marijuana-induced disability for brief periods in critical situations.

But he is not greeted with the almost universal nonchalance by the law enforcers that the drunk is when he is stopped for wandering all over the highway and perhaps slaughtering a child in the process. Tests for marijuana use did not exist a few years ago. They are still inexact compared to the very clear test for alcohol (and the very clear standard set nationally to determine drunkenness, the .10 standard which indicates the amount of alcohol in blood content). It is not hard to tell when someone has been smoking dope, but it is hard to determine if he is stoned. Still, the law enforcers do not have to be so concerned with convictions. There are laws nationwide against the use of marijuana. The majority of judges are not dopers and will convict.

The next great highway/driver/car problem the federal establishment must face is a problem the federal government imposed upon itself.

In pursuit of saving fuels, the Congress passed the Energy Policy and Conservation Act which became law in December 1975. Among other things, it required that cars built in this country achieve a fleet-weighted average of 20 miles per gallon by 1980 and 27.5 mpg by 1985. Although this is not an NHTSA edict, it amounts to a design standard. For unless someone invents a magic elixir or an alchemist discovers a formula for transmuting gizzards into gasoline, there is only one way in which that fleet-weighted average can be achieved: by building much, much lighter and smaller cars. The process has already begun. Cars introduced in model year 1977 were hundreds of pounds lighter than the '76 lines and many of them were smaller. By 1980, cars coming off Detroit production lines will be mere shadows of their former hulks.

This serves as introduction to two terms dearly loved by engineers and safety freakos alike: "volatile highway mix" and "aggressivity." To an engineer specializing in safety, one car can be more "aggressive" than another. The principle is not hard to understand. A big, heavy object is likely to damage a small, light object to a greater degree than it itself is damaged if they encounter one another. An AMC Matador smashing into a Volkswagen will survive better than the VW. A Cadillac smashing into a Matador will come out, most likely, in better shape than the Matador. A diesel locomotive will almost surely win in the first round against a Cadillac. Add a few sharp edges to the heavier object and you increase its "aggressivity."

"Volatile highway mixes" are the results of putting Cadillacs and VWs on the same road. Heretofore, this has been a problem but not a critical one. Market penetration by little cars—subcompacts—has been relatively small in most states except for California.

But now, with Detroit forced to abandon ultra large crude carriers, the highway mix is going to change. Instead of an 85/15 ratio, large to small, which approximates the 1976 conditions, the new, light Detroit cars will reverse the ratio by the mid-80s. In the meantime, during those ten years it takes to get rid of existing cars on the highway through scrappage, there are going to be a lot of big cars hitting an increasing number of small cars. The highway is going to be an aggressive and dangerous place, even more hostile to humans than it is now. Former NHTSA administrator Gregory sees this as America's "next great safety crisis."

The final problem also originated with the Congress. But it is only a problem to the driver and not to the government. In fact, NHTSA has taken up the 55mph speed limit as its special darling.

The intent of the national 55mph speed limit was fuel conservation according to a panicked Congress which passed the law at the request of the President after the OPEC embargo. There was not much attention to any other effect the law might have.

It was not expected by most to save lives. It seems to be saving about 10,000 a year.

It was not expected by most to cause strikes, boycotts, and blockades. It prompted independent truckers to do all those things.

It was not expected by *anyone* to cause the common shares of manufacturers of citizen band radios to soar on the stock exchanges. They have gone clear out of sight.

First returns showed a great fuel saving as well as a saving of lives. But it was not clear whether either was attributable to less travel or lower speed. In 1975, passenger miles driven began to approach, and in some cases to exceed, the figures for 1973, the last year before the embargo. We were not, it turned out, saving much fuel, if any. We were still saving lives.

That was not because people were driving 55mph, however. People were *not* driving 55 (truckers call the limit the double nickel). What had happened was that average speeds were coming down, not down to 55, but down. So instead of highway numbers of 67mph (or about 75 in Nevada and some other western states) they were hovering around 62. Fewer people were dying of injuries sustained in car crashes, but more were dying of boredom, and a couple were dying of rage.

Among them was State Senator Warren "Snowy" Monroe of Nevada. A member of the transportation committee, he was a staunch opponent of ratification of the 55mph limit. "Not in my lifetime," septuagenarian Monroe proclaimed, in between boasts of being able to drive from his hometown of Elko to Las Vegas in five hours at an average speed of about 105mph. But Snowy Monroe, like state legislators in North Dakota and Oklahoma, caved in when the Congress threatened to cut off all federal highway aid.

Although it is universally unpopular, although it seems irreversible, although it echoes the unworkable prohibition of alcohol, the double nickel law seems here to stay.

It saves lives. So long as lives are saved no argument is going to prevail against it. Not the argument of distances that need to be traveled in the West. Not the argument of money lost by time consumed on the part of long haul truckers. Not even the argument that no one is driving fifty-five miles an hour. Because the NHTSA is determined that people *will* drive fifty-five, and to that end they are funding all sorts of Buck Rogers devices to make every cop in the country Tom Swift with his electric radar.

The circle is complete.

When there was no effective traffic safety establishment in the nation, blood on the highway was the fault of the nut behind the wheel. Now that we've altered the car at great cost and established national and state bureaucracies to monitor traffic safety in responsible fashions, we're back in our new, enlightened state to concentrating on the nut behind the wheel.

Not to teach him but to ticket him.

7 : Chasing Our Own Tailpipes

If we are indifferent about safety and ignorant about our own inability to drive, we are spectacularly apathetic about how the automobile fouls the air we breathe.

There is little difficulty in understanding the reasons for that apathy. We know *something* has been done already, since the cars we have bought in the last five years in particular are plumber's nightmares in terms of the pipes and tubes and bowls and jars and pumps and exhaust system bulges. They get rotten mileage, which we are told over and over is due to emission control devices. The catalytic converter used on most cars, we are warned, gets so hot that we must not under any circumstances park our catalytic cars in open fields or national forests during the summer for fear of burning down the nation.

The information that we are doing something about the car as a disease spreader, a kind of Johnny Cancerseed, is with us ever.

So is the debate between Detroit and Washington on newer, tighter controls. We don't understand any of it. All we do understand is that Detroit keeps saying it can't meet the strict requirements that Washington wants to impose by the deadline Washington has set. We read about CO_2 and HC and NO_x and ppm and gpm and airborne lead and carcinogenic particulates.

We don't know what they're talking about except it all means we now have to buy unleaded gasoline which costs up to 7 percent more than regular.

We don't *see* our cities getting any cleaner. Our eyes still smart in the summer smog.

If we live in California, there are some cars we cannot buy that everyone else in the country can buy. The same is true if we live in cities or towns or in the countryside at altitudes over 4,200 feet.

But because we are confused by all the absurd technical language of emissions; or because we are sick and tired of the endless, whining wrangle between Detroit and Washington on what standards should be met when; or because we don't *see* any improvement in the quality of urban air; or because we are resigned to paying for non-leaded gasoline forever; or because the whole bloody mess has gotten too confused to keep up with, much less understand, are these sufficient reasons to decide to hell with it all, let the industry and the bureaucracy fight it out?

Six years ago the Mitre Corporation, a think tank, did a wrap-up of how we are affected by automotive emissions for the President's office of science and technology. If we persist in being apathetic, we can look at Mitre's report and at least be aware of what we are being apathetic about:

> Many of the industry's approximately 850,000 jobs are directly on the line in this debate. To meet standards, says Detroit, car prices are going to skyrocket, fewer cars will be sold and people will be laid off.
> A further 15 million jobs could be affected as a result.

> In 1975, total health care expenditures stemming from our dependence on the car cost the country $80 billion. The projected figure for 1985 is $130 billion. Of this, in 1968, a study by the Ad Hoc Committee on the Cumulative Regulatory Effects on the Cost of Automobile Transportation, RECAT, attributed $16.1 billion to pollution.*
> In 1975 the cost to the consumer of emission control plumbing on each new car was about $500.

* This is an aggregate estimate of damage from *all* pollutants.

The great emissions debate affects an industry whose total value in plant, equipment, and assets (as of a decade ago) was $40 billion (or about half what it cost the nation ten years later in treating medically the damage its products caused). This is $1 billion more than the sum values of the primary iron and steel·industry.

If we view emissions as part of the whole environment/resources problem, we might stop to consider that manufacture of the car consumes (as of 1968) 21 percent of all steel used in the United States, 10 percent of all aluminum, 55 percent of all lead, 37 percent of all zinc, and 65 percent of all rubber. These figures have since increased.

We spend (as of 1970) 13 percent of our personal annual outlay on our cars. That has increased a great deal. (For example, cars cost about half again as much in 1977 as they did in 1970.) As noted, a good deal of that goes for emission control devices.

Inspection of emission devices on cars including periodic replacement of required parts costs about $40 a year for each car.

The cost assigned just to monitor the quality of air amounts to $1 a car for each of the 109 million cars in the country.

The cost of administering national and state air quality programs is about $4 for each of the 109 million cars in the country.

It cost the oil companies about $4 billion to convert to the refining of non-leaded gasoline, which is required in cars using catalytic converters to reduce emissions.

It cost the consumer about five cents a gallon more to buy unleaded gasoline for a total of $2.2 billion annually, and rising.

Cost to society for painting, cleaning, and the market devaluation of property damaged by air pollution was (in 1970) $14 billion.

In 1970, the average mile per gallon figure for all cars—in part thanks to emission control devices—was 13.8.

If you are numbed by this staggering recitation of costs, you are supposed to be. But you are not supposed to *remain* numbed. Perhaps it's time you contemplated becoming angry. There is ample reason, and it does not all have to do with your pocketbook. The stuff a car spits out of its tailpipe is not recommended as a health cure. " . . . cars . . . fill the air with the foul odor of burning fossils, and so day by day our lungs fill up with the stuff of great ferns and dinosaurs who thus revenge themselves upon their successors, causing us to wither and die prematurely," said Gore Vidal.

We are discovering more and more exactly in what fashion "the stuff of great ferns and dinosaurs" is affecting us and, as we discover, we find ourselves in the middle of a new debate. Is it really all that bad? Or have we come far enough now so that any more expense by the industry and the consumer would be a dreadful violation of the cost/benefit ratio concept? This is an argument that, because of its potential direct and indirect cost to you (when you buy a new car or when you pay your chemotherapy bill), you should be debating actively. Thus far, it seems, it has been all too much of a bore for you to have bothered; perhaps if you were aware of the principal assumption that began the great emissions control crusade, you would be annoyed enough to take interest.

The argument for tough standards originally went something like this: Chemicals come out of the rear end of an automobile. We know what most of them are. We think we have established with some accuracy that they have a good deal to do with smog. Although we do not know in what manner nor to what degree smog, or its components, affects human life, it is better to be safe than sorry. Therefore, admitting we do not have measurements or test studies to back up what we are about to do, we are going to establish standards that will restrict the amount of stuff that an automobile puffs out. This will cost money, no doubt. It may have other adverse effects (we shall see that for a long time one of them was a worsening of fuel economy), but until we know something is harmless, we are not going to take any chances.

This also has meant that we have not known exactly how to *set* specific standards. If you do not know that "y" amount of carbon monoxide in the air will affect an urban population in "x" fashion, how are you to know for sure whether you want to set standards that will bring about a "y" concentration or a "y minus r" concentration or maybe even leave the concentration as it is?

Thus, the inability to quantify damage done by air pollution from "mobile sources" (as air pollution mavens call the automobile and its bigger brothers) has meant that our judgments have been essentially political. We *think* this would be a good thing, even though we can't prove it. So we'll do it.

It would seem that one of the problems in quantifying all this is the minute quantities of pollutants with which the people in the laboratories deal. For example, if you dressed nine women in red coats, gathered the entire population of Columbus, Ohio on a rather large lawn (large enough to accommodate one million persons) and made them wear gray, you would be able to see the ratio of carbon monoxide to everything else a single car spits out running a continuous eight hours: "CO, 9ppm—8hr. max," says the Federal Primary CO Standard. But that is not really the trouble at all. The trouble is we don't know for sure whether we want 9ppm (parts per million) or .9ppm or 9.9ppm. We simply haven't done enough testing.

The Congress decided, in amending the Clean Air Act in 1970, that it would approximate the findings of Dr. Delbert Barth, then director of the Bureau of Criteria and Standards of the National Air Pollution Control Administration of the Department of HEW. But Barth and his people based their studies on some ivory tower criteria. First off, they took 1990 in urban areas as the baseline to measure what they wanted to accomplish. They then decided that what they wanted to achieve was a quality of air that would pose no danger to the health of any single American living in a city in 1990. So far as the automobile was concerned, Barth's boys decided they would choke it down to a point that would bring this Utopian condition to a city with the *worst imaginable* conditions as of 1990. Now remember, although the automobile (and its bigger brothers) are the principal factors in contributing to foul air, they are not the only ones. So Barth was envisioning a city that would certainly suffer pollution from "stationary sources" as well as mobile sources—oil refineries, steel mills, incinerators. The trouble here, of course, is that few cities could be presumed to have air as bad as Barth's ideally disgusting atmosphere, and yet *all* cars would have to conform to standards based on reducing that extreme level to a point where *no one* could possibly suffer. Further, even by 1990 less than half the nation will be living in large SMSAs, although everyone will have to buy and pay for emission controls designed to protect urban air basins.

This projection was done on the premise that to do something was better than doing nothing, and since the data weren't there, Barth and his people could ignore cost in good conscience. From a study of this called *The Automobile and the Regulation of Its Impact on the Environment,* and in particular the chapter done by David Harrison, Jr. and John F. Kain, comes this quote (as well as a great deal of the information in Part I of this chapter): "[Barth's analysis] assumes that the cost of achieving these gains is of no consequence and that the congressional intent in setting emission standards is to avoid *any* adverse influence of air pollution on human health whatever the costs."

Since the Congress seems to have relied a great deal on Barth, his work is a measure of the severity of the standards set. Congress did not stop there. It assumed a larger growth in the auto fleet than seems likely. It assumed that this would unduly affect urban areas, ignoring the real geographic distribution of the automobile. It also compressed the standards in time, so that instead of reaching an ideal goal by 1990, which Barth's study implied might be the manner in which they should be implemented, the Congress cranked them down to 1978.°

Was there sufficient reason?

Cars emit five pollutants that have been identified as harmful to one degree or another. Three of these are subject to control. In 1972, the Council on Environmental Quality estimated these five contributed to nationwide air pollution from automotive sources alone in the following percentages: carbon monoxide, 75.4 percent; nitrogen oxides, 51.5 percent; hydrocarbons (producers of photochemical oxidants), 56.2 percent; sulfur oxides, 2.9 percent; and particulates, 2.8 percent. (Because of their low concentrations, the last two are uncontrolled.) In each case, we'll examine the dangers of the pollutants so far as they have been established, but at a glance those numbers seem to be a pretty solid case for Congress's having mandated the Environmental Protection Agency to take immediate and strict action on CO, HC and NO_x. Health effects of the five pollutants are of greatest concern, but there are others. Pollutants obviously have some impact on materials and on vegetation. They also cast a visible pall; they are not aesthetic contributors to our lives.

It is hard to determine just how deleterious the effects of the grim five are to our lives, since we can hardly lock volunteers in a laboratory and pump them full of nitrogen oxides. We have

---

° As of this writing (January 1977), it seems likely that the Congress, which has already relaxed the schedule, will extend the deadline even further. It is certain also that control of NO_x the toughest standard to meet, will be less harsh than first proposed.

assumed in our epidemiological studies, through an analysis of deaths and sicknesses in highly polluted areas, that pollution is a cause of Los Angeles being a dangerous place in which to live for someone prone to upper respiratory diseases, as opposed to San Francisco. The problem here is that we don't have data enough to tell us whether the Los Angeleno who expires in the middle of a fit of coughing is dead from the burden of his atmosphere or any one of a million other causes. Still, we know something about the pollutants themselves and how they affect us. Perhaps that alone, perhaps that in combination with their urban concentration and the ratio in which they are spewed into the air by the car, is reason enough for regulation.

Carbon monoxide is so well known as a harmful byproduct of the internal combustion engine that it is high on the list of choices as death agents by suicides. It is absorbed in the lungs and reacts with hemoglobin. Hemoglobin is the substance that carries oxygen throughout the system. The result is twofold: the blood can no longer carry sufficient oxygen (or at least a much reduced amount) and the hemoglobin-carbon monoxide mix impairs the release of what oxygen there is to the tissues.

This is not particularly helpful to the human body, specifically the body driving a car. Ohio State University recently conducted experiments using old and young drivers treated with zero to 12 percent of the carbon monoxide-hemoglobin combination. (It is called carboxyhemoglobin and its symbol is COHb.) After treatment, the drivers were put out on the highway in order to determine their responses to freeway driving, reading highway signs, car following, driving with vision partially impaired, cornering ability (driver, not car), and ability to estimate time and speed. The experiment included five young, healthy nonsmokers and five healthy, older (60 to 65) nonsmokers.

The Ohio State people discovered that when concentrations of COHb were approximately 12 percent, nighttime vision was affected in both groups, although in different ways. The young suffered significantly decreased visual activity; they didn't search the road as much as they had during the day. The old parties had a problem with peripheral vision. The striplings' heart rate was increased, while their elders' remained the same as it had been. Concluded the report, "In general, CO effects on the road are much less than those found in the laboratory. The results indicate the CO effects are first manifested in the visual system before driver control or vehicle performance measures are affected."

In addition to impaired vision, *laboratory* tests have shown that COHb affects the nervous system in a way that impairs vigilance and overall performance. *The Automobile* . . . speculates that perhaps COHb concentrations are responsible for a measurable number of auto accidents, but deplores the lack of sufficient study. We know that high CO concentrations are deadly in their effect on the heart and circulatory systems. As for the less dramatic effects of CO, it gives you a headache or other indifferent discomforts. It is particularly dangerous to those who smoke heavily (they have already restricted the oxygen in their systems) and to those prone to cardiovascular diseases. Carbon monoxide is dangerous, and it can be fatal.

Of the nitrogen oxides (NO_x), nitrogen dioxide (NO_2) is the villain. It affects the respiratory system. "The basic . . . response is an inflammation of the lungs, accompanied by various chemical and cellular changes in lung tissue, including damage to lung proteins, rupture of mast cells, and development of pre-emphysematous lesions." In other words, if you wish to continue to breathe, nitrogen dioxide inhalation is bad news.

Laboratory animals have also suffered tissue damage to organs other than the lungs. Heart, liver, and kidney have been affected; changes in the composition of the blood have resulted as well. NO_2 encourages chronic lung disease and it increases the possibility of respiratory tract infection.

Hydrocarbons (HC) are on the EPA enemies list not because they are wicked substances if they stay home alone, but because they conspire to produce photochemical oxidants, the most damaging of which is ozone. Nobody seems to know exactly how ozone works on the body, but such small amounts as one part per million have been proven to increase susceptibility to infection of the respiratory tract, to cause lung damage, lower resistance to infection, and induce changes in other organs of the body. "A few experimental studies," reports *The Automobile,* "[have shown] human pulmonary function is impaired by exposure to concentration of oxidants ranging from .5 to 1ppm for one or two hours." That is a very short time and those are not very great amounts.

Further, ". . . industrial workers exposed to moderately high (.3ppm) to very high (3ppm) levels of oxidants for periods ranging from one to one and one-half hours are reported to have unusually frequent nasal and throat irritations, distinct irritation of mucous membranes, coughing, irritation and exhaustion, and sleepiness."

Oxidants are also demonstrably unhelpful to high school football, basketball, baseball, track, and water polo championship aspirations. All of this is unpleasant, but at least it isn't fatal. Further, what has been done, has been done on short-term exposures. "There are no adequate studies of the long-run effects of high oxidant concentrations on health."

Sulfur dioxide, which was highly suspect, has been let off the hook a little bit recently. There was much concern (there is still substantial concern in some circles) that catalytic converters are the source of sulfur dioxide which, like the nitrogen oxides, affects breathing mechanisms. It could also be carcinogenic and it may increase heart disease. But late studies are putting to rest the contention that catalytic converters are particular villains in the sulfur dioxide assault on the human body. This is not to say that auto emissions are free of the stuff. They are not.

We do not like sulfur dioxide primarily because of its stink. Carbon monoxide has the manners to be odorless, colorless, and tasteless. Although that makes it the more deadly, it is deadly without intrusiveness. Sulfur dioxide is the rotten egg gas. When it's there, you know it's there. It is sulfur dioxide, by the way, to which the legendary atmospheric disasters in the Meuse Valley in 1930, Donora, Pa. in 1948, and the great London death fog of 1952 are attributed. There is some quarrel with that since there were few measurements taken and not many of other pollutants. Part of the quarrel also centers on the fact that many of the fatalities in all of the incidents were among the already very sick. If this seems praising by faint damnation, at least we know that if you are very sick, sulfur dioxide is not going to be of much help. Whether it'll make you sick if you are healthy to begin with, we cannot document, however strong our suspicion.

The fifth identified (although not yet prohibited) substance that a car emits comes out in the form of solids. They are tiny little pieces of matter called particulates. It seems clear that particulates, of which there are many kinds, affect respiration and the respiratory tract. They can also be carcinogenic. At the moment, one of the highest priorities of The Sierra Club are the tiny dust particles of asbestos that are put in the air as a result of the use of the substance in brake and clutch linings. Asbestos *is* carcinogenic, and the car puts a lot of it in the air, but the official emissions establishment dismisses it as a serious threat in terms of automobile exhausts. Perhaps that is because it comes from a part of the car that is not at its tail end.

Carbon monoxide and particulates are of no great concern to farmers, but NO_x kills vegetation. Its effects include cell collapse and patterns of localized death or necrosis, according to laboratory studies. Real-world studies have shown damage to tobacco, spinach, orange trees, and soybean plants in Los Angeles.

And, says *The Automobile*, "The economic loss to farmers and nursery men resulting from photochemical oxidants (HC-produced) may be the largest of any of the air pollutants." This was first noticed in Los Angeles in 1944 when the first systematic study of pollution on crops was instituted. Ozone bears the greatest burden of blame. Again it is localized death of cell tissue. This is a well-known phenomenon to the tobacco growers in the East. For the farmer, there is little to be sanguine about, no matter where he lives, so long as there are cars around.

Anyone who has flown over the Los Angeles basin knows very well what the aesthetic effects of auto-produced pollution are: ugly, yellow smudge covers the city. Curiously, eye irritation is considered an "aesthetic" effect of pollution, since it is not harmful and doesn't last long.

Perhaps the most overlooked damage done by auto emissions, by pollutants in general, are their attack on things that are inanimate. This is unpleasant and costs money, as for instance when a building or a home requires repainting because its surface coating has been eaten or covered with filth. But it also can cause potential death or injury. One of the materials most affected—by ozone again—by automobile leavings is rubber. Ozone makes rubber brittle. The result can be a cracked sidewall. The result of *that* can be a fatally weakened tire and a car thrown into a bridge abutment.

So now that we know very roughly what we're dealing with, back to the question of whether it's really all that bad. That is to say bad enough to continue the argument, bad enough so that you should get exercised about automobile emissions. Bad enough so that the cost/benefit ratio question is not clearly answered.*

Thus far we have dealt with the harm produced by components of car emissions. But we have done a great deal to mitigate that harm. From an uncontrolled car, we have reduced emissions as of 1977 by something over 90 percent for hydrocarbons, something more than 83 percent for carbon monoxide, almost 50 percent for oxides of nitrogen. The industry viewpoint is that it is already costing the consumer $500 to do that just in the initial purchase of a car. From here on costs get exponential. To meet standards that are much tougher than the current ones will cost amounts that go off the scale.

In addition to increased costs to the consumer, decreased fuel economy, and potential unemployment, the claim is made that our mobility is being restricted. The government, according to this view, is telling communities how to use their land. States and municipalities are restricting driving (California tried a diamond-lane experiment, since abandoned and then partially revived, in which lanes on its freeways were reserved for cars occupied by three or more persons). Cities—Berkeley, for example—are being blocked off to the automobile and parking is being restricted.

The industry is angry because "... emission standards are written directly into the Federal law allowing little administrative flexibility." This is to be taken as meaning lobbying with the monitoring agency is worthless and that the government means what it says.

The essence of the argument is that consumers should put the burden of proof where it belongs for further control of automotive emissions. If the government wants us to go further, at far greater cost for far less benefit, it should document its case. Yes, there are some communities that need all the help they can get, but they are in the minority and they are mostly in California anyway. In the interim, why penalize everyone else?

---

* *The New York Times* (February 9, 1977), citing a federal task force report informally known as the 300 Days' Study had a dramatic perspective: "... if all automobile pollutants were eliminated, or nearly so, stationary sources would still be emitting enough hydrocarbons and nitrogen oxides to create a health hazard. In fact, if all automotive nitrogen oxides were eliminated by 1990, cities such as Los Angeles, Chicago, and New York would still exceed the clean air standards."

Particularly since the federal government is clearly at odds with itself on this one. First it wants clean air, which costs a lot of money and, at least according to the industry, cuts down on fuel mileage. Then it enacts a law requiring all Detroit products to more than double their fuel economy average, which *also* costs money and requires the removal of emission control equipment. You can't have it both ways, says the industry. In which direction do you want to go?

There is one man who knows whereof he speaks who wants to go both ways and says there's no problem at all getting there.

II

Which direction do you want? "The answer to that question, is that it's absurd. The question is ridiculous. There aren't *any* fundamental reasons a car can't be clean and efficient at the same time."

We are in Sacramento at the California Air Resources Board on a hot summer's day, in a low brick building that looks like a planter's box covered with great ferns and huge, protective trees. Tom Austin's office looks out on Q Street through a wall of glass, which almost certainly has been put in during the conversion of this building from a cola bottling plant.

Austin is deputy executive director (technical) of California's ARB. It is late afternoon, and Austin is sitting in a white Eames chair at a round, white Eames table at the far end of his office, away from his desk. He swings his lower legs as he talks. He is coatless. His clothes are faintly eastern, but unidentifiable in terms of giving any clue about who Tom Austin is.

The only indicator Austin offers is that his language is that of the technocrat. He is the latest in a long line of California Air Resources Board Turks. His is the last bastion of the hard-line air-quality-at-all-cost philosophy in the country.

Austin will not tolerate the presence of a tape recorder.

"Look at cars," he goes on in carefully controlled outrage, answering the question the industry poses about the mutual exclusivity of economy and clean exhausts, "in any weight class. Segregate them according to their 0-60mph acceleration times. Then look at the ones that get good fuel economy." It is a fairly enigmatic statement since Austin is skipping at least five essential facts in the drawing of his argument, assuming that if the listener has gotten this far, he can fill in his own blanks. What Austin seems to be saying is this: Since all cars must conform to federal standards, they are "clean." (In California, the standards are stricter.) Therefore, that they are reasonably pollution free is a certainty. Given that, acceleration times from 0-60 will serve for the basis of a test that can show us cars that are not only clean but that get good gas mileage and that have good performance as well—that are, in other words, efficient. And Austin is right. For among the quickest accelerators are lightweight cars with sophisticated and carefully controlled fuel metering devices such as the fuel-injected Audi Fox. It is almost as fast as the big-engined Pontiac TransAm and gets at least twice the mileage. He is making his argument for light weight. But it is not a very fair argument since, like the assumptions of Dr. Barth, it doesn't take cost into consideration. Never mind fair. It isn't fair that people should breathe polluted air either.

Tom Austin's spiritual and intellectual progenitor in California—in the whole auto emissions debate as a matter of fact—was Dr. Arlie Haagen-Smit, a biochemist. It was Dr. Haagen-Smit who discovered the link between the auto exhaust and the photochemical smog in Los Angeles eighteen years ago. Under sunlight, he concluded, automotive hydrocarbons react with oxides of nitrogen to produce the smog. The Los Angeles Air Pollution Control District had already been at work on the problem, and their findings, coupled with Dr. Haagen-Smit's, just about nailed the culprit.

Ralph Nader points out that the auto industry had been aware that auto exhaust was a problem but had never done anything about it. "It is significant," he said in *Unsafe at Any Speed*, "that the major role the automobile plays in the creation of smog was discovered by someone outside the automobile industry," referring to Arlie Haagen-Smit. Nader, like Tom Austin a decade after *Unsafe* was written, is absolutely unswayed by industry arguments. In fact, he makes a convincing case (as Austin does) that industry indifference was deliberate.

Nader quotes testimony before the California legislature in 1959 given by Paul Ackerman, then chairman of the Engineering Advisory Committee of the Automobile Manufacturer's Association. The "... unique characteristics of the California atmosphere came to our attention in the 1920s, when we noticed that tires and other rubber products cracked and deteriorated in the Los Angeles area," said Ackerman. (Austin, when asked questions about what kind and how much research had gone into determining whether this ozone effect on rubber could be related to safety standards in an attempt to bring safety and emission approaches together, seemed astonished at the notion. Of course, he was aware of ozone's effect on rubber. But it had never seemed to occur to him that here was an issue on which differing departments within California's transportation bureaucracy might find common ground, saving time and money and being more effective in the process.)

Nader traces a chilling history of indifference by the industry to air pollution. For example, he cites industry testimony before the Ribicoff committee in 1965 that "control of vehicle emissions has no relation to driver safety." This comes as a Naderian punchline after carefully establishing that freeway traffic in Los Angeles often had to be slowed down or diverted because of visibility-diminishing smog concentrations and that Dr. Haagen-Smit had recorded CO concentrations of up to 120 parts per million in bumper to bumper traffic in the L.A. basin, four times what the California State Health Department determined was an "adverse" level.

Then Nader quotes a 1953 letter from a member of the Ford engineering staff to a Los Angeles supervisor ". . . The Ford engineering staff, although mindful that automobile engines produce exhaust gases, feels these waste vapors are dissipated in the atmosphere quickly and do not present an air pollution problem. Therefore, our research department has not conducted any experimental work aimed at totally eliminating these gases." Or eliminating them at all for that matter.

When Haagen-Smit was discovering the cause of half the smog in the Los Angeles basin, Austin says the automobile industry was denying that emissions had anything at all to do with anything else, but it had already begun looking around in its research and development laboratories for answers. One answer it found, it immediately rejected: The catalytic converter, which is a kind of chemical scrubber using a ceramic plate and rare metals to detoxify emissions. "In 1952, the catalytic converter existed but the industry decided it wasn't feasible to use. In the early '60s, our predecessors at the ARB decided catalytic converters could be mass produced."

This less than modest estimate about the rectitude of the ARB's past judgments is a byproduct of Tom Austin's career. He is a mechanical engineer with a degree from the University of Michigan, he did engine design for the Army's propulsion system laboratory, and then spent five years with the Environmental Protection Agency hovering over the problem of emissions from mobile pollutant sources before coming to this Sacramento building a year ago. "Things started to slow down at the EPA," says Austin ruefully. "The pressures of the recent [Gerald Ford] administration and the loss of a strong administrator caused the EPA to back off."

Tom Austin is impatient with *The Automobile and the Regulation of Its Impact on the Environment,* that rather critical study of the car and its leavings which, as indicated in the first part of this chapter, clearly pointed to some basic damage the car is causing us. "It is not what I consider in tune with the latest available [information]. Its bias is conservative. It is pessimistic about what can be accomplished through control."

He is impatient with any hope that alternative fuels (such as methanol, an efficient and clean-burning additive for gasoline and the stuff Indianapolis cars race on) will be used. He does not think the diesel will ever be a significant factor in the mix of cars or that its fastidious manners concerning the dumping of HC and CO are of much consequence. It will not meet future nitrogen oxide standards, according to Austin, so the diesel is no solution.

He holds little hope that new cars, despite the fact that the whole 109-million American passenger car fleet is replaced every ten years, are going to help much either. The problem in California, the Department of Motor Vehicles tells him, is that people hang on to old, uncontrolled cars far longer than they do elsewhere, probably because they are not ravaged by weather and Californians seem to *like* old cars. "Old cars don't get retired," Tom Austin says almost savagely, as though their refusal to die were in personal defiance of him.

Austin is impatient with those who point to the cost of emission control devices and say their effect on the economy of the industry has a devastating effect on the economy of the nation. In the first place, he says, the control devices cost only $250 per car. Further, even if they did cost more (which they don't) it's not California's fault, it's the industry's.

So long as California, with its tough Air Resources Board, stops the sale of AMC and Chrysler cars with certain engines, and fines them both hundreds of thousands of dollars for failure to comply with California standards, and then sues them for millions for failing to pay the fines, Detroit is going to be forced into sainthood. "GM and Ford [no mention of the other two companies, as though they had put themselves beyond the pale] will be a hell of a lot more efficient in terms of cars," says Austin. Is he implying that efficiency in terms of *cars* is distinct from efficiency in terms of profits?

Perhaps not. Because one company has just come to California with an offering to Tom Austin's boss, Tom Quinn the ARB chief, of a car that proves, absolutely once and for all, that the American car industry has for all these years been screwing California—and incidentally everybody else—on the subject of emissions.

If Volvo can be more efficient *right now,* so can Detroit. Volvo discovered its miracle car by accident, according to ARB chief Quinn. The company was trying to develop an emission system to meet California's strict new standards and at the same time improve fuel economy. Said Quinn, "Volvo had no idea that its new control system would result in a nearly pollution-free car." That's what happened, though. According to the ARB, the Volvo submitted for California testing was ten times cleaner than cars sold in the rest of the country (so called "federal" cars) and nearly seven times cleaner than current California cars. Volvo's system did not require any dramatic change at all. It even used American technology, a three-way converter developed by Engelhard Industries of Edison, N.J. According to the ARB the controls cost only about $25 to $50 per car *and* the best of all (well, almost the best) is that Volvo achieved its second objective: tests showed that the California Volvo got 10 percent better gas mileage.* "The technology to meet the standard we are proposing for 1981

* Detroit's cost estimate for the three-way converter is about twice the ARB's.

actually exists right now," says Quinn, "but past foot-dragging by Detroit may make it impossible for some domestic auto makers to immediately adapt the new system for their cars." *

Current federal NO_x standards are 3.1 grams per mile. California's mandates 1.5 gpm. The three-way catalyst on the '77 Volvo is said to emit only .17. And it is nitrogen oxides that are the big stumbling block, according to Detroit, in meeting even the federal standard.

California, which started the whole emissions control program and implemented regulations well before the federal government got around to it, shows impressive decreases in pollutant readings in critical urban areas. Total organic gas emissions including oxides of nitrogen, sulfur dioxide, and carbon monoxide have been dramatically reduced in the South Coast Basin; carbon monoxide emissions in single car hour/parts per million have been halved, from sixteen to eight in the decade 1965 to 1975.

Was the Volvo discovery a genuine accident? Have we reached an acceptable level in air quality despite the striving for perfection of the Tom Austins, having reduced the dinosaur's vengeful effluents to 10 percent or so of what they used to be? If Volvo's accidental discovery really happened, did it come somehow as a result of Tom Austin and the California ARB's feet to the fire approach? In the course of that search, was it the consumer who was underwriting the ARB crusade? If Volvo isn't for real, won't he still be?

---

* It should be said that the ARB story is only one side of a debate on the three-way catalyst. The system is called Lambda Sond, and was actually developed by Bosch, a German electronics company. It requires sensors in the tailpipe to read mixture, and a somewhat more complicated catalyst, containing rhodium as well as platinum, than the one American cars use now. Bosch selected Volvo—and another Swedish car builder, Saab—to try the Lambda Sond system because of their relatively low production. This meant that Bosch could keep a careful eye on manufacturing controls. It could also have a fleet of cars that was neither too large nor too small to supply data for a final evaluation of the three-way catalyst. The Lambda Sond-equipped cars for sale to the public, by the way, are the California versions of the Saab 99 and the Volvo 242.

8 : To What End the Highway?

I

The average motorist, particularly when he travels an unfamiliar road, constantly finds signs, signals, road configurations, and roadside clutter that create confusion and indecision. Even familiar streets and highways contain features that can become booby traps for the unwary. The motorist need only stray from the traveled way to learn firsthand how easy it is to be led afield.

There is a peculiar phenomenon present here. The motorist knows it, expects it, but rarely, if ever, thinks seriously that anything can be done about it. He accepts the highly imperfect driving environment with a resignation that is inconsistent with the vigorous assertion of his "rights" in other areas and the pursuit of social reform that characterizes so much of contemporary society.

Wait a minute. "Highly imperfect driving environment?" "Highways [containing] features that can become booby traps for the unwary?" America has the best goddamn highway system in the world! The American Interstate is the envy of civilized men everywhere. Who in hell are these radical, commie, pinko critics of everything right and good about America, land of the concrete miracle?

Will the Subcommittee on Investigations and Review to the

Committee on Public Works of the House of Representatives do?
Are you prepared to accept its report about highway safety,
design, and operations subtitled "The Need for a Safer Driving
Environment"?

The federal government bore 90 percent of the costs of
building the Interstates, 50 percent of the roads designated
primary, secondary, and urban until 1974, when the percentage
rose to 70. Now the same federal government is telling us a lot of
that money was spent on the wrong things, many of which are
either literally misleading us or luring us into danger.

The first significant governmental action—after the invention
and wide use of the automobile—came in 1916 with the passing of
the Federal Aid Road Act in July. The basis in law of the federal
government's moving into the construction business was its
established power to build post offices and post roads. The
Congress appropriated $75 million to be spent over a five-year
period, but there was, of course, a string attached. Only those
states that had created their own highway bureaucracies were
eligible for federal money. It was not difficult to predict the result:
by 1920 all states had highway departments of their own.

In 1921, the Congress again acted in the matter of highways,
this time with tightened strings and more of them. The purpose of
the Federal Highway Act of 1921 was to improve interstate
travel—to a point. Thus, each state highway department could
designate roads to be improved but only so long as their length did
not exceed 7 percent of the total national highway mileage.
Interstate travel was the principal goal of the act, but it also
applied to the improvement of both primary (interstate) and
secondary (intercounty) roads. This time, however, the federal
government required that the states share the cost on a fifty-fifty
basis.

In the meantime, led by Oregon in 1919, the states had
descended upon gasoline as a taxable commodity in order to raise
the money needed for their own roads and for money to constitute
the matching funds that the government was asking. By 1929, all
states had such taxes on gasoline (Oregon's innovative tax had
been one cent a gallon) and by that time about $431 million had
been accumulated in various state treasuries, thanks to this
ingenious device. The average tax by then had tripled.

Professor James Flink *(The Car Culture)* concludes that the two federal road aid acts had brought a highway system to the nation that was very likely about as good as it should have been. From the late '20s on, it was not the highway that was the problem, in his view; it was Detroit. By building ever faster cars in ever greater numbers in response to a demand to travel roads that were built to accommodate existing cars, Detroit had reversed the highway dynamic. It was now the federal and state governments that had to rush to keep up with what was coming out of Detroit. Since Detroit was now setting the pace, that task was a hopeless one. Indicating how far behind we might fall, Professor Flink quotes the President's Committee on Recent Social Trends as saying in 1933, "Should there be no further increase in the volume of motor vehicle traffic, the utility of new construction and improvement projects would naturally diminish as present highway programs approached the period of completion. This in turn would lead to a more careful weighing of the relative advantage of additional highway facilities as against a reduction of highway taxes." It was very clear we were neither aware nor particularly concerned about what the car was doing to us.

Nor did there seem to be much enthusiasm about new roads. More specifically about public underwriting of new roads, for Flink cites the difficulty that the Pennsylvania Turnpike Authority had in the '30s finding a market for its bonds.

Flink credits (or blames depending on your view of our highways) Franklin Delano Roosevelt for the spurt in road building during the years of his administration. Highway construction and improvement was a natural category into which to stuff allocated funds in order to create Depression jobs, and that's just what FDR did. "Convenient and noncontroversial," is the manner in which Professor Flink categorized the highway as a make-work project.

The Congress acted next in the late years of World War II, appropriating at first $500 million a year in 1944 for three years of road building in the Federal Aid Highway Act (actually, the Interstate and Defense Highway Act). In 1948, these appropriations were extended for two years, but the amount was cut to $450 million a year.

But the great boondoggle act, the legislation that enrages anti-highway people was certainly the Interstate Highway Act of 1956, for it established the Highway Trust Fund. The purpose of the fund, fed by taxes on such automotive necessities as gas, oil, and tires by the federal government, was to build 41,000 miles of toll-free express and urban freeways—the Interstates. The Pennsylvania Turnpike (which was ultimately funded) had demonstrated the public's willingness to pay for and use improved, limited-access high-speed roads, and the federal government was now funding 90 percent of this new cross-country system. Under some conditions, it was paying for as much as 95 percent of the system.

The quarrel of the anti-Interstaters was that the trust fund was inviolable. It was there to build the Interstates and only the Interstates. It was a commitment by the government to the automobile to the exclusion of every other means of surface transportation. To hell with the city dweller, said the Highway Trust Fund. Let him take a cab, let him walk, let him suffocate or wait his life away in antiquated busses and subways. The people-moving system of the future is the automobile. Let us give praise, and up to 95 percent federal funding to it. In 1956, the year after the great auto sales blitz, perhaps there were some honest men in the Congress who truly believed that they were doing the right thing. But there were certainly an equal number of national legislators who received the lavish favors of the Road Gang—the legislators, highway builders, and automobile industry who had pushed for the great roads. It was not until almost twenty years later, in 1973, with the oil embargo hovering about them, that the Congress realized a mistake of the most enormous proportions had been made by their predecessors, and opened the Highway Trust Fund to access by the advocates of mass transit.

So the Interstates were built. And they are still being built. Not many miles of them any more, but the system is almost complete. In terms of safety, the great highways that crisscross the land are marvels; they are, by a factor of seven, the safest roads in the nation—probably in the world. They are the pride of the Federal Highway Adminstration. They are the envy of nations less foresighted than ours with smaller road lobbying establishments. The great roads are also replete with instances of incredible stupidity by their planners; with miles of death traps; with mistakes so elementary an eight-year-old child with a jar of paste and a sheet of cardboard would not have made them.

All of these are chronicled in the report to the Committee on Public Works of the House by its Subcommittee on Investigations and Review entitled, *Highway Safety, Design and Operations (The Need for a Safer Driving Environment).* It is certainly one of the most curious documents in the Government Printing Office's inventory.

" 'There is nothing more terrible,' wrote Johann Goethe almost two hundred years ago,' " quotes the Subcommittee reports, " 'than activity without thought,' " and goes on to cite some of those activities in the building of the Interstates:

> Who could believe, for example, that millions of dollars' worth of guardrail has been incorrectly installed along the nation's highways, some of it actually endangering rather than protecting life?
>
> Or the clearance distances marked on overpasses are so unreliable that some trucking firms make their own measurements and publish their own guides for drivers?
>
> That a maintenance crew assigned to remove a hazardous roadside tree would cut it off so high as to leave an equally hazardous stump?
>
> That a commonly used minimum standard for lettering on road signs is so small that 20 percent of the driving population can't read the message?

The Subcommittee indictment of the highways lists: utility poles along the outside of curves that are hit and knocked over and replaced in the same place they were before; the use of fragile guardrail that collapses instantly on impact; exposed trees and bridge abutments; spearlike guardrail ends; guardrail without washers so the bolts pull right through the metal; ditches and culverts that direct an out-of-control car into a fixed object or over an embankment; gaps in guardrails that "snag" veering cars; muddy, soft, or rutted shoulders, sometimes with severe drop-offs; narrow walks on bridges that do not protect the stranded motorist and subject the car wandering out of its lane to an undue hazard; unguarded open spaces between parallel bridge spans where a spinning car could catapult into a river or the highway below. "It is imperative that overall and not just the initial costs of sometimes expensive safety-related design be considered. A thousand or a million dollars in construction costs are not 'saved' in any sense if subsequent losses through accidents, lawsuits, and design corrections add up to more than the initial paper 'saving.' One way or another, society pays for doing it wrong—and often many times over.

"Ironically . . . doing it right in the first place is frequently no more expensive. . . ."

The Subcommittee's revelations resulted in corrections costing the *new* Interstate system $383,178,313 in four years from 1967 to 1971, ". . . truly a sad commentary on wise stewardship of the taxpayer's dollars."

Roadside hazards are just one of some ten categories of complaint the Subcommittee had with the Road Gang's Interstates, as well as with government subsidized primary and secondary state roads.

There was "signing"—the verb for the design, manufacture, and hanging of signs on highways. A nice quote from a veteran automotive journalist says it all, "The important thing to understand about highway and freeway signs is that their logic is perfectly clear only to the highway engineer." The Subcommittee breaks this one down, too. Highway signs on federally funded roads are written in type so small they can't be seen; they are too close to the point of decision; signs often mark places nobody is going and ignore major areas nearby; signs don't bother to use the language the driver uses. (For example, "New York Thruway" or "Bayshore Freeway" are anathemas to sign makers—they're simply too clear.) There are often no signs at all at points where a driver must make a decision on which direction he needs to go; signs are often hung in such clusters that "a motorist traveling at a normal speed is befuddled; [there are] signs [that] have confusing shapes, symbols, and colors; often signs are filthy, concealed, lost in roadside clutter or unlit." In sum, said the Subcommittee, "Studies confirm that the lack of advance route information is probably the most glaring deficiency on the nation's freeways."

So you can kill yourself if you don't treat these fine new freeways as potential ambushers and you can get lost if you think you're going to make any sense of the signs on them. What else has the Highway Trust Fund contributed to our welfare?

The federal-aid system has produced even worse conditions on roads that aren't freeways. The list of the Subcommittee's criticisms goes from advance warning signs that are right in the middle of intersections instead of upstream of them, to the use of red signs meant to signal "go." In one series of lunatic usages an octagonal sign, which is supposed to indicate "stop" by its shape, has been used for "slow," which is not all that bad, as well as for "crosswalk," which begins to get whimsical, and "beware of flying golf balls," which is downright bizarre.

The Subcommittee didn't like accident investigation techniques. It said the investigations were too often conducted by police whose mind-set was to establish driver error instead of making a real attempt to interpret what had happened so that it might be corrected.

The Subcommittee was incensed at the failure of the states to be sympathetic to a uniform code of safety regulations.

Back on the subject of freeways, the Subcommittee was appalled at the failure of designers to understand that road surfaces present hazardous conditions when they are wet and to compensate by specifying grooved highways and gentler curves. Examples presented during the six years of testimony are terrifying.

There was a clear lack of leadership within the highway establishment both on federal and state levels; nobody wanted to make decisions, and decisions that were made weren't passed along to all those who needed to know them, complained the Subcommittee, so that if there were to be any change, it would be extremely hard to implement.

There is a real problem in resolving value conflicts, the Subcommittee conceded, but this shouldn't prevent some effort from being made. A value conflict as applied to the highway is much the same as a value conflict anywhere. Do we take environmental considerations inside the highway engineer's office, or do we leave them out howling in the cold? How about community priorities when it comes to widening a bridge for safety's sake? Perhaps that community would rather pave its gravel roads.

Finally, and with good reason, the Subcommittee was critical of the public, the people who use the highways. "Progress in protecting individuals from the carnage of the motor car must be achieved against [a] backdrop of ambivalence and apathy . . . The dedicated public servant must, in a sense, strive to protect the highway user and the pedestrian in the face of their classic indifference and non-cooperation."

You argue against that one. And while you're doing it, cast your mind back to the last trip you took on an Interstate. Think about conversations in the car (distractions), overloading, whether you checked the tires before you left, whether you were drunk or sober or somewhere in between, how fast you were going; think about the degree of your concentration. If suddenly a voice from nowhere had sounded offering you $1 million if you could call out the make of the last car you passed, even its color, would you be a millionaire today? There is a driver's test in England for the Institute of Advanced Motorists that takes five hours and requires its subjects, without warning, to list the last four signs the car has gone by. Could you list the last *one?*

So do not be too sure the Subcommittee was off base in classifying the driver a hazard as great as a highway that turns to a black ice-like nightmare at the first sign of a summer's sprinkle because an engineer in an office somewhere simply hasn't thought to put grooves in it, or has specified the wrong materials in the first place.

There is one criticism the Subcommittee did *not* consider. Those great concrete ribbons are deadly in a fashion that does not fall within the consideration of the bureaucrat. In a sense, despite the Subcommittee criticism, the builders of those roads succeeded too well. The great roads are alike, all of them.

Traversing their endless spans, the traveler loses the sense of the richness of the country. It is blanked away by the Stuckey signs, the Howard Johnson's, the rest stops, the Holiday Inns, the Shell Islands that occur and reoccur with numbing regularity as the miles spin out.

It used to be that a cross-country traveler could sense the atmosphere change as he went from state to state. We are a diverse people, and it shows not in macrocosm but in those details which make the landscape: the red Georgia clay; the lush green branches that close down on Connecticut roads making them into macadam trails; the bleak sand of the high Nevada desert cloaking the climbing two-laner from Las Vegas to Carson City in a sense of loneliness without end.

The Interstate has homogenized the landscape. There is no

Ohio as distinct from Indiana as distinct from Pennsylvania; there is only like-colored, like-marked, like-serviced highway. Route 80 in the Poconos is the same Route 80 that pierces the Donner Pass. The Delaware Water Gap and the summit of the Sierra stand strong enough in our history and our topography to resist the insidious cultural erosion of the great highway. But elsewhere on 80, the fine, rich mixture of America turns into a pale broth.

The Interstates take not only our lives, they take our heritage. The Subcommittee could not answer that one, but it did have solutions to the overall problem which it defined this way:

"We on the Subcommittee contend that the old maxim 'everyone loves a surprise' should not hold on the nation's highways."

In contemplating how to eliminate those deadly surprises that were killing and injuring so many people, the Subcommittee leaned heavily on Charles Prisk. Prisk, who had spent thirty-eight years in highway safety work, served the Subcommittee on Investigations and Review in much the same capacity that Ralph Nader served the Ribicoff Committee. Looking at Interstates in all nine Federal Highway Administration Regions, the Subcommittee advanced a variety of solutions.

The Subcommittee concluded it is more important to take some time to determine all the factors involved in the highway, and plan to include safety factors that will enhance the chance of survival of its user rather than risk his life. That may entail somewhat higher initial costs (although there is no certainty that it will), but it will save money in the long run and lives now.

In dealing with the variety of contractors and suppliers of a highway project, the Subcommittee suggested, make some effort to see that each knows what the other is up to. Signs, guardrail and drainage facilities, for example, interact. It is not only helpful, but indispensable, that they be integrated into a system rather than stuck on a ribbon of road like model railroad accessories.

If there is a problem between sign makers and guardrail manufacturers, there is an even more dramatic failure of coordination between the engineers who design the bridges of the great Interstates. Going from road to bridge and bridge to road is often a roller coaster experience. It can also be a game of chicken on one-lane rural roads. Neither of these is a desirable state of affairs.

There is a real need for a multidisciplinary approach to

highway design. Design, construction, traffic, and maintenance people should be in on the building of the road from the beginning. There is even room on such a team for a behavioral scientist. They should be active in its planning, its building, and they should make a thorough review of the road when it is complete. All too often, they will discover, it is not complete at all.

Ample room should be left on either side of an Interstate—thirty feet is a good distance—absolutely clear of any obstruction. This means new standards for planned roads; more important, it means that for roads that already exist, fixed barriers such as trees, unmovable poles, and killer guardrail must be removed. Exits and entries have to be equally antiseptic, and since Americans seem to have trouble keeping traffic flow moving on other than platter flat land, 6:1 grades should be thought of as an objective.

In addition to the removal of major killer barriers, we should not be so preoccupied that we ignore the lesser assassins: the signs that misdirect; the tightrope-wide walkway on the bridge that is threatening to the pedestrian and whose curb is a built-in trip for the motorist; the flared guardrail end which can skewer a motorist like a Thanksgiving turkey. We should as well pay attention to small enhancers of life on the hostile highway: the breakable signpost; the lowering of concrete footings so that they are flush with the ground; and the removal of all unnecessary curbs.

Somehow, researchers and road builders are not in touch with each other, said the Subcommittee sadly. The result is a series of little enclaves, totally out of touch with one another, unaware of what each is doing—perhaps duplicating efforts, perhaps going in opposite directions. All too clearly their work is in evidence on the highway: stoplights visible from several directions at once; a sign that points in multiple directions to indicate a single route to a single place.

And when all these things are done, there remains one further effort to be made. The new highway must be inspected when it is complete and then put in use as soon as possible so as to divert traffic from hazardous roads to safe ones.

"No single device ... should be viewed as a silver bullet solution to any traffic control problem. The overriding criterion to be applied is, what will work in dealing with people?" Those are the words of public servants who understand there is a real world out there and who wish to serve its needs. And so are these: "The motorized world that mixes people and cars is a complex one. We must act to simplify it wherever we can."

II

If cars are unsafe, if they pollute, if the great highways were born of boondoggle and midwived by scandal and are now characterized by disgracefully dangerous conditions and are only there at all because the Road Gang wanted to perpetuate a monolithic system of transportation—the private automobile—people moving by car works *despite* its excesses and its deficiencies.

In contrast virtue must lie in mass transit, we are told by many so-called experts. There is at least one expert who is *not* in the least so-called, the philosopher/urbanologist Lewis Mumford, who joins the mass transit chorus and chooses to meet the mass transit vs. automobile confrontation head on. He goes straight to the automotive temple, Los Angeles, to make his case. (The *City in History* was written in 1971):

> The reductio ad absurdum of [the car as people mover] myth is, notoriously, Los Angeles. Here the suburban standards of open space, with free standing houses, often as few as five houses to the acre, has been maintained; likewise the private motor car, as the major means of transportation has supplanted what was only a generation or so ago an extremely efficient system of public transportation.
>
> Los Angeles has now become an undifferentiated mass of houses, walled off into sectors by many-laned expressways, with ramps and viaducts that create special bottlenecks of their own. These expressways move but a small fraction of the traffic per hour once carried by public transportation, at a much lower rate of speed, in an environment befouled by smog, itself produced by the lethal exhausts of the technologically backward motor cars. More than a third of the Los Angeles area is consumed by these grotesque transportation facilities; *two-thirds* of central Los Angeles are occupied by streets, freeways, parking facilities, garages. This is space-eating with a vengeance. The last stage of the process already beckons truly progressive minds—to evict the remaining inhabitants and turn the

entire area over to automatically propelled vehicles, completely emancipated from any rational human purpose.

Mumford does not propose that we must reconsider that "extremely efficient system of public transportation" for Los Angeles. But others do. At this moment a debate rages in Los Angeles about the investment by the city in a new public transportation system as well as about why the old one vanished.

Setting the stage for the proponents of revived mass transit in Los Angeles is James Flink's summary and analysis of the destruction of the old system:

> National City Lines (the GM et al holding company) in 1940 began buying up and scrapping parts of Pacific Electric, the world's largest interurban electric rail system, which by 1945 served 110 million passengers in 56 smog-free Southern California communities. Eleven hundred miles of Pacific Electric's track were torn up, and the system went out of service in 1961, as Southern California commuters came to rely narrowly on freeways. By 1974 Los Angeles was struggling to reestablish the viable mass-transit system it had lost. Mayor Tom Bradley complained before the Hart committee [Senator Philip A. Hart's antitrust subcommittee investigating the restructuring of the automobile and ground transportation industries] that GM had restricted competition and thwarted technological advances in bus manufacture. He anticipated that the Southern California Rapid Transit District alone needed 1,400 new buses, while nationwide production was only 3,700 in 1973. San Francisco Mayor Joseph Alioto, an antitrust lawyer, charged that a once fine electrical rail system in the Bay Area also had been destroyed by the "terrifying power of the auto monopoly." He alleged that "the basic monopolistic practice in the auto industry is the interlacing and interlocking control of competing modes of transportation."

There stands the indictment and the unspoken case for a great new system. It says, in effect, mass transit was killed in Los Angeles in order to shift people out of public transportation and into automobiles. That view—and the consequent brief for mass transit—does not go unchallenged. In April of 1976, the Institute for Public Policy Research of the University of Southern California's Center for Public Affairs gathered a group of distinguished experts to discuss transportation alternatives for the area.

In its published report, there was unanimous disagreement with Flink.

Professors Peter Gordon and Ross Eckert, both economists, gave the introductory perspective, summarizing the views of the scholars at the symposium.They noted that Los Angeles took over its public transportation system in 1946 as an "almost reflexive response" to disinterest in it by private entrepreneurs. This, they documented, was no unique phenomenon. It was a common occurrence in the United States, and it had begun in the '20s. As economists, they felt it important to say that it was not only a common solution but an unusual one, since it is rare that subsidies are given to an enterprise that fails the market test. It was done because public transportation was thought to confer special benefits on the population of a community that were important to preserve: Lack of congestion on the streets and highways; less cost to build new highways; lower maintenance for those already built; an improvement in the quality of the community's air; and lower demand for fossil fuels. Finally there was an overriding social benefit. Public transportation served the "transit-dependent" citizen. But there was a caveat. If the community operation of public transportation systems were to be successful, it had to be able to divert auto travelers away from their cars. "Diversion is *the key* issue: a transit system that does not divert drivers in droves will not have 'mass' patronage, without which it cannot offer the intended external benefits of less congestion, pollution, or energy consumption."

That is getting ahead of things, but by reversing Gordon and Eckert's question of diversion, we're back on the tracks again. Were the big red cars of the Pacific Electric Railway diverted by conspiracy, or by any other intrusive happening? Or would they have gone into museums eventually anyway?

There is some reasonable quarrel with the contention that the big red cars ever constituted that "highly efficient" system their mourners proclaimed on their behalf. George W. Hilton, a UCLA economics professor, does not like the conspiracy theory. Particularly he does not like the Snell Report which "has argued that General Motors maliciously brought about the conversion of the

Pacific Electric to bus operation through control by its partly owned subsidiary, National City Lines."

One of the problems with the National City Lines theory is that the National City Lines never owned Pacific Electric and its big red cars. P.B. was controlled by the Southern Pacific Railroad.

In a sense that begs the question about the survival of the system. The central Los Angeles rail system was owned by the Los Angeles Railway, a streetcar line. Its gauge and the gauge used by Pacific Electric were incompatible. Pacific Electric shared track with the Southern Pacific.

The Pacific Electric system *was* comprehensive. (As an interurban, says Professor Hilton, it had no equal for size. It represented about 10 percent of the investment of all United States interurbans. It had over 1,000 miles of track and 700 route miles.) But it had some problems. It was highly centralized from downtown Los Angeles and spread out radially from the city's center (with whose streetcar tracks its own were not compatible, remember. This was partially solved by widening the streetcar tracks with the addition of an outside third rail so both the trolleys and the big red cars could use some of the same rights of way). This meant two things: there was a great deal of surface street running, which did not allow for even reasonable speed; secondly, with the rail running on the surface for by far the greater part of its length, there were many grade crossings, which were "greatly troubling."

For a while the company's operations were profitable. But in 1923 business began a decline that continued for the duration of the line's life. The Depression was a particular blow; it was a killer to many city streetcar and interurban lines in the nation. The big red cars lost half their business from 1929 to 1933. Five years later, the Southern Pacific began cutting back on its passenger service which represented about three-quarters of its business; the other quarter was devoted to moving freight. By 1950, most of the passenger service was gone and in 1954 SP sold the remaining passenger lines to the Metropolitan Coach Lines—like National City, a GM et al inspired company. It is interesting that Metropolitan Coach applied for permission to convert to bus passenger service, but got it only for the Hollywood and Burbank lines it had bought. Why, if the city was so eager for public transportation?

The last route—Los Angeles–Long Beach—was abandoned April 9, 1961.

That it lasted at all is remarkable. In Chicago, the five interurban routes were similar. They spread out radially from the city's center. The first succumbed in 1927; the second in 1933. The third, which went into sprouting suburban areas, lasted until 1957; the fourth continued two years after the abandonment of the Los Angeles–Long Beach service. One remains—the Chicago South Shore and South Bend—and it would like very much to get out of the passenger business. The point to the Chicago comparison is that Chicago distances are long, although by no means as long as those in Los Angeles. But Chicago is approximately three times more densely populated than L.A. and has about the same factor of business concentration in its downtown area, the center of the system, as the one in Los Angeles. Further, as Professor Hilton says, "It has a large financial community, water barriers on three sides of the central business district and a harsh climate . . ." which is not encouraging to drivers.

Professor Hilton thinks some blame for Pacific Electric's death can be placed upon its very nature. Los Angeles didn't grow along the radial routes of its interurban, as did Chicago. Separate communities grew in clumps around the routes, but they were pretty much self-contained and, to a degree, they coalesced. This made downtown Los Angeles a less and less important center, since the communities served by the big red cars had their own centers, most of them preferred to Los Angeles as shopping areas by their residents. It was inevitable, then, that use of the Pacific Electric should decline, as it did.

These are solid reasons to question the conspiracy theory. At the very least they are reasons to conclude that if there had been a conspiracy it would have been redundant; there were too many factors at work undermining the continued health of Pacific Electric to have allowed it to survive. The question left is, should Pacific Electric have been subsidized in order to grant Los Angelenos the benefits of public transportation despite the railroad's inability to survive on its own?

In support of that view was the fact of Pacific Electric's right of way, its company-owned geography. It was so laid out that it could have been converted into an effective rapid transit line. And that, given an effective job of upgrading, might have diverted drivers to rapid transit riders, relieving road congestion and cutting down on air pollution.

Professor Hilton does not entirely believe even that could have happened. Although the right of way of the big red cars invited upgrading, there was no guarantee that however upgraded it became it would have taken drivers out of their cars. As an economist, Hilton resorts to a discussion of "elasticity" when he talks about why this is so. Elasticity reflects the response of one factor to a change in another one: use to price. The automobile has "a strongly positive income elasticity of demand." When income goes up people want to use their cars more. Mass transit has positive income elasticity of demand only in low income brackets, below $4,000 a year. As between cars and mass transit, the "cross elasticity of demand ... which is to say the responsiveness of consumers of one service to a change in the price of the other, is so low as closely to approach zero."

This is esoteric stuff. But the infamous case of the Bay Area Rapid Transit District project is not. A good man through whose eyes to examine BART is Martin Wohl, professor of transportation system planning at Carnegie-Mellon University.

Wohl's BART-as-failure argument begins provocatively: "... if rail rapid transit was even *a* way—much less *the* way—to 'cure' the traffic congestion and pollution problem, then why is congestion and pollution so bad in New York, Chicago, Boston, and Philadelphia? And why, if rail rapid transit is so attractive to people, are the five older U.S. rail rapid transit systems *losing* patrons—even as both capital and operating subsidies are increasing and as new lines and stations are being added?" The standard answer, that these are in fact the older, unattractive systems—slow and dirty—is simplistic.

A good system of rail rapid transit would be fast, clean, up-to-date to attract people to ride it. This would lure people from their automobiles and it would help the transit dependent. It would have a high capacity—30,000 to 40,000 people per hour per track.

Those were exactly the virtues BART promised when it came before the people for approval. "The main purpose of Rapid Transit is to eliminate the oppressive traffic congestion," the BART people proclaimed as BART went on the market. "To accomplish this, the BART system must be so appealing that commuters will choose, most willingly, to ride the trains to and from work each day, instead of struggling along crowded traffic arterials in their cars. The trains must be competitive with the private automobile in terms of comfort, speed, cost, and convenience."

Only part of the routes BART promised the people were funded. Its highly automated systems are working sporadically; some have been abandoned. BART, despite space-age cars gleaming in white and blue, handsome as Apollo rockets, is carrying far fewer people than expected. On all lines, BART is carrying about 120,000 persons a day, instead of the expected 30,000 to 40,000 an hour. The great tube beneath San Francisco Bay is transporting only about 26,000 persons in each direction per day. Meanwhile, the Bay Bridge, that anachronistic monument to the automobile, is carrying 110,000 persons each day in each direction.

Traffic congestion continues in the San Francisco Bay Area. BART didn't even hit its principal target, the Bay Bridge or its approaches. A BART impact study reported, "Traffic levels at the *busiest* hours showed only small reductions."

The new, hugely expensive rail rapid transit system San Francisco hoped would be a model for the world *may* be cheaper to ride than the private auto is to operate, although that is not absolutely certain, but it is *not* an improvement in speed. On the surface, BART's fare is cheaper than the cost of running a car over the same route. But as we shall see, that fare is highly subsidized. At the same time, it takes longer to ride BART trains than it does to drive a car from one place in the Bay Area to another. Transbay BART riders lose thirteen minutes in the trip. Only those who have spent a decade or more commuting have an understanding of what an added twenty-six minutes a day consumed by travel really means.

As for the so-called transit dependent, he hasn't profited much either. Forty percent of BART's users come from families who have incomes of $20,000 or more. In addition, only 40 percent of BART users get to the trains by method other than auto. This surely does not speak strongly for BART's usefulness to the transit dependent.

At least in terms of BART's original promise, it is a failure. Is it the only such?

There are two new rail rapid transit lines in Chicago, the Dan Ryan and Kennedy lines. They run in the median or adjoin highways. In the case of the Ryan, rail rapid transit carries 110,000 persons each day. The highway adjacent takes 160,000. The figures should at the very least be reversed. The numbers for the Kennedy are even worse: 60,000 for transit, double that for the highway.

But those are the most optimistic of examples.

The Lindenwold Line from New Jersey to Philadelphia is automated and high speed. It carries just 20,000 persons per day each way. Just 10,000 persons per day use the South Shore Line to Boston and the same number back. The airport extension from Cleveland draws 5,000 persons daily each way.

A BART team looked at these three lines and decided the same thing they decided about the San Francisco–Oakland Bay Bridge traffic. "No perceptible changes in traffic congestion were recorded on [the parallel highway] facilities," notes Wohl, whereupon he asks the crusher questions: Why are we providing such facilities? What can we do to improve them?

We have already discussed much of the "why." It involves fuel savings and aid to the transit dependent and the reduction of traffic congestion. But there is another reason. Somehow we know deep down in our hearts that mass transit by rail is the cheapest form of transportation, particularly when it is compared to the automobile. Wohl would have us all take another look. ". . . the record is sordid, to be blunt about it, and it seems high time to blow the whistle on the high-priced PR experts and fancy analysts who estimate and bandy about the expected costs and revenues for these modern-day urban saviors."

The Lindenwold Line was going to cost $54 million. It ended up costing $92 million. The South Shore Line was going to be $74 million going in. Coming out it was $111 million. Their cost overruns were cab fare tips compared to BART's and the Washington, D.C. Metro's.

Revised figures for D.C. Metro, offered in 1969, after the project was sold to the Congress and local and state governments had been required to give approval and become involved, were $2.5 billion for capital outlay (including 30 percent built in for contingency and inflation), and annual maintenance and operating costs to come to some $32 million. Six years later, the Metro folk were back with some revised revised numbers. They had made this little mistake, the figures were *not* actually $2.5 billion and $32 million respectively; they were, in fact, *$4.5* billion and *$129* million instead. "Very tidy! " notes Wohl. "Only an 80 percent mistake on the capital outlay side in six years and a 300 percent 'slip' with respect to maintenance and operating costs."

BART was going to cost $1 billion to build and $13 million a year to operate when its district director said ebulliently in 1964, "We are obligated to complete this system within the funds made available by the voters." When completed, BART cost $1.6 billion to build and $57 million a year to operate. BART had promised the people of the Bay Area a $10 million a year surplus. It has suffered annual financial reversals of $40 million instead. Professor Wohl points out that while the BART fare-payer is getting something of a break in comparison to what it might cost him to drive his car, it is costing the public about $5.40 for each BART trip instead of the estimated $1.30. "Put differently, with an actual average fare running about 60 cents (not 30 cents as planned), each BART rider is subsidized to the tune of $4.80."

A Sierra Club spokesman, quoted by James Flink, has said, "Time has shown [the freeway advocates'] vision was inadequate. They have put us in a horrible kind of box, committing us to a transportation system that was fundamentally evil."

A transportation system that relies entirely on highways and cars is bad—perhaps not fundamentally evil, but certainly bad. But are those who wish to commit us to their vision of rail rapid transit so much more virtuous?

III

"Modal mix" is the term used to describe the immediate solutions to our complex, dangerous, and expensive problems of moving people and goods around. "What an effective [transportation] network requires," says Lewis Mumford, "is the largest number of alternative modes of transportation, at varying speeds and volumes, for different functions and purposes."

That is modal mix. It includes cars, busses, rail rapid transit, commuter airlines, bicycles, pedestrain "aids" (escalators, for example), motorcycles, para-transit (mini-busses and jitneys), and computer car pooling. "To have a complete urban structure capable of functioning fully, it is necessary to find appropriate channels for every form of transportation; it is the deliberate articulation of the pedestrian, the mass transit system, the street, the avenue, the expressway, and the airfield that alone can care for the needs of a modern community. Nothing less will do."

It is not only an "urban structure" we are compelled to think about, it is a village, a suburb, a farm. Ninety percent of our private transportation is now by automobile. That will no longer do. What will we use instead? Of the systems we now have, how will we make them more used, more efficient, more prominent in the mix?

We know cars are going to change their shapes and their sizes, but it won't be until the '80s that there will be measurably less congestion on the highways as a result of smaller cars and fewer of them—the inevitable consequence of energy conservation legislation.

We can look to an increase in the use of large busses both in urban areas and in commuter service between suburb and central business district. There is already a striking example of how such service is attracting people who used to drive. It tells us that busses, which are cheaper and quicker to build than new rail systems, can take up a good deal of the burden of mass transit if only we are willing to try them and if only we give incentives to use them. Upper-income drivers are now going to their jobs in Washington, D.C. using the Shirley Highway Service, a system in which busses collect people from the areas in which they live and then zip downtown on freeways with special express bus lanes. Surveys of riders on the Shirley Service show they are using it because the schedules are reliable, they need go to minimum inconvenience to get to the busses, and the amount of time it takes to get to work compares favorably to that taken when they drove. "Interview studies showed that 82 percent of those electing to use the busses in the corridor did have a car available for the trip, whereas nearly half the users of conventional pre-existing bus service in the corridor did not have cars available," says Professor Martin Wachs, head of the Urban Planning Program of UCLA's School of Architecture and Urban Planning. Three-quarters of the Shirley patrons who drove to the bus stops had incomes greater than $15,000 a year. Over half of those who walked to the points of pickup had equally high incomes. There were more men than women on the Shirley busses, important because women tend to be more transit dependent. This statistic led observers to the conclusion that Shirley busses represented a conscious choice in travel mode. The sum of the Shirley study was that the people riding the service's busses into Washington were more like auto commuters than bus commuters. "The most impressive statistic is that of all the commuters in the Shirley Corridor who lived in areas served by the busses and worked in areas served by the busses, some forty percent have elected to ride the bus transit system rather than driving to work." The Shirley Highway Service also provides the two amenities that travelers seem to want: the busses are air-conditioned and there is a high probability that a seat will be available. (Interestingly, commuters who have been polled do not list exquisite environmental surroundings very high on their list of desirables. They want reliable service above all things.)

To the degree that we do not invest enormous amounts of money in them, we can and must upgrade existing rail rapid transit routes and equipment. We have them. They carry demonstrably significant numbers of people. They are relied upon by those people to take them along predictable routes that often mark the boundaries of their riders' lives. We must abandon neither the routes nor the people. In every way that we can upgrade trackage and equipment to provide metrospeed interurban rail transit, we should also do that.

Computer car pooling is embryonic in the sense that it is only now beginning to be recognized as a solution to congestion on the highway. We could not only encourage it, using municipal computers and employees, but we could open the system to allow the owner of a car who wants to use it as a kind of private minibus to charge for his services. This would require some regulation, obviously. But it would also go some way toward solving the disgraceful waste of transporting a single 175-pound man to work in a 4,000-pound car.*

---

* A significant new step is van pooling. In its Febrary 28, 1977 issue, *Business Week* called the subsidy of ten to twelve-passenger vans for the transport of employees to and from work by corporations, "A new type of mass transit network."

Within urban areas, or higher population density areas, there are numbers of solutions we could implement right now. The first is the encouragement of so-called "para-transit." Para-transit refers, essentially, to demand/response vehicles: the mini-busses, the taxis, and the jitneys. Jitneys are actually outlawed in many cities. There is no sensible reason why one car or limousine can't carry a number of people picked up at a variety of spots and delivered at a variety of other destinations. The "outlaw" jitney is an anachronism. It is time we made it an integral part of our transportation system.

We can and should encourage the use of motorcycles. They are efficient transportation devices. The anti-motorcycle argument is that they are dangerous and noisy. That is true. But we have begun to set national and state standards for equipment to be included in their manufacture. We can and should (California and several other states to the contrary) require the use of helmets by those who ride motorcycles. We can and should encourage the use of small displacement engined motorcycles and discourage the use of the big-engined bikes.

Bicycles are an overlooked and important part of any rational transportation system. They are odorless, colorful, and efficient. They do not pollute. They are inexpensive. They take up little space. They offer the added benefit of conferring an opportunity for exercise to their users. But, like motorcycles, they are dangerous. Anyone who has traveled in a car in a college town such as Palo Alto, California or Eugene, Oregon knows that a bicycle that wanders out of a bike lane or is ridden at night without its rider wearing reflective clothing or without the bike's showing a light, is a dreadful hazard. Fortunately, standards are being contemplated for bicycles, shocking as that might seem. A fall from a bicycle is as potentially dangerous as a head-on automobile accident. Few, if any, bicyclists think to wear protective headgear. The result is injury to the skull, and that in turn results in much higher than reasonable fatality or serious injury rate to the rider.

We can and should encourage walking. This is a city planning function. Cities must be made safe and attractive places in which to walk. There must be mini-parks in which to rest or picnic. We can build ramps and escalators. We can even use those moving sidewalks beginning to be common in airports across the land. These devices are called "pedestrian aids" by transportationists. The point here is that we often forget the pedestrian is a part of the transportation mix. He should be encouraged.

All of this seems reasonable, but the technology and the devices and the ideas have been around for a while and they have yet to work. So the problem posed is this: How do we "divert"? We divert by making it easy to use things other than the automobile. At the same time we make it expensive and inconvenient to drive. These things, too, are in our power to do immediately.

Some of the ways of diverting are clear and have been mentioned: Continued (but not increased) subsidy for rail and bus; upgrading of equipment and trackage; discounts on use, including subsidized out-of-central district parking. But we can also have open exchange systems for cross-use of public transportation to a far greater extent than we have now. And we can fill the work years of present seasonal or part-time labor to insure that the equipment used in mass transit systems is clean and functioning.

We have failed, not so much in offering incentives for use of public transportation as in not levying penalties on the use of the automobile. The most important penalty of all is the most reasonable: we can charge the driving public for the full cost of the automobile. For example, in the Los Angeles basin, planners who focus on the car estimate about $800 million a year in visible revenues and expenses—while ignoring as much as four times that amount in hidden costs. Ward Elliott, of the Rose Institute of State and Local Government at Claremont Men's College breaks down the hidden costs into the difference between what is collected and what is spent by governments on auto-generated expenditures, smog costs, and costs of congestion. According to his estimates, and he admits they are rough, the motorist is subsidized to the tune of about a penny a mile in budgetary services and tax exemptions. He is subsidized three times that amount in free pollution rights, depending on where he drives and what time of day. It *could* go as high as fifteen cents a mile if he has an old car and drives during peak traffic hours near, say, the Los Angeles International Airport. In terms of the "time cost" of peak hour driving to everyone concerned, the "average hidden-public costs" can be 6.3 cents a mile, *"five times* conventionally reckoned public costs of 1.2 cents a mile in state and federal taxes for a compact car . . . a peak-hour driver enjoys hidden subsidies of about $2 per workday in the summer and $1 per workday in the winter." Congestion costs are reckoned on travel time's being calculated at half the value of working time. ". . . congestion, like smog, is a common problem," says Elliott, "where the road user imposes more delay on others than he incurs for himself . . ." According to Elliott's figures in Los Angeles, hidden subsidies amount to about twelve cents a gallon. Included in that is the exemption of freeway land from the tax base.

So what the experts call a "disincentive" to the use of a private automobile in Los Angeles would be the adding of twelve cents a gallon to the price of gasoline. That would disincent a lot of people. Parenthetically, if this revenue were not used to clean up the mess the car makes, it could well be allocated to subsidy of public transportation.

Great chunks of Berkeley, California are already closed to cars. Parts of many other cities have their central business districts (known in the transportation trade as CBDs) converted to walking and shopping malls. Clearly, if there are no streets on which to drive a car, cars will not enter the cities. More communities must be closed to automobiles, and soon. Much of this depends on having alternative means of transportation. Amsterdam has city-owned mini-cars, low polluters and a source of revenue to the community. That seems a little way off for most of this country, although the system is being studied carefully in a number of states and cities.

In addition to closing the central business districts to auto-mobiles, municipalities could deny access to truck delivery during the daylight hours. That is not too great a hardship to impose. For centuries, farm produce was delivered to Paris's central market at night. That is still the practice in many European cities and a good number of American ones.

A whole series of "little diverters" make use of the car less convenient than it is now. California seems bound and determined to cut the use of the automobile by about a quarter, largely using these systems.

One such little diverter is the ramp meter. It is nothing more than a stoplight (or golight) leading onto a freeway. Using sensors, it regulates the flow onto the freeway and therefore *on* the freeway, feeding cars out in time with the pace of the traffic. It is often easier and quicker to opt for underused surface streets than to wait for the golight during rush hours.

A variation on the diamond lane is the toll lane for car pool vehicles, and that seems to work quite well, particularly when coupled with diamond lanes on the bridge onto which the booths feed.

Many communities are putting increasing money into enforcement of parking laws. They are upping fines (a source of revenue not to be overlooked) and making it very expensive indeed to park within their confines.

Cities are charging high tolls to enter and nothing to leave where access to them is by bridge or tunnel. Early results of both these devices—the high toll and the high parking costs—looked at by themselves or together, seem discouraging. New York is a prime case of failure of either or both of these "solutions" to bring much relief. To cross the Triboro Bridge from the Bronx or Queens into Manhattan costs seventy-five cents in toll. To park in the city can cost $9 a day. To park illegally *could* result in having your car towed to a police impound garage in which you might as well leave it forever if the car is worth $200 or less. The price of bail is just too high.

Singapore has a little diverter that seems to be working well, one which we have not tried in this country. Should you need or wish to drive during peak hours, you are required to buy a colored sticker that costs about $2 and must be displayed on the windshield. For those who drive at saner times, a sticker is still required, but it is of a different color and costs less.

There is no guarantee, of course, but if you close central business districts to cars, provide alternate means of transportation, charge the real costs of car use to the driver, and institute a system of traffic management through the use of many and integrated "little diverters," you might look forward to a significant decrease in auto usage as well as an increase in revenue.

None of this is blue sky. We are doing much in this direction right now; we simply need to do more of it. We have closed some cities, and we have closed many areas within many other cities.

We have legislated away the big car. We are providing incentive for cars that do not pollute (Oldsmobile should be announcing a diesel-powered car as you read this); we have computer car pools. We have grasped, but we must extend, the concept of staggered work hours and the four-day work week. We should do a great deal more investigation into parking management. Electric vehicles are being made, some of which could be easily converted into city-owned fleets. Others have been delivering mail in urban areas for years. There is even one route—between Chicago and Detroit—that has intermediate stops geared to recharge electric cars.

In contemplating the future, let us understand "future" can as well mean tomorrow morning as it can the year 2000. There is no need to surrender control of the car or the highway to mystical federal agencies run by remote bureaucrats. The building of the car, its design and its sale can be determined by market pressures; whether Detroit is willing to admit that or not. Recent consumer influence is clearly evident in the industry's triple design and conversion plays of the last three years: big cars to small cars to big cars. As for emissions control, highway building, safety (to air bag or not to air bag), and mass transit, you may be sure state and federal agencies alike are waiting, somewhat fearfully perhaps, to hear from you. Nonetheless, Detroit and the government confidently expect to go on doing as they please.

They haven't heard from you thus far and not much tells them they ever will.

Part Four

(with Tom Mandel)

"Futurism differs from planning . . .
by reaching beyond economics to embrace
culture, beyond transportation to include in its
concerns family life and sex roles,
beyond physical and environmental concerns
to include mental health. . . . ". . . without
broad-scale citizen involvement, even the
most conscientious and expertly drawn
plans are likely to blow up in our faces."

—ALVIN TOFFLER,
The Eco-Spasm Report

9 : 2001: A Continuing Odyssey

I

As far as the eye of the futurist can see—perhaps as much as fifty years out—the car will remain what it is today: the principal module in our transportation system.

That is not to say it is going to be the car as we know it. For one thing, we can't expect the future to be a simple extension of the past. Many different variables are affecting the future of our society, and the shape of society will inevitably affect the automobile. We cannot, for example, now predict absolutely what effect the great winter freeze and drought of 1977 will have. Mainly it made us aware of problems with getting enough natural gas for heating and generating electricity. That, and gradually declining domestic oil production, mean that *probably* we will end up importing more oil because, when we can't get enough natural gas, oil is our next favorite fuel. Perhaps the federal government will soon be able to fashion a comprehensive energy program; *probably* it will be frustrated in implementing it, and we will continue to import almost half our oil for some time to come. But foreign oil means more expensive fuel and, if it is unreasonable to speculate about $1.00 a gallon gasoline in 1978, to suggest $1.50 a gallon in a few more years is betting on a sure thing. Eventually we know we will have to find some substitute for

237

gasoline. How soon and at what price are unknowns directly affecting the design of automobiles and how we use them. Now if one oil embargo and one season of dramatically bad weather can make so profound a difference in the price of a commodity critical to the automobile's future, what could happen if the great high pressure ridge off the Pacific Coast that seems to have caused this curious change in our climate were to remain there for several years? We don't know. We can assume devastating social consequences: people fleeing frozen northern cities; midwestern agriculture shuddering from drought followed by drought; and huge amounts of oil allocated by fiat to keep our power plants running and our homes heated; and, indirectly, profound impacts on personal transportation. But what might they be?

Or, alternatively, the climate remains favorable; OPEC decides that inexpensive oil is to everyone's benefit; and Detroit comes up with a clean, thirty-five miles-per-gallon, six-passenger car. What then?

When you're in the prediction-making business, one way of dealing with not knowing is to suppose alternative situations. Stanford Research Institute has done a lot of predicting lately, much of it about transportation. In a report prepared for *National Transportation Facts and Trends* by the Department of Transportation, SRI said, "Since there are an infinite number of possible futures, the first problem is to select some manageable number for analysis . . . it appears that three futures based on the dimensions of goals and success subsume most of the futures regarded as really likely in the next several decades. These are: Traditional values successfully realized; traditional values attempted but not realized owing to external causes; and a major shift away from traditional values." SRI calls these three, "Success," "Distress," and "Transformation."

Here are the three SRI future scenarios described and renamed:

BLUE SKIES, HIGH PRESSURE ALOFT; MODERATE TEMPERATURE, NO PRECIPITATION: A LOVELY QUARTER DECADE FOR A DRIVE. (SUCCESS)

All credit to Herman Kahn, the father, mother, and midwife of the alternate scenario for this one. There are others who agree with him in his optimism. This one says we used to be poor, now we're rich. Although much of the world is still poor, it has the same, perhaps better opportunities than we had and soon it will be rich, too. We are not going to be bothered *in the long run* with overpopulation, energy shortages, resource shortages, food shortages, permanently bad weather, or war. Of course there are many problems to solve, and a good many of those have to be solved in a very short period of time. But in the long run, we will look back on all this turmoil we seem to be having and wonder, "Why were we so upset?"

LOW MOVING IN WITH LOWER AND LOWER LOWS BEHIND IT. RAIN FOLLOWED BY SLEET FOLLOWED BY HAIL FOLLOWED BY BLIZZARD FOLLOWED BY AN ICE AGE. STAY HOME IF YOU VALUE YOUR LIFE. (DISTRESS)

For this we depend on Paul R. Ehrlich and Anne H. Ehrlich, primarily from their book *The End of Affluence*. A little *Future Shock* and a lot of *Eco-Spasm Report*, both by Alvin Toffler, tend in the same direction as the Ehrlichs, but with substantial modifications. This is the doomsday scenario. It says we have already experienced the leading edge of catastrophe with the great fuel shortage of 1973. Growth has gotten out of control, it is already too late to save the world from famine, energy depletion, overpopulation, economic collapse. There are some things that we can do as individuals to ameliorate our situations, but we cannot look to the lives of our children with anything but dejection. A century from now the survivors will be looking back and asking, "Why did we let it happen?"

ROSY-FINGERED DAWN: RAIN FOLLOWED BY SLEET FOLLOWED BY THE QUESTION, "WAIT A MINUTE, WHY DON'T WE DO A LITTLE EXPERIMEN-TATION IN WEATHER MODIFICATION?" (TRANSFORMATION)

This, too, in all likelihood begins with dark clouds, shortages, and depression. But before the avalanche achieves critical momentum, a significant group in society is able to escape it by embracing values that put them out of its path. Since they are not caught up in the problems of overpopulation, overuse of energy despoiling of the land, and callous disregard for the environment, they are able not only to sidestep many of the effects of the doomsday scenario, but also (which is perhaps more important) to reduce the impact of disaster on the rest of the world. This scenario says we have pursued affluence too long, that its product has resulted in a great, fat overdependent land; that affluence has brought with it all the evils of obesity: immobility where there should have been mobility, addiction to consumption where there should have been freedom to be ascetic. It says that we have come to take the obesity as a given; that we would not dream of examining its real cost, its crippling effects on us. But the time has come to do just that.

In this sense, a "futures" chapter could easily be called a "warnings" or a "solutions" chapter.

Our preference is in the direction of a solution, for we think there is a solution based on a modification of the use of the automobile, which as should be clear, is historically and realistically the major transportation device in the United States and can and should remain so for at least the next quarter century. Rosy-fingered dawn is appealing also because it suggests that engaging in active forecasting can be accompanied by self-determination. We can decide to alter our lives and alter our futures in consequence. This is what the third scenario represents. The first two imply surrender to overpowering forces. We do not see the inevitability of such surrender. But take the warnings if you wish. Doomsday is not a course we anticipate with glee, but we are not so sanguine as to conclude it is less possible than the other alternatives.

In our judgment, it is the Kahnian view, the success scenario, in which the danger lies. For although it is the most complacent, should it be accepted without question by the majority of Americans, the possibility of difficulty or disaster would turn into certainty. There is a consensus that the problems are out there waiting. It is our view that you do what you can to anticipate them.

II

To the many members of the Society of the End-of-the-World, the facts of survival are grim. The keys, they say, are energy supply and population. The first is draining away, the second turning into a flood.

The Blue Sky People shake their heads reprovingly and wonder how the End-of-the-Worlders can be so wrong. It is clear we have lived and grown on cheap energy during the period in which the western nations developed as industrial states. That was necessary, or at very least convenient. But we are no longer simply industrial, and energy is no longer cheap.

Still, that need not deter us from continued growth.

Pausing to lay the foundations of such growth is worthwhile and Herman Kahn's book, *The Next 200 Years,* is helpful in formulating the stages through which we have passed, are passing and will pass, on our way to permanent Blue Skies.

At first the economic process is based on extraction; that is to say resources are exploited. Crops are planted, grown, and sowed. Mines are dug and their ores brought out. The seas and the forests are harvested. City dwellers are few in such a society; the ratio is perhaps 20–1 in favor of those who live on farms. Whereupon society shifts to one in which the important activities are construction and manufacturing, the processing of those goods taken from the land. This results in a population shift from farm to city.

The third stage—an agonizing one we are now passing through on our way to serenity—is the transformation from an industrial to a service economy. Here emphasis is placed on the affairs of the work force that support both the exploitation of resources (the primary stage of the economy) and their conversion into goods (the secondary stage). People are engaged in transportation, finance, education, and regulation. From this tertiary postindustrial society the step is into a quaternary society, in which people do things for their own sake. In its emphasis on activities that satisfy human needs and a new kind of value that is nonmaterialistic, the quaternary stage so resembles the chief characteristic in the third scenario (Rosy-Fingered Dawn), that we will delay its specifics until we arrive there. Not to minimize quaternary, but under Blue Skies, it's a "ways out," which is futurese for "not immediately foreseeable."

We are tertiaries, you and I, in this view of the development of society, and we can afford to be.

For example, population growth on the planet will peak by the year 2050. If Blue Skies is right in its guess that there will be adequate supplies of everything, it suggests the slowing of the rate of population growth will be the result of a reduction in demand. Essentially, we will see the same pattern in the rest of the world as we have seen in the United States. Given affluence, children have a lower economic value than they do in a primary society; it costs more to bring them up and educate them; and there is an intrusion of a variety of religious and family anomalies—at least in traditional perspective—all of which lessens the interest in and pressure for large, cohesive families. Birth rates are already leveling off in the United States and so are death rates; thus we reach population equilibrium.

The underdeveloped countries grow, in the Blue Skies view, through the action of at least ten devices: the availability to them of capital markets and technology; their own export to over-developed countries of a labor force who save their money and send some home (all the while learning important skills abroad); the import of export-oriented industry—an example of which would be moving an auto assembly plant to the Philippines where labor is cheap; tourism; technology transfer, primarily agricultural technology; the availability of "useful examples" (quixotically, OPEC based its organization and embargo quota systems on those invented by the Texas Railroad Commission in the '30s); the importation of activities the developed countries feel they can no longer afford to have carried on within their own borders; substitution of home grown industry for import industry; the existence of strong internal stability resulting from the possession by underdeveloped countries of materials which the postindustrial states need; and finally, foreign aid.

Thus, the Blue Sky argument goes, there will be a leveling off not only of population, but also of economic growth. That is, because there will be a stable number of people in the world, production will reach a point where it is as costly in what we now think of as underdeveloped countries as it is in large, rich ones. The shift to service means that the ancillary activities of postindustrialism—insurance, finance, education—will take care of the needs of most people and therefore they will alter their goals somewhat from pure acquisitiveness to matters more contemplative. Finally, there will come an antigrowth sentiment of some proportion in direct consequence of this shift in values.

All this is based more on the continued availability of energy than almost anything else. What is there to tell us that we can be sanguine on that score? And how about raw materials, another source of agony to the doomsayers?

We'll have to deal here (so that the entire chapter is not taken up with zeros) in quads (q) and quints (Q). A quad is a quadrillion British Thermal Units (BTUs)—one followed by fifteen zeros; a quint is a quintillion—one followed by eighteen zeros. A billion barrels of oil (forty-two gallons per barrel) contains about 6q (or .006Q). One million barrels per day consumption of crude oil means 2.1q per year.

To supply the infinite pie (Kahn's term) the world will require .6Q per year for the year 2000 which assumes a population of 6.6 billion persons and a gross world product of 17.2 trillion dollars. Taken from 1975, the cumulative consumption of energy at the end of the century for that twenty-five-year period would be 10Qs. Where's it all going to come from?

From fossil fuels alone (oil, natural gas, coal, including lignite, shale oil, and tar sands) proven United States reserves total 27.6Q; world reserves total 120Q. *Potential* nonrenewable resources allow the United States 185Q and the world 2,200Q. These numbers (quoted in *200 Years*) come from *Exploring Energy Choices, A Preliminary Report* done by the Ford Foundation; *U.S. Mineral Resources,* a U.S. Geological Survey project; and *Resources and Man,* done by the Committee on Resources and Man of the National Research Council.

So *proven* resources are enough (if we are willing to pay the price of their extraction) from the fossil fuels alone for the energy needs of the world for about one hundred years. *Potential* resources double the length of time we have.

None of this takes into consideration the resolution of the problems surrounding the use of fusion power. A solution to that means energy Nirvana. To all intents, then, we are going to have Blue Skies without the nuclear reactor stirring up the friends of the earth.

Of course there are going to be short-term problems with energy. When are costs going to come into balance; that is to say when is oil going to become so high in price (but still "inexpensive") that it is sensible to spend the money to liquefy coal and plumb the tar sands and extract the oil from shale? And what are the environmentalists going to say? How about the people who live in the states where these resources lie? Will they object, and if so, how violently?

There is, as well, the possibility of making a costly mistake somewhere along the way, and such mistakes, "... may create serious temporary local or regional supply problems lasting perhaps five to ten years, higher costs, rationing, brownouts, and similar troubles. In retrospect, the developed world's present vulnerability to OPEC appears to be attributable to a mistake of this kind."

But the energy is there.

How about the raw materials?

Well, matter is indestructible, so no elementary substance can be used up. We'll recycle and reclaim because we'll be able to afford the energy to do so. Besides which, there are substitutes for almost everything we use. Take aluminum, which is going to be an increasing element in the manufacture of cars since they are going to have to become lighter. Substitutes for aluminum ore (bauxite) include kaolinite, dawsonite, alunite, anorthosite, nepheline syenite, saprolite, and coal ash.

Yes, we are dependent on imports of critical materials. But that is in the short run, and anyway we're a whole lot better off than Western Europe or Japan. For a short while the import dependence figures can be taken literally, but looking out a decade or so we don't have to worry. The reason is simple. We're dependent now only because import is the cheapest way of acquiring these critical stuffs. When the prices get high enough, we'll find our own or we'll go to some sort of substitutes.

As for metals cartels similar to OPEC, we are not to worry. The copper cartel didn't work very well. The Conseil Intergouvernmental des Pays Exportateurs de Cuivre, CIPEC, which included Chile, Zambia, Peru, and Zaire, was a moderate success in raising copper prices. But in 1974 commodity prices began weakening, Japan dumped its copper reserves, nations began using substitutes and recycling copper, and CIPEC's program became all but fruitless.

And so it goes. We're not going to be concerned with food supplies because we'll have the energy to generate the fertilizer to go with the water that we will garner through the digging of new wells, "harvesting" rainfall, using rivers better, recycling waste, and desalinization. We're going to expand tillable acreage, increase multiple cropping, and multiply yield. All of this is about to happen.

Heretofore, we've talked about how the car has affected society. Now, since we're postulating multiple societies, we're going to have to get some kind of grip on societal forces to understand, as *they* vary, how they are going to have their specific impacts on the car. Blue Skies will determine that the automobile and its use will be of very particular kinds; Doomsday will tell us the car is going to be quite a different creature indeed; and Rosy-Fingered Dawn carves out yet another shape for the automobile.

This means some preliminary examination of alternative social values in each scenario before getting down to examining the shapes, sizes, and uses of the car as it will exist—depending on what kind of world we are to live in.

Blue Skies is affluent. It is materialistic. We are hard working. Our goals will continue to be measured by the same kind of achievement standards as in (almost) recent memory. Blue Sky people are going to be making a lot of money, and with that money they will be buying the same things they were buying at the height of the Sloanist boom, and they will be buying other things as well: cars, of course, but also swimming pools, sophisticated home electronics games, solar-heated ski chalets, SST round trips to Frankfurt and Tokyo.

Energy will cost more, but not that much more. Its cost remains in equilibrium with the rise in income. So our acquisitive Blue Sky society continues to be fueled not with people (it is not labor intensive) but with this fairly inexpensive fuel.

Imagine then, an industrial economy moving into a postindustrial economy, a service society, funded by Saudi Arabian money as well as that which we generate ourselves. An upwardly moving society in which affluence is the dynamic and service the instrumentality.

In such a society, says the Stanford Research Institute in its "Facts and Trends" chapter, "The transportation system performs well ... with most facilities and services increasing considerably by 1990 to meet expanded demands ... in and between cities and internationally. The intercity rail systems, after pruning of excess capacity, are in good health. The major problem areas, remaining from earlier periods, are the high levels of traffic noise, congestion, and traffic-generated air pollution . . . and still excessive levels of highway traffic accidents . . ."

SRI solves the urban problem with Space Odyssey devices: automated guideways, group rapid transit, moving way systems, and automatic mixed traffic systems ". . . in which the vehicle may be guided on concealed wires and may incorporate sensors for detecting objects in their paths." The Institute also foresees as possible, "tracked levitated vehicles, evacuated [pneumatic] tube concepts [and] automated or electric highways . . ."

But what of the car?

It is going to be much smaller and lighter; we will be concerned even in Blue Skies with wasted materials and lost efficiency, and this concern will be reflected in overall vehicle design. Wheelbases will range *downward* from ninety-six inches. Maximum weights will be around 3,000 pounds. There will be about as many styles and models as there are now. Fad cars (and cars to fit specific new functions such as true urbocars) will come— and sometimes go. There will be as much emphasis on simulated luxury as we see in the 1977 showroom windows, but real luxury— leather seats and burled walnut dashes—as well as high technology will be expensive and available on a very few models. The car will be expensive enough already. Twenty years from now, a Lincoln Versailles (whatever it is to be called) which costs about $12,500 today will probably sell for a little over $42,500 in 1997 dollars.

Performance improvements will be in the area of handling— particularly braking—not acceleration or speed. Top end will be 90 mph or so; 0–60mph will take about seventeen seconds. Cars will be infinitely safer, new technologies (electronic devices that will assume control of the car when an accident is imminent, for example) will become economical and available. Moreover, the consumer will be more and more willing to pay for better occupant packaging as education pays off. The car will be vastly more durable. Because of higher materials costs, cars will be designed to last longer and to be more economical to service. Modular design and repair will both be important factors in serviceability and longevity of the car of 1997. Gasoline costs will be very high (about $2.50 a gallon). The real use of electronics to monitor engine performance (micro processors) and then respond in a closed loop system by adjusting fuel metering for optimum performance will be universal. The turbocharged diesel-engined car will have captured about 25 percent of the market, while alternative engines—mainly the Stirling cycle and the rotary with moving parts made of ceramics rather than metal—will move into full production only after 1990. Taxes on large, wasteful cars will have reduced their use so much they will be about as common as Ferraris today.

And the 1997 car will be clean. As material standards of living improve, we can afford to pay attention to health and spend more and more money on the public good. Wide recognition that cancer and lung disease can be traced to pollution will lead to acceptance of strong legislation. The industry, making record profits, will be willing to recognize that living customers are better than dead ones.

Initial price is the principal reason Detroit will be forced to make cars longer lived. Not only will they be more expensive to manufacture but societal costs will at last be properly apportioned; so cars will be more expensive to operate. Warranties will be extended by federal government mandate and the cost of that will be added to the price of the car. Insurance will go up as well, as, in 1997, the nation will be coming out of an horrendous period of high insurance claims resulting from the awful damage done by almost two decades of change in highway mix: armadas of big cars running into shoals of little ones.

This new 1997 shape of the car will be achieved without dramatic breakthroughs in technology. The Otto-cycle internal combustion engine as we know it will still be the dominant power unit in the American passenger car fleet, although that $42,500 Lincoln will probably be a turbodiesel—but free of the horrible clanking and intrusive odor current diesel engines inflict upon us.

Not only alternative engines will still be in the future (albeit the immediate future); so will alternative fuels. We will almost certainly be relying more and more on synthetic crude made from liquefied coal. But such exotic essences as alcohol will not be powering our cars, except in small proportions with conventional fuels (perhaps 15 percent methanol with 85 percent gasoline).

The car's very sophisticated 1997 electronics will be mere

extrapolations of 1977 hardware. Dashboard digital read-outs will indicate the current state of tune of the engine; perhaps there will be a full route display on an instrument panel map. We will solve our emissions problem by use of exhaust sensors which will measure the pollution content of the waste gasses and "instruct" the engine to adjust if the indices go too high.

The real "travel" revolution may come in communications and not in transportation at all. There is a view that shuttling around in personal modules is at best very primitive communication. This view holds that most of our business will be conducted long distance by telephone lines, cathode ray tubes, and home terminals. A Blue Skies future would encourage research in communications technology. Further, it would result in a society rich enough so its members could afford the complicated gadgetry that would change community habits of visiting, recreation, and doing business, allowing many people to accomplish all these things at home.

But that is really Blue Sky.

In the meantime, we can only expect that increased affluence will be seen as it has been seen for the first seventy-five years of this century in America: reflected in the shiny finish of the ever-increasing number of cars on our highways.

III

The Doomsday scenario is popular for a very good reason; there is a cruel likelihood of its coming to pass.

In the underdeveloped countries of the world, populations have been growing at a rate of between 2 and 3 percent a year. That means by the end of the century (perhaps a little later) their populations will have doubled. The people of those countries have no food and are not able to buy any, while the consumption in an overdeveloped country such as the United States is five times per capita as much as it is among the poor and starving. In the United States we are not growing in numbers of people, but we are eating (and wasting) enormous quantities of food. Thus, in those countries with by far the largest proportion of the people in the world, populations are increasing at stunning rates, food supplies are simply not keeping up, and there is no machinery for worldwide food distribution between the haves and the have nots.

"In the global [food supply] situation, *the* major factor will be the weather. . . . Should monsoon failures persist in south Asia . . . no solution is possible. Well over one billion people live in countries affected by the Asian monsoon, and no conceivable transfer of food could make up for the inevitable shortages . . ."

This is the beginning of the Doomsday *Blueprint for Your Future,* the subtitle of the Paul R. Ehrlich and Anne H. Ehrlich disaster trace, *The End of Affluence.*

Blue Skies may be totally sanguine about food supplies, energy availability, overabundance of resources or their substitutes and population control; Doomsday, etched in the Ehrlich's blueprint, is heading hell-bent in the opposite direction.

Doomsday begins with a permanent change in climate. Bad weather is nothing new, but now natural changes are being exacerbated by man-made changes: air pollution; the cutting of timber in immense quantities; the cancer spread of the megalopolis from which great heat radiates upward; and the overfarming by agribusiness which exposes the land and leads to the introduction of immense quantities of dust in the air.

Since we are aware merely of the fact that even the lightest change in the gaseous envelope which surrounds and supports us can later alter a benign atmosphere into one antipathetic to man, we have, in a very real sense, only the dimmest notion of what changes we are causing.

But at the University of Wisconsin, *Affluence* tells us, there is a a man who is grim indeed about climatic changes. Professor Reid Bryson suggests that the adding of CO_2 through stabile and mobile pollution sources and adding dust as well are operating to change atmospheric conditions so that we can be very pessimistic about the dependability of the monsoon. Here is his reasoning: The great rains of the Asian subcontinent come from moisture-rich air that moves north from the Indian and South Atlantic oceans each summer. But the carbon dioxide and the dust are combining to form a kind of wall which is screening the monsoon rains from the land where they have been the source of water for crops that have fed, historically, a huge part of the world's population. At the moment, perhaps half a billion persons depend on these monsoon rains. Professor Bryson doubts that we can ever count on the monsoons again.

But that is not the disaster scenario's most ominous portent. We have based all our agricultural research and development of high yield genetic strain crops on the weather as it has been analyzed from the period 1930 to 1960. Yet it is precisely these three decades which have seen the most extreme weather conditions the planet has experienced in a millennium. So we can throw out our new, tough winter wheat, because winter is going to be far more severe. And the same for soybeans and for corn; in fact, for just about everything, since agribusiness has managed nearly everything we raise and in managing it changed it to be more "productive."

Nor can we look to the sea for food. There is agreement, says Doomsday, that we have reached maximum catch; plunder will go on, but will become less productive each day. Fish yields increased steadily until 1970 when they began a chartable decline, attributed by the Ehrlichs to pollution, overfishing, and the destruction of the estuaries.

Even should the fish return, the overdeveloped countries would continue to use fish protein wastefully as animal feed instead of allocating proper amounts to the underdeveloped countries ° to which it would be a bonanza. In any case, fish provides only about half the food worth of meat.

Nor can we count on the great grain basket of the American Midwest; the weather again haunts us. We have always been able to produce a surplus from this bountiful granary, enough to store for ourselves, enough to export to a hungry world. But the Midwest has been subject to drought cycles every twenty years. There were major droughts in this decade at, of course, exactly the wrong time. A Midwestern drought is no longer, in the context of Doomsday, a problem of supplying the world with surplus; it is an immediate problem for the United States. "A lasting midwestern drought, difficulty in importing what we need, and the increased demand created by foreign purchases could combine to make food

---

° It seems worthwhile to use the Ehrlichs' definition of overdeveloped and underdeveloped countries exactly as they do. "Overdeveloped countries (ODC) are those in which population levels and per capita resource demands are so high that it will be impossible to maintain their present living standards without making exorbitant demands on global resources and eco-systems. Underdeveloped countries (UDC) are those that are unable to provide even the basic necessities of life—food, clothing, shelter, and health care—for the majority of their citizens." It is a loaded definition, but this is a loaded scenario.

shortages a reality in the United States," is the way *The End of Affluence* puts it.

If the environment is our barrier in the solution of the food problem, it is the absolute killer of any hopes to the solution of the supply of energy. This is the argument: Suppose we find further sources of energy (which we won't); suppose we solve the nuclear energy supply problems (which we won't); we are still faced with the ultimate crisis, the amounts of heat and humidity man can afford to pour into his environment.

"All human activities produce heat as a consequence of the second law of thermodynamics [roughly, any energy conversion process results in some amount of unusable waste heat; the process is called entropy], and no technological gimmickry can prevent humanity from heating up the world as human energy use increases. If worldwide energy consumption [were to continue] to increase at the rate that prevailed during the 1960s, it would probably be less than a century before the heat produced caused unacceptable climatic changes." That's the Ehrlichs' and the world's Catch 22. Population and food control depend on climate; affect the climate and you unalterably and tragically change global climate so that survival is improbable—at least survival as we know it. And yet food production and availability of energy would mean its use and its use would mean the generation of such amounts of heat and humidity and their injection into the atmosphere that the climate would change and—Catch 22.

But what if we could get around Catch 22, *could* we find sufficient energy supplies? Of course not.

Premise one: We are going to continue to depend on petroleum until hell won't have it. After all, we have been running this nation on oil for as long as any living man can remember to the point of granting unheard of subsidies to an industry that is perhaps more rapacious than Detroit itself.

Premise two: Petroleum demand in the United States has been growing at about 4.2 percent a year (extrapolated by *Affluence*). This translates into 24 billion barrels a year by the year 2000. Using only the known Alaskan reserves, this rate of consumption would exhaust them in twenty weeks. Using *potential* Alaskan reserves, the time until exhaustion is extended to two years.

"Can we expect to discover and develop the equivalent of a

new Alaskan field every two years by the turn of the century?" the Ehrlichs ask. "One every year by 2020?"

The Middle East offers not much more. With proven reserves of 350 billion barrels °, we can expect that we will have exhausted that supply in sixty years. *We,* the United States, will have exhausted it. That is not even taking the rest of the world into consideration.

Proven global reserves total 640 billion barrels. That stretches United States supply to about 110 years, again ignoring the rest of the world. But if we are altruistic and allow others to share in what they own or what they have at least as great a claim to as we have, there is about 35 years' supply left.

Premise three: Coal won't work either; nor will oil shale. We're going to be desperate enough not only to strip-mine coal but to ignore the environmental consequences of mass ravaging of the land. At least one result will be further irreparable damage to the production of food. The rain will leach poisonous substances from the leavings of the strip miners and contaminate the water in once pure rivers. So right away, coal strip mining is going to present a food and a pollution problem.

We won't care because we are going to need that coal. All we will be able to think of is that there is enough coal and enough oil shale to last us indefinitely.

But wait a minute. Coal is dirtier than petroleum and in gassifying it or liquefying it, we lose about a quarter to a third of its potential energy. As for oil shales, the extraction of oil will produce far more rock than oil; in fact, far more rock than there was to begin with, since in the process of extraction the shale expands. In trying to dispose of the shale waste, we will surely create pollution and dust bowls. More effect on the climate.

Both the extraction of oil from shale and the conversion of coal to a form equivalent to petroleum products so they can be used in modified energy producing machinery, is energy intensive itself.

Notice then with coal: Use energy to get energy. But that energy is diminished by a fourth to a third as a result of its conversion. Moreover, it is far more expensive than the energy we

° Herman Kahn uses quads and quints in the Blue Sky scenario when talking about energy. A million barrels of petroleum per day equal 2.1 quads per year.

have now. Further, it pollutes, and pollution is a byproduct of its extraction. Not a very good solution, perhaps not a solution at all.

Every consideration, every tendency, every indicator points to our government's solving the petroleum problem by a "crash" conversion to nuclear energy.

Would you like to know what's wrong with nuclear power technology? The Ehrlichs will be glad to tell you:

1. Thermal [heat] pollution;
2. Low-level routine releases of radioactivity from power plants and subsidiary fuel-processing plants;
3. Radiation exposure of people involved in the mining of uranium, the primary fuel for nuclear fission power plants;
4. The possible contamination of the environment by large amounts of highly radioactive wastes, which must be flawlessly contained in storage for many thousands of years if such contamination is to be avoided.
5. The chance that a catastrophic accident might release the enormous inventory of highly radioactive materials in a reactor core;
6. The possibility that terrorists may sabotage facilities or steal sufficient fissionable material to make a nuclear bomb.

So much for energy and Doomsday. How about the availability of raw materials? We're not going to get them. In 1972, the Secretary of the Interior reported to the Congress that we imported 100 percent of our platinum group metals—mica, chromium, and strontium. We imported over 90 percent of our manganese, aluminum, tantalum, and cobalt and importations of materials that reached fifty percent or more included zinc, mercury, potassium, gold, antimony, columbium, nickel, bismuth, tin, asbestos, titanium, and fluorine. We even brought in almost 30 percent of our iron.

Those who hope to substitute for these critical materials count heavily on plastics. But plastics are largely petroleum derivatives, and we have already discovered what is going to happen to petroleum. Another argument is that we will be able to continue to import if only we are willing to pay the price. Well it is almost certain that the prices are going to skyrocket. What is not so certain is what we are anticipating paying with. Now we are counting heavily on grain. But we are not going to have the grain to consume, much less export.

For his part, Alvin Toffler tells us Doomsday can come in a number of forms.

We could have a "Depression on the Installment Plan," a random collapse of segments of the economy with none of them returning to their previous levels of health.

Or a "Sleeper Depression" in which we go out almost without realizing it, sleepily, in ignorance, but with a nagging suspicion that since we can't eat and can't buy anything and can't heat our houses, something, somewhere is wrong.

Or a "Magic-Formula Depression," a repeat of 1929, in which we collapse, but a man on a white horse arrives in Washington with a bag of economic tricks and suddenly all is right with the world. Toffler also calls this the "Don't Count On It Depression."

Or a "Super-Crash," much the same kind of thing the Ehrlichs predict. The bottom falls out and half the nation sits around unemployed.

Or the ultimate "Armageddon Depression," a sharp decline followed by the ultimate solution, nuclear war.

Whatever the Doomsday specifics, the Stanford Research Institute study is cheerfully pessimistic about transportation:

> The depressed level of the economy restricts the need for business travel, and lack of disposable income reduces demand for recreational and educational travel and car ownership per capita. Energy shortages increase the cost of travel, and fear of crime and terrorism acts negatively on the desire to travel. Travel to remote resorts is significantly reduced, use of urban parks and nearby recreational areas is greatly increased, and backyard vacations are in vogue.
>
> International travel plummets ... and demand for cruises and SST travel all but disappears.

There will still be cars, and the Doomsday car will look a lot like the Blue Sky car—only more so. It will be *much* smaller and *much* lighter, there will be many fewer models and styles, and it will be hugely more expensive. But our view of the car will be different in Doomsday, as will the government's attention to it. And the industry—in fact the aftermarket and the entire economic community—will be deeply affected by those views and that attention.

Because of material and fuel shortages, the government will step in to tax and regulate the car. High prices and regulation will force a move to mass transit—at first busses and trains and then, beyond 1990, new generation BARTs, funded by the government as parts of massive make-work programs. Auto tax dollars will be diverted from highway building and maintenance completely into these projects.

In the suburbs, where it will not be practical to build enormous public transportation systems, people moving will shift to massive van pool and car pool programs mandated by local governments.

Although staggering unemployment will lead to much leisure time, the high cost and regulation of travel will restrict the car's role in leisure. A single exception will be motor racing, which will grow enormously as a spectator sport, becoming an outlet for societal pressures that will result from crowding and economic deprivation. Likely to emerge will be some sort of "Rollerball" auto sports—perhaps a combination of today's destruction derbies and motorcycle motocrossing.

The only special-purpose vehicles upon which research money will be spent are those meant for public officials, police, and public welfare agencies. What variety there will be in the few plain-jane standards offered to the public will come from high dollar add-ons for the wealthy. Luxury will still be important to the rich, but there will be many fewer of them and the split between rich and not rich will be widening. Utility will be the marketing theme of the manufacturers.

The car will not be so important to mobility since movement will be restricted in what will amount to a totally managed economy. Nor will the American be able to look to his car to grant him privacy. Autos and travel will be too expensive to be relied upon to support such a value; instead people will find privacy by remaining inside their own homes.

The energy crisis will persist, with the federal government taxing *and* rationing fuel, diverting it from private transportation to essential business and mass transit. The government's role in public health and safety will increase with the emphasis on pouring money into welfare programs to stimulate the economy. This will be reflected in increased rigidity by the government on safety and emission standards with the manufacturers.

In Doomsday, the government will serve another function: Through some form of quasi-public agency it will become a major insurer of automobiles. Coverage will be standardized and sub- sidized by taxes. No Fault will be universal and the day of the $5 million personal injury suit will be long past.

The auto industry will not be so boldly intruded upon as insurance, but Detroit will be federally subsidized—at least in part. Technical know-how and capital will be available mainly from public sources. This will go a long way toward allowing the government to control auto design. And the highway system will be managed as an arm of the bureaucracy. It will be redesigned and reconstructed, not only as a make-work device, but also to emphasize the increasing importance of the transportation of goods and materials instead of the movement of people.

As Detroit employment shrinks, unions will resist, but they will be unsuccessful. Any lingering thoughts of public control of the marketplace will have long since been dispelled. Anyway, Doomsday will be a totally managed economy in which market- place pressures literally do not exist.

It will be almost as if Henry Ford the Original were still building black cars and only black cars. In the sense that standardization of the car is symptomatic of standardization throughout the whole economy, the industry will help to set tastes and standards, but the real role here will belong to the federal government. If there is innovation to be done, it will be done by the government. In order to survive, private industry will follow docilely along.

None of this will provide incentive to management or labor. Chronic absenteeism, shoddy workmanship, stagflation, and cyclic disturbances in the economy (in spite of government planning) will keep productivity low. In this new planned economy—short of jobs and short of solutions to problems—management will be centered in the government and a relatively small group of professional planners. The union will weaken. It will be forced to go along with the federalizing of the industry because jobs will be cherished, and taken where they can be found

Anywhere you look in Doomsday, you will see shadows. The car will be among the least of society's worries. What are wheels when the question is survival?

IV

Even the doomsayers see *some* possibility for a silver lining; even the blue sky forecasters warn of freakish thunderclouds. *The End of Affluence* on food and starvation in the United States: "The United States undoubtedly *could become* self-sufficient in food, unless its population grew subtantially larger. There would, of course, be a high energy cost and some sacrifice in the variety of foods available, but the nutritional quality of the average diet would remain high."

The *Eco-Spasm Report* on energy, resources, and technology: "The old resource/energy bargain basement is closed. . . . While it does not mean the end of technological advance, it does mean radical conservation policies. It means a high order of imagination. And it means that tax and other incentives ought to be placed on the rapid development of low-energy and resource-conserving products. Instead of awarding indiscriminate tax credits for corporate investment, why not target these specifically for investments in new, ecologically sound, socially valuable technologies?"

The End of Affluence on the *possibility* of population control: "But there is a brighter side. When *The Population Bomb* [Paul R. Ehrlich] was written six years ago [1968], few people were deeply concerned about the population-resource-environment crisis the world was entering. Today we might take heart because people *are* worried; getting people concerned about a problem is half the battle. And concerned people have taken action. Since *The Population Bomb* was published, millions of Americans have made responsible personal decisions to limit the size of their families . . ."

So Doomsday is not necessarily all bad. Is Eden necessarily all good? *The Next 200 Years* on the worm in the apple ". . . we do not expect economic growth to continue indefinitely; instead, its recent exponential rate will probably slow gradually to a low or zero rate." We had best be warned that the human condition requires dues to be paid. Thus, if we have affluence, we also have "relatively little need for self discipline"; if we have continuous growth, we also have "unrealistic expectations"; if we have mass consumption, we also have "aesthetic ... standards ... determined by the masses"; if we have economic security we also have "emphasis on relative poverty, hence a desire for radical egalitarianism"; if we have physical safety, we also have "a neurotic concern with avoiding pain and death." It goes on—a long, long list of the "failures of success."

If *The End of Affluence* provides the philosophic backbone of Doomsday, and *200 Years* does the same for Blue Skies, where are we to look for support of Rosy-Fingered Dawn?

First off, there is the SRI's *Alternative Transportation Futures* study for DOT's National Transportation Facts and Trends.

Its summary of the scenario's characteristics is crisp. There will be a mild shortage of raw materials; there will be only a limited rise in the price of gasoline (80 cents a gallon in 1976 dollars); the climate will be favorable; unemployment will be about 5 percent (but with much underemployment); productivity relative to the 1975 figures will increase by thirty-five percent; the real gross national product (again using 1975 numbers as the baseline) goes up 44 percent; inflation is very low, 1 to 2 percent; population does not rise much, reaching about 246 million in the United States at the end of the century; terrorism and crime moderate; and there is strong but controversial support for environmentalism.

SRI thus comes down just about in the middle of the other two scenarios in characterizing Rosy-Fingered Dawn; but it does *not* (as the other two do) make a judgment about the likelihood of its coming about.

There is an additional face to SRI's "transformation" society that follows on the Institute's refusal to take an advocacy position. The very first listed characteristic delineated is a split in the community, with 70 percent of the population struggling for prosperity and 30 percent placing value on frugality.

Advocacy is nice; *Affluence* and *200 Years* help in the writing of strong scenarios; but if it's probabilities we seek, the SRI approach is more reassuring. It's not because it takes a comfortable middlish position, but rather that it seems to understand that society and the world are not monolithic. Still *Transportation*

Futures is a bit antiseptic to provide a rich enough loam in which to discover the philosophical roots of what the jargonists call the future of "voluntary simplicity."

E. F. Schumacher's *Small Is Beautiful* suffers no such nutritional deficiency, and has the blessings of the governor of California besides.

Small Is Beautiful begins by telling us about "our inability to recognize that the modern industrial system, with all its intellectual sophistication, consumes the very basis on which it has been erected . . . the irreplaceable capital which it cheerfully treats as income. . ." which is to say: Fossil fuels, "the tolerance margins of nature," and "the human substance."

Schumacher wants us to get off this collision course and his prescription is to understand the problem—to understand it *now*—to act on our understanding, and to evolve a new life style. Specifically, he wants us to research and implement biologically sound methods of producing foodstuffs and to create a technology "with a human face." A technology with a human face is one that takes the worth of the job and the reward it offers the worker into equal consideration with the product that is the result, and then forms a partnership between the producers and those who underwrite them with capital.

That said, Schumacher is free to address resources—the same resources that so bother the Ehrlichs and so elate Herman Kahn—and comes to a conclusion about how they are to be viewed in a philosophical fashion that turns out to be as pragmatic as the others. There is a limit to what the world has; particularly in the way of energy, and it is widely and randomly scattered around the globe. Given that, the ruthless exploitation of these resources—coal, oil, and natural gas—is not simply self-defeating, but is an act of violence against nature. The next step is inevitable: Do violence to nature and the historic consequence is violence between men.

Here, then, is the introduction of a new perspective as well as a new resource. "Violence to nature" brings to us a consideration we have not yet faced. Underlying the concept is a belief in a natural order; in turn this must suggest a role for man to play in such an order—a duality between man and nature.

Man's role is clear. Like energy and metals, he is a resource. He is a part of nature. He must cultivate himself as carefully as he cultivates nature so that he does violence to nothing. "It is man, not nature, who provides the primary resource: . . . the key factor of all economic development comes out of the mind of man."

This is accomplished through, and is the result of, education, which is "the transmission of values." When people ask to be educated, they are really asking what things mean—not what things mean in some absolute scientific sense; not what things mean in some abstract philosophical sense, but what things mean to *them*. They ask this question in order to determine how to put themselves into perspective with the world they see around them.

If we exploit this resource—man—properly, we will shape our teaching so the result is each man's understanding of his own life. He will therefore be able to conduct that life in an enlightened fashion, with sense, conscience, and responsibility. "Our task . . . is to understand the present world in which we live and make our choices." The result of this exploitation, this teaching, is that we will make choices that will be responsible toward not only ourselves but toward nature, our neighbors, and our world. This is the ultimate and only solution to the distribution and the exploitation of the nonsentient resources of the planet.

Here is the appeal of Rosy-Fingered Dawn. The pragmatist will recoil at Schumacher's excursions into mysticism. He will properly decline to believe that simply because man has certain pieces of information he must therefore act in an enlightened fashion. But unlike Blue Skies or Disaster, the third scenario does not consign us to the mercies of an inevitable fate. If Rosy-Fingered Dawn says nothing else, it tells us that man has some influence on his own destiny. We may decide to be intimidated by the future and lie passive until the world overwhelms us. We may conclude there is nothing to worry about, and by accident of new discovery, never understand there was. But the rational course, says Rosy-Fingered Dawn, is to view the future with concern and to mold it by our own decision. Moreover, this third scenario admits the reality that society does not act in concert. Nor need it. Given only the conviction of at least a recognizable group of people that they wish to lead a frugal life and to seek rewards other than materialistic, there is every expectation that such a segment of the population can succeed. In succeeding, they will have influence over the remainder of the group. The scenario does not require a natural miracle to come to realization. It does not need mass conversion. It relies merely on the continuation of an already existing trend. And it looks to the human animal to maintain that trend or to shape it in a direction that may differ from its present form but will always suit the needs of the shapers. For instance, *Small Is Beautiful* tells us, as we have been told before, that the real problem is energy. A human solution to the energy problem would take into consideration the needs not only of the consumer but the producers. It simply won't work to complain there isn't enough petroleum so that the reserves that do exist must be taken out with haste and efficiency. How does that permit a reconciliation with the needs of the owners of that resource?

The oil-consuming nations understand there is no immediately available substitute for petroleum. They would also understand that what they have to offer in exchange for the petroleum falls very short of supplying what the oil-producing nations need for their economic growth—time to build new sources of livelihood for their people.

So a human solution, which would be available if only we were willing to exploit the principal resource—the mind and imagination of man—would quickly conclude that the critical element here is time. For if we are patient in our demand for oil, a "wasting asset," we will discover that a cadenced removal of oil from the land of its owners will not only stretch the time available for the oil user to find and develop new sources of energy—oil substitutes—but will also give the oil producers time to develop a new way of life for their people. It is a matter of prolonging the life span of the remaining oil in the world.

"Catastrophic developments on the oil front could be avoided only if the *basic harmony of long-term interest of both groups of countries* came to be fully realized and concerted action were taken . . ."

It is this basic harmony which is the theme not only of *Small Is Beautiful*, but of Rosy-Fingered Dawn. Of course there are going to be problems, but that is our lot; our goal is to harmonize with nature so that we find some solace in the very inevitability of problems. We are resource-full. It is up to us to understand where we are placed, each in his own life and his own time, without doing violence to nature or himself. In this, we will find answers to the reconciliation of our problems. This is the manner in which we might pursue each reconciliation:

> ... the intelligent laymen ... must work on public opinion, so that the politicians, depending on public opinion, will free themselves from the thralldom of economism and attend to the things that really matter.
>
> What matters ... is the *direction* (of research), that the direction should be toward non-violence rather than violence; toward a harmonious cooperation with nature rather than a warfare against nature; toward the noiseless, low-energy, elegant, and economic solutions normally applied in nature rather than the noisy, high-energy, brutal, wasteful, and clumsy solutions of our present-day sciences. ...

If this seems terribly vague, *Small Is Beautiful* has a specific prescription: Do away with a great deal of modern technology— automated styrene cup machines, for example; computerized popsicle shapers; mechanized pantyhose weavers. Substitute people. Give a man useful work he can do with his hands and his mind, give him something creative: perhaps group assembly of an automobile so that a single group sees the car to completion rather than each member spending his working day in an endless, mind-numbing repetitive job. Increase the *amount* of work a man does from the 3.5 percent of total social time actually spent in production to six times that, and you have gone a very long way to a solution.

"An incredible thought! Even children would be allowed to make themselves useful, even old people." If we redefine productivity to preserve the notion of total work done or total goods produced, but excise the part of the equation that requires that this must be accomplished by requiring one man to produce a specific amount in a rigidly fixed period of time, we have suddenly solved the malaise of man-as-machine and man *thinking* of himself as a machine.

We would, in this fashion, also be given back the time to do a really good job, to pause and enjoy the execution of quality, "... even to make things beautiful." Not to mention that we would be acting in a therapeutic fashion toward society. "No one would then want to raise the school-leaving age or to lower the retirement age, so as to keep people off the labor market. Everybody would be welcome to lend a hand. Everybody would be admitted to what is now the rarest privilege, the opportunity of working usefully, creatively, with his own hands and brains, in his own time, at his own pace . . .

"People who work in this way do not know the difference between work and leisure."

What is Rosy-Fingered Dawn saying here—at least to that 30 percent of the people during the next quarter century who awaken to it? There is worth in inner exploration, in contemplation, in doing something for its own sake. There is tolerance of both the harsh reality of nature and the harsh and jarring behavior of the majority of the population who pursue a grinding, stress-filled acquisitive life. Technology, as a device for getting more work out of a single human unit, is of no value; it is dehumanizing, it denies any opportunity to relish accomplishment.

Using these principles and concentrating on the human Rosy-Fingered Dawn ends with the best of all transportation worlds, according to Stanford Research Institute: "Transportation in the Transformation society performs generally well . . . This is due in part to the prosperous achievement sector that maintains high productivity and consumption rates, and in part to the strong support from the voluntary simplicity sector for efficient and low-energy ways of moving people and goods."

One of those low energy ways will be the transformed automobile. The world car will have come into its own. American and overseas multinational auto companies, already in 1977 producing cars with engines and transmissions sourced in countries other than where the car is built and marketed (Mustang II with its Brazilian engine, for example) will have taken the pattern to its ultimate form. The 1977 Chevette started life in Brazil in 1969; a future Chevette will be built from parts manufactured all over the world. It will appear in the same form in a dozen different countries under a dozen different names, but it will be the same car. In order to appeal to widely different markets, it will be basic and appealing to the least affluent buyer. It will be easy to build and easy to fix. It will be cheap.

Both Ford and General Motors produce a 1977 Third World car that is very basic and adaptable to a variety of needs. Both can be converted from passenger car to jitney to pickup truck to stake truck. Both have small, fuel-stingy, inexpensive engines. This will be the shape of the voluntarily simple Rosy-Fingered car of 1997.

In the high technology countries, the world cars will bristle with all the electronic circuitry of their larger brothers: closed loop control of mixture, tune, and emission; controls that will hold automatic transmissions in optimum gears to correspond to engine revolutions; dashboard read-outs of malfunctions; antiskid devices for braking; and drug-defeat systems. With the appearance of the world car the voluntary simplicity sector will finally have its ethical automobile; with the world car tricked out in its ultimate gadget-filled version, the prosperous sector will have an ethical car that also satisfies the need to spend a lot of money and wallow in the fruits of technology.

Big cars (but not nearly so big as 1977 cars) will continue to be built in large numbers, but will benefit from advances in use of lightweight metals and plastic. This will mean that cars will be able to stay about the same size as the current Chevrolet Nova and still be economical to operate, a very important consideration since imported fuel will have risen in price as much as 5 percent per year since 1977.

In Rosy-Fingered Dawn, Stanford Research sees a substantial change in mass transit:

> The focus is now on neighborhoods, districts, and small communities rather than on entire regions. Under "local autonomy" legislation passed in 1980, it became possible for a local interest group of any kind to establish a special public transportation district for a small area. Examples are residential or mixed neighborhoods of a few square miles; central business districts; university communities; and parts of rural counties.
>
> These special districts are popularly called transit territories (TTs). TTs have definite boundaries, set their own service standards, conduct transit and paratransit operations, restrict or exclude automobile traffic as warranted, deal with unions, raise tax revenues ... and obtain subsidies from higher levels of government ...
>
> The more densely traveled TTs seek to constrain automobile

travel. . . . Urban and local travel in non-TT areas remains much like [1977] with even heavier dependence upon automobiles as the quality of transit service declines.

Heavier use of the car will underscore the transformation society's awareness of the car's social cost. The automobile will take into account prevailing aesthetic considerations. Rosy-Fingered Dawn will rise on very few billboards, but there will be great attention paid to such things as highway design and landscaping. As for the looks of the car, ostentation will be frowned upon. Lifestyles will be—as they are now—reflected in the styling of the car, and this will be a society that values tranquillity and meditative and reflective activities.

There will be much public discussion of the societal merits of the car. The mass media will mirror the concern expressed by the voluntary simplicity sector toward technology's intrusion into the natural order of the universe. The government will undertake frequent and saturating advertising campaigns to warn against misuse of the car.

But the automobile will remain important to the American way of life. The labor force will have grown by 22 percent by 1990 and cars will be owned by more people. Passenger miles driven will increase. We will be enlightened, and we will demonstrate our new enlightened state by driving new enlightened cars; but for most of us, the car will still shine in the driveway as a symbol of achievement.

V

Whatever 1997 has in store, Americans are certain to be far more aware of the car than they are now. It will have to be brought under control, and a prerequisite of control is understanding.

We betray ourselves and our children by our present failure to understand the car; these are facts the American car owner does not know or simply will not recognize:

Ninety percent of our personal travel is by car.

We spend more on our cars than we do on clothing or medical care.

Never mind the 15 percent of the work force who can thank the car for their jobs; the industry alone accounts for 4.7 million persons employed.

The automobile is the single largest consumer of petroleum in America, using about 31 percent of our supplies. Any reduction in this amount within the next fifteen years by use of an electric car is "remote," according to the government's own report on the future of the automobile.*

We can reduce car pollution-caused "projected excess cardiac deaths and person days of discomfort to *zero*," accomplish the stunning goal of bringing down attacks of lower respiratory disease in children by nearly 600,000 cases a year, and cut person days of chest discomfort by 5,000 by the end of this century if only we maintain our present carbon monoxide standard, reduce hydrocarbon emissions to statutory level (from the present 15 grams per mile to .41), and bring oxides of nitrogen down to levels proposed (from 3.1 grams per mile to 2.0).

These last are some of the substantial benefits to be had if we choose to acknowledge that our cars are causing many of our problems.

In examining how the car came into our living rooms; in discovering what the car costs in lives; constraints on our freedoms as a result of the government regulation it brings on our heads; in the part of our precious and shrinking budgets it takes to buy, repair, operate, and resell; in examining its effects on the relationships we have with others in our families and our communities; in calculating all the drains on our bank accounts, our life expectancies, and our patience attributable to the car; perhaps we can come to understand what it really means to live in a nation driven by automobility.

Having calculated cost, we are then able to *add* what the car has given us in terms of freedom to move about, privacy, a shiny

---

* This estimate, as well as most of the statistics on the page, comes from a report by the Federal Task Force on Motor Vehicle Goals beyond 1980 chaired by Elliot L. Richardson, the so-called "300-Days' Study" released in September 1976. The study was undertaken to determine whether the industry could meet fuel conservation goals and if so with what difficulty and at what cost. It concluded the industry could indeed meet the standards and with current technology. Detroit, predictably, disagreed.

object for adoration, a recreational device, a broad horizon, and a dynamic in the economy.

We will have externalized the car. And that is something we must do and do immediately.

"How can the American public be convinced of the need for changeover to more fuel-efficient motor vehicles, and be induced to accept the types of automobiles which will achieve desirable fuel economy?" the *300-Days' Study* asks. "How should the nation handle the risk which the automotive industry must accept in motor vehicle changeover . . .? How may the federal government effectively balance the sometimes conflicting objectives of reduced energy, increased safety, and improved environmental quality . . . especially when these requirements are imposed by several independent agencies with separate authorities? How far should passenger safety and emissions control be mandated into automobile designs?" The federal government asks the question, but it doesn't supply the answers because it doesn't know what they are.

It does know that the American car owner must be brought into the process of making the decisions because he will be profoundly affected by them.

That would be you. But your willingness to join in arriving at the answers depends on more immediate understanding than you have heretofore been given. It depends even more on your willingness to accept that many of these decisions are yours to make.

"Our task . . . is to understand the present world in which we live and make our choices," E. F. Schumacher has told us.

Taking the car for granted, dismissing it as a necessary evil or God-given blessing is not understanding but ignoring our present world.

So long as we continue to do that, we have no choices to make.

Bibliography

There is an endless amount of material on the automobile—and there is almost none. By which I mean serious, comprehensive studies of the car in America are few. There are many works such as John Keats' *The Insolent Chariots,* amusing but thin, and enough technical papers in every discipline to cover the earth in documents. But we need more autobiographies and biographies by and of people now in industry or recently retired from it. Most of all, we need more James Flinks and Emma Rothschilds to write important books like *The Car Culture* and *Paradise Lost: The End of the Auto-Industrial Age.* I have relied heavily on taped interviews, and more than I would have liked on magazine pieces. There is some irony here, since I have been critical (properly, I think) of the enthusiast publications for their bias, and equally of the general media of their failure to pay proper attention at all. Thus, I cite *Car and Driver,* a buff magazine, and *Automotive News,* a trade journal because, if nothing else, at least they deal with the automobile. My preference would have been, say, the *Atlantic Monthly* and the *Washington Post.*

Below, the most useful sources.

Books

Boorstin, Daniel J. *The Americans: The Democratic Experience* (New York: Random House, 1973).
Commager, Henry Steele. *The American Mind* (New Haven: Yale University Press, 1950).

Dulles, Foster Rhea. *The United States Since 1865* (Ann Arbor: The University of Michigan Press, 1959).

Ehrlich, Paul R. and Ho, Anne. *The End of Affluence* (New York: Ballantine Books, 1975).

Flink, James J. *The Car Culture* (Cambridge, Mass.: The MIT Press, 1975).

——*America Adopts the Automobile, 1895-1910* (Cambridge, Mass.: The MIT Press, 1970).

Ginger, Ray. *People on the Move: A United States History Since 1860* (Boston: Allyn and Bacon, Inc., 1975).

Grand, Frank P., et al. *The Automobile: and the Regulation of its Impact on the Environment* (Norman, Okla.: University of Oklahoma Press, 1975).

Gustin, Lawrence R. *Billy Durant: Creator of General Motors* (Grand Rapids, Mich.: William B. Eerdmans Publishing Co., 1973).

Jerome, John. *The Death of the Automobile* (New York: W. W. Norton & Company, Inc., 1972).

Kahn, Herman and Wiener, Anthony J. *The Year 2000* (New York: The Macmillan Company, 1967).

Kahn, Herman and Brown, William and Martel, Leon. *The Next 200 Years: A Scenario for America and the World* (New York: William Morrow and Company, Inc., 1976).

Keats, John. *The Insolent Chariots* (Philadelphia and New York: J. B. Lippincott Company, 1958).

Labatut, Jean and Lane, W. J., eds. *Highways in Our National Life: A Symposium* (Princeton, N.J.: Princeton University Press, 1950) and in particular Francis E. Merrill, "The Highway and Social Problems."

Lynd, Robert Staughton and Lynd, Helen M. *Middletown: A Study in American Culture* (New York: Harcourt Brace & Co., 1929).

——*Middletown In Transition: A Study in Cultural Conflicts* (New York: Harcourt Brace & Co., 1937).

McCluggage, Denise. *Are You a Woman Driver?* (New York: Grosset and Dunlap, Inc.)

Mahoney, Tom. *The Story of George Romney* (New York: Harper & Brothers, 1960).

Nader, Ralph. *Unsafe at Any Speed* (New York: Grossman Publishers, Inc., 1965).

Rae, John B. *The Road and the Car in American Life* (Cambridge, Mass.: The MIT Press, 1971).

Randall, Donald A. and Glickman, Arthur *The Great American Auto Repair Robbery* (New York: Charterhouse, 1972).

Rothschild, Emma. *Paradise Lost: The Decline of the Auto-Industrial Age* (New York: Random House, 1973).

Sampson, Anthony. *The Seven Sisters: The Great Oil Companies & the World They Shaped* (New York: The Viking Press, 1975).

Schumacher, E. F. *Small Is Beautiful: Economics as if People Mattered* (New York: Harper & Row, 1975).

Sloan, Alfred P., Jr. *My Years With General Motors* (Garden City, N.Y.: Doubleday & Company, Inc., 1964).

Turner, Frederick Jackson. *The Significance of the Frontier in American History,* Harold P. Simonson, ed. (New York: Frederick Ungar Publishing Co., 1963).

Widick, B. J., ed. *Auto Work and Its Discontents* (Baltimore and London: The Johns Hopkins University Press, 1976).

Winther, Oscar O. *The Transportation Frontier, 1865-1890* (New York: Holt, Rinehart and Winston, 1964).

Monographs, Occasional Papers, Technical Papers and Magazine Articles

Analysis of the Impact of Selected Technological, Economic, and Political Forces on Ford's Future Automotive Business. By the Staff of Battelle-Columbus, Battelle-Geneva, Battelle-Frankfurt and Battelle's Seattle Research Center, to Ford Motor Company. Battelle Columbus Laboratories, Columbus, Ohio. February 28, 1975. Final Report.

Appleby, Michael R. and Bintz, Louis J., Automotive Engineering Development. *Vehicle Safety Improvements Using Vehicle Characteristic Ratings.* Engineering & Technical Service Division, Automobile Club of Southern California, Los Angeles. March 1975.

Barry, Patricia Z. *Individual Versus Collective Responsibility for*

Safety: An Unexamined Policy Issue. University of North
Carolina, School of Public Health. May 15, 1975.

Bedard, Patrick J. *We Have Seen the Engine of the Future and It's
in Your Car, Esquire,* March, 1976.

Burks, J.M., et al. *Human Volunteer Testing of the Inflatable Belt
Restraints.* Automotive Research Division, Southwest Re-
search Institute. And National Highway Traffic Safety
Administration, U. S. Department of Transportation.

Burns, Marcelline and Sharma, Satanand. *Marihuana Effects on
Driving Performance and Personality.* University of California, Los Angeles.

California Air Resources Board, *Non-Methane Organic Gas Emissions, South Coast Air Basin.* Bar Graph. Jan. 20, 1976.

California Air Resources Board. *Total Organic Gas Emissions.* San
Francisco Bay Area Air Basin. Bar Graph. Feb. 25, 1976.

California Air Resources Board Bulletin, Vol. 7, No. 5, May 1976.
Sacramento, California.

Cooke, Conrad H. *Decision Making Criteria for Ranking Motor
Vehicle Safety Standards.* National Highway Traffic Safety
Administration. July 14, 1975.

Cooley, Peter. *Fire in Motor Vehicle Accidents.* Highway Safety
Research Institute, the University of Michigan. April, 1974
(revised April, 1975).

The Economics of Automotive Safety. Comments by Dr. Henry L.
Duncombe, Jr., Vice President and Chief Economist, General Motors Corporation, at the Fourth International Congress on Automotive Safety. July 14, 1975.

Elgin, Duane, et al. *City Size and The Quality of Life-An Analysis
of the Policy Implications of Continued Population Concentration.* Prepared for NSF, Research Applied to National
Needs (RANN) Program, under NSF Contract GI. 138462,
by The Stanford Research Institute. November 1974.

*Evaluation of Mandatory Vehicle Inspection and Maintenance
Programs.* Summary Report. State of California Air Resources Board. May 1976

Faigin, Barbara M. *Societal Costs of Motor Vehicle Accidents for
Benefit-Cost Analysis: A Perspective on the Major Issues and*

Some Recent Findings. Office of Program Planning, National Highway Traffic Safety Administration.

Faulkner, David. *Staff Report on Methanol Fuels.* California Air Resources Board, Division of Implementation and Enforcement. September 1, 1975.

Fourth International Congress on Automotive Safety. Abstracts of Papers. Session 2A. Fourth International Congress on Automotive Safety.

Gordon, Peter and Eckert, Ross D. *Transportation Alternatives for Southern California.* Conference Proceedings of Symposium. Sponsored by The Institute for Public Policy Research, Center for Public Affairs, University of Southern California. April 12, 1976.

Gotoo, Kenichi and Serizawa, Yoshio. *Tomorrow's Automobile Safety and the Role of Legislation.* Nissan Motor Co., Ltd., & Japan Automatic Transmission Co., Ltd. July 15, 1975.

Gray, Paul and Helmer, Olaf. *California Futures Study—Analysis of Impacts for Transportation Planning,* Summary Report. Sponsored by Division of Transportation Planning, California Department of Transportation. Prepared under Contract B 134411. Center for Futures Research, Graduate School of Business Administration, University of Southern California, Los Angeles. November 30, 1974.

Hart, Stanley. *A Code of Standards for the Auto Industry.* Stanley Hart Associates, Altadena, California

Hartman, Charles H. *The Evaluation and Improvement of Motor Vehicle Safety Through Regulation.* Motorcycle Safety Foundation. May 15, 1975.

Hemphill, Robert, Jr. and Difiglio, Carmen. *Future Demand of Automotive Fuels,* Presented at the General Motors Research Laboratories Symposium of Future Automotive Fuels. October 1975.

"Henry Ford on Autos, 'A Look Down the Road,' " Interview with the Chairman, Ford Motor Company. *U.S. News & World Report.* October 20, 1974.

"How the Automobile Has Altered Our Lives." *New Scientist.* May 24, 1973.

Huelke, Donald F. (ed.). *Proceedings of the 19th Conference of the*

American Association for Automotive Medicine. San Diego, California, November 20-22, 1975. American Association for Automotive Medicine, Lake Bluff, Illinois.

Husted, Robert A. *Automobile Transportation Cost Tradeoffs.* U.S. Department of Transportation, Office of the Secretary, Energy and Environment Division. May 15, 1975.

Jacobsen, Willis E. *A Technology Assessment Methodology— Automotive Emissions.* Prepared in cooperation with and for the Office of Science and Technology, Executive Office of the President. MTR 6009, Vol. 2, PB 202778-02. The MITRE Corporation, June 1971.

Jense, Donald W. *Considerations in Determining Priorities Among Motor Vehicle Safety Standards.* Vicom International, Inc., Vehicle Research Design & Production Engineering. May 12, 1975.

Johannessen, H. George and Pulley, Charles H. *Safety Belt Restraint Systems: Comfort, Convenience, Use Laws as Factors in Increased Usage.* Abstract of the General Session, Fourth International Congress on Automotive Safety. July 14, 1975.

Kraft, Hans-Joachim and Fellerer, Jorg. *Opportunities to Enhance the Cost Effectiveness of Safety Regulations.* Abstract of the General Session, Fourth International Congress on Automotive Safety. July 14, 1975.

Little, Joseph W. *Modes of Standard Setting Behavior: Judicial Versus Legislative,* University of Florida, College of Law. May 15, 1975.

Lundstrom, Louis C. *Integrating Vehicle Safety, Costs, and Consumer Attitudes.* General Motors Corporation, GM Technical Center, Warren, Mich., June 18, 1975.

Mackey, G.M., et al. *European Vehicle Safety Standards and Their Effectiveness.* Accident Research Unit, Department of Transportation and Environmental Planning, University of Birmingham, Birmingham B15 2TT, United Kingdom. May 1975.

Man, Automobile and Road. Mercedes-Benz Of North America. Safety Seminar. Stowe, Vt. July 17-18, 1974.

Merrill, Stephen A. *Political Determinants of Feasibility Among*

Safety Standards: The Case of Occupant Restraint. U.S. Senate Staff. July 1975.

Moffatt, Edward A. *Occupant Motion in Rollover Collisions.* General Motors Engineering Staff, Warren, Mich.

Mitchell, Arnold. *Trends in Ways of Life.* Stanford Research Institute.

"More or Less Regulation?": The Wrong Issue. Remarks by Albert Benjamin Kelley, Senior Vice President, Insurance Institute for Highway Safety, General Session Panel, Fourth International Congress on Automotive Safety, San Francisco. July 14, 1975.

Morrison, Mike. *The Realities and Unrealities of Energy Economics.* Reprinted from the *Sierra Club Bulletin,* May 1973, Sierra Club, San Francisco.

"The National 55 mph Speed Limit," *Fact Sheet,* U. S. Department of Transportation, Office of Public Affairs, Washington, D. C. May 14, 1976.

Nearly Smog-Free Car Developed. California Air Resources Board, Sacramento, California May 29, 1976.

The Need for Public Policy Dialogue. Comments by William D. Eberle, President and Chief Executive Officer, Motor Vehicle Manufacturers Association of the United States, Inc., at the Fourth International Congress on Automotive Safety, San Francisco, July 14, 1975.

1976 MVMA Specifications Form—Passenger Car. Chevrolet Motor Division, General Motors Corporation.

1976 MVMA Specifications Form—Passenger Car. Pontiac Motor Division, General Motors Corporation. Sept. 1, 1975.

O'Neill, Brian, et al. Insurance Institute for Highway Safety. *Evaluating Motor Vehicle Safety Performance Standards.* June, 1975.

Proposed Motor Racing Vehicle Noise Regulations, Chapter 8: Noise Regulations, Part 5; Proposed Rules and Regulations for the Control of Noise from Motor Racing Vehicles. Submitted by the Illinois Environmental Protection Agency. August 10, 1975.

Pulley, Charles H., President, American Safety Belt Council. *Motor Vehicle Safety Belt Use Laws on the National and*

International Scene. Abstract of the Paper of the American
Association of Automotive Medicine.

Rau, John G. *Cost-Benefit Considerations in Safety Standards
Versus Energy Consumption.* Ultrasystems, Inc., Newport
Beach, California. June 10, 1975.

*The Report by the Federal Task Force on Motor Vehicle Goals
Beyond 1980,* Draft, Executive Summary. September 2,
1976.

Rockwell, Thomas H. and K. N. Balasubramanian. *Carbon Monoxide Effects on Highway Driving Performance: An Investigation of the Effects of 12 Percent COHb on the Nighttime
Performance of Young and Aged Drivers.* Department of
Industrial and Systems Engineering, The Ohio State University, Columbus, Ohio.

Saunders, A. Bryan and Benson, David A. *The Practical Application of Social Costing in Road Safety Policy Making.* Road
Safety General Division, Department of the Environment.

Schmidt, Ruediger. *Accident Investigation in the Evaluation of
Safety Standards—A Survey of Methodology and Applicability.* Volkswagen Research Division. June 20, 1975.

Seargeant, Janet C. and Hodge, Bruce E. *California Pedestrian
Accidents.* Public Safety Department, Automobile Club of
Southern California, Los Angeles.

Seiffert, Ulrich W. *An Analysis of the FMVSS-Standards in
Respect to Safety of the Vehicle Occupant.* Volkswagenwerk
AG, Germany.

Selzer, Melvin L. and Vinokur, Amiram. *Driving and Psychosocial
Characteristics of Drunk Drivers.* The University of Michigan, Ann Arbor.

Sharma, Satanand and Moskowitz, Herbert. *Marihuana Effects on
a Critical Tracking Task.* Department of Psychology, University of California, Los Angeles. Southern California
Research Institute.

Show Room 20—Longevity of Passenger Cars in Sweden. Volvo of
America.

Smith, R. P. *Consumer Demand for Cars in the USA.* University of
Cambridge Department of Applied Economics, Occasional
Paper 44. Cambridge University Press, Cambridge, 1975.

Smith, Russell A. and Moffatt, Charles A. *Accident Experience in*

Air Bag-Equipped Cars. Office of Statistics and Analysis, National Highway Traffic Safety Administration.

Social Effects of Government Energy Conservation Policies and Programs. Part I—Technical Proposal, Proposal No. URU-75-33. Prepared for Office of Energy Conservation and Environment, Federal Energy Administration, Washington, D. C., Reference: Request for Proposal No. 50223. Submitted by Arnold Mitchell. April 15, 1975.

Struble, Donald E. *Societal Costs, and Their Reduction by Safety Systems.* Minicars, Inc. July 1975.

Special Subcommittee on the Federal-Aid Highway Program of the Committee on Public Works, House of Representatives, 90th Congress, 2nd Session. *Highway Safety, Design and Operations, Freeway Signing and Related Geometrics.* May 7, 8, 9, July 9, 10, 11, 16 and 18, 1968, available from Superintendent of Documents, U. S. Government Printing Office.

Subcommittee on Investigations and Oversight of the Committee on Public Works, House of Representatives, 92nd Congress, 2d Session. *Highway Safety, Design and Operations*—Operational Deficiencies. April 11, 12, 13, June 20, 21, 22, 1972, 398 pp, available from Superintendent of Documents.

Ventre, Philippe. *Proposal of Methodology for Drawing Up Efficient Regulations.* May 7, 1975.

Wakeland, Henry H. *An Array of Social Values for Use in Analyzing the Need for Safety Regulation.* Bureau of Surface Transportation Safety, National Transportation Safety Board. July 15, 1975.

Warner, Charles, Y., Ph.D., et al. *Societal Priorities in Occupant Crash Protection.* For publication at the Fourth International Congress on Automotive Safety. May 30, 1975.

Magazines

Automotive Age and Kelley Blue Book Reporter, Autoweek, Automotive News, Business Week, Car and Driver, Consumer Reports, Road Test, Road and Track.

Newspapers

Despite my feeling that newspapers in general don't take serious
notice of the car, there are exceptions. Detroit newspapers
give equal priority to news from the automobile industry
and the White House—at least so it seems. The best is the
Detroit *News*. The *Wall Street Journal* does a marvelous job
and not only from the industry's point of view. I am also
partial to the Los Angeles *Times*.

Index

Accident simulators, 184-85, 187
Accidents, auto, 5, 7, 163-64, 180, 190, 199
Ackerman, Paul, 204-05
ACRSs (Air Cushion Restraint Systems). See Air bags
Adolescents, and autos, 14-18; work/reward system, 15-17, 18
Advertising Age, 72
"Aggressivity," 189
Air bags, 176-79
Air Pollution Control, National Center, for, 56
Alioto, Mayor Joseph, 220
AMC. *See* American Motors Corporation
American Association of Motor Vehicle Administrators, 164
American Bar Association, 164
American Historical Association, 63
American Historical Society, 62
American Motors Corporation, 90-91, 98, 154-55
Americans: The National Experience, The, 70
Anderson, Winston L., Jr., 3-5, 7-8, 29
Annual model change, 28, 85, 86
Anthony, Earle C., 122
Apperson brothers, 81
Are You a Woman Driver?, 9
Assembly line, work on, 110-13
Austin, D. W., 150
Austin, Tom, 203-04, 205-07
Auto Industries Highway Committee, 164

Auto racing, 46-47, 82, 104, 255
Auto Safety Foundation, 164
Auto Work and Its Discontents, 110n
Automobile and the Regulation of Its Impact on the Environment, The, 197-98, 199, 201, 206
Automobile Industry. *See* Detroit
Automobile industry, threats to, 57-58
Automobile Manufacturers Association, 72, 161-62; Engineering Advisory Committee, 204. *See also* Motor Vehicle Manufacturers Association of the U.S.
Automobile Safety Foundation, 175
"Automobility," 81
Automotive News, 87, 120, 132, 135, 147, 149, 150, 172
Autos: adolescents and, 14-18; beginnings of, 80-84; and blacks, 23; buying on time, 118-19; and cultural homogeneity, 84; diverting from, 230-33; doing without, 24-29; and drinking, 7, 188; and drugs, 187-89; and environmental pollution, 56, 58-59, 192-208; future of, 237-38, 245-48, 254-57, 263-67; "healthfulness of motoring," 83-84; injuries, 5, 7, 191; Los Angeles and, 3, 93, 204-05, 219-20, 231-32; and mass transit, 20, 22, 23, 219-20, 264-65; model proliferation, 90-92, 131; number of, 82, 88, 102, 124; and population migrations, 52-54; and privacy, 21-22, 255; the problem of, 29-30; psychology of owner-

Autos: adolescents and *(cont.)*
ship, 19-20, 23, 265; selling methods, 88-92, 125-31; and social consciousness, 104-07; social benefits
of, 20-21; speeding, 4; trading, 3-4;
and vacationing, 6; women and, 9-
14; world car, 263
Autoweek, 149, 151

Badge Engineering, 91
Ball State University, 36, 39, 42, 50,
51, 58
Balloon payments, 147-48
BART. *See* Bay Area Rapid Transit
District
Barth, Dr. Delbert, 196-97, 204
Bay Area Rapid Transit District
(BART), 224-27
Benton, William, 149
Better Business Bureaus, 117
Better Homes and Gardens, 152
Bohn, Joseph J., 150
Bondurant, Bob, 181-83, 185, 186
Bondurant, Bob, School of High Per-
formance Driving, 181-85,; acci-
dent simulator, 183, 184-85; skid
pad, 183-84, 186; trailing brake,
185
Boone, Dan, 151-52
Boorstin, Daniel J., 70-72, 73, 74-75,
76, 87
Bradley, Mayor Tom, 220
Brown, Richard Kimball, 97-99, 101-
02, 103, 154
Bryson, Reid, 249
Bulkeley, W. M., 150
Bumpers, 173, 175-76
Burham, John C., 81
Burman, Wild Bob, 82
Business Week, 72, 149-50, 151, 229n
Buyer/dealer/builder   relationship,
146-57
Buyer protection plan, 154
Byrne, T.A., Chevrolet (dealership),
134-35, 147
Byrne, Tim, 134, 135-36, 139-41, 142,
147

Cafiero, Eugene, 97
California, 180, 187, 190, 193, 202,
204-05, 206-08, 230, 232; Air Re-
sources Board, 101, 203, 206, 207;
Auto Repair, Bureau of, 143, 145-
46; Business and Transportation
Agency, 187; Highway Patrol, 182;
State Health Dept., 205; Traffic
Safety, Office of, 178
Car and Driver (magazine), 94, 152,
167
Car Culture, The, 81, 211
Carmania, 3-8, 46
Carmichael, Gil, 156
Catalytic converters, 101, 192, 205-
06, 207, 207n; Lambda Sond sys-
tem, 208n
Census, Bureau of, 52, 73, 79
Census of Manufacturers, U.S., 81
Chapin, Roy, 79, 110
Character, American, 73-76
Chevrolet, Louis, 82
Chicago World's Fair (1893), 62
Christian Science Monitor, The, 150
Chrysler Corp., 57, 88, 96-100, 107,
108, 149, 153; Dealer Development
(DD) program, 139; management
philosophies, 96-100
CIPEC. *See* Conseil Intergouverne-
mental des Pays Exportateurs de
Cuivre
City in History, 219-20
City Size and the Quality of Life, 52-
53, 56
Claremont Men's College, Rose In-
stitute of State and Local Govern-
ment, 231
Clean Air Act, 196
Coleman, William, 178
Commager, Henry Steele, 73, 74, 75
Commerce Committee, Senate, 170
Compromise Energy Bill, 55. *See also*
Energy Policy and Conservation
Act
Conestoga wagons, 68
Conseil Intergouvernemental des Pays
Exportateurs de Cuivre (CIPEC),
244
"Consumer Demand for Cars in the
U.S.A.," 148
Consumer Reports, 74, 152-53
Consumerism, 74, 146-47

Contingent reserve, 118
Cosmopolitan, 152
Cost/benefit ratio, 180, 187, 195, 202
Crain, Keith, 132, 135
Cumberland Road, 65
Cuming, Fortescue, 65-66
Cumulative Regulatory Effects on the Cost of Automobile Transportation, Ad Hoc Committee on (RECAT), 193

Dahlquist, Eric, 101
Daimler-Benz, 166, 178
Dan Ryan Line, 226
Dealers, auto, 89, 115, 116-57; factory stores, 139; franchised, 121, 133, 135, 137, 138, 147; NADA, 132-33, 137-38; parts and repair racket, 141-46; post World War II shortages, 123-24; price pack, 127; relations with Detroit, growth of, 121-23; selling with dignity, 132, 133; System, The, 125-31; under-table bribes, 124, 137
Death of the Automobile, The, 89-90
Demise of the big city, 56
Detroit, 28, 36, 40, 42, 45, 72, 74, 79-115, 121, 122, 123, 125, 133, 146, 149-50, 156, 161-65, 167-70, 171, 172, 175, 178, 190, 192, 193, 207, 208, 211, 234, 256; crash (1973), 94-96, 99, 101-02; Imperium, the, 80, 87, 89, 94, 114, 124, 128, 132; public disenchantment, 162-65
Detroit News, 151
Dobbs, Hull, 125
Dodge Adventurer (magazine), 153
Dole, Charles E., 150
Donner, Frederick, 169
Donner, George and Jacob, 61-62
Donner party, 61-62
Drag racing, 46-47
Drake, Edwin L., 73
Drew, Daniel, 69
Driver education, 16, 17-18, 181-88; attitudinal problem, 186
Drivers, auto, 164-65, 181-91, 215-16; attitudinal problem, 186, 216; and drinking, 188; and drugs, 187-89
Du Pont, Pierre S., 85

Durant, William Crapo, 80, 81-82, 85, 86, 121, 122
Duryea, Charles E. and J. Frank, 80-81

Eaton Corporation, 177
Eckert, Ross, 221
Eco-Spasm Report, The, 235, 239, 257
Ehrlich, Paul R. and Anne H., 239, 249-53, 257, 259
Elliott, Ward, 231-32
End of Affluence: Blueprint for Your Future, The, 239, 249-53, 257, 258
Energy, availability of, 242-44, 251-53
Energy Policy and Conservation Act (1975), 55, 171-72, 189
Englehard Industries, 101, 207
Environmental pollution, 56-57, 58-59, 192-208, 247, 248, 249-51, 252, 253, 266; carbon monoxide (CO), 192, 195-96, 197, 198-99, 200, 201, 202, 205, 206, 208; hydrocarbons (HC), 192, 197, 199-200, 201, 202, 202n, 206; nitrogen oxides (NO$_x$), 192, 197, 199, 200, 201, 202, 202n, 206, 208; ozone, 199-200, 201, 205; particulates, 192, 197, 200-01; smog, 193, 204, 205; sulfur oxides, 197, 200, 208
Environmental Protection Agency (EPA), 57, 79, 101, 154, 197, 199, 206
Environmental Quality, Council on, 197
Esquire, 152
Estes, Pete, 135
Eugene, Ore., 26-27
Executive Reorganization, Senate Subcommittee on, 161, 167-69
Experimental Safety Vehicles, 174-75
Exploring Energy Choices, A Preliminary Report, 243

Federal Highway Administration, 212
Federal Primary CO Standard, 196
Federal Task Force on Motor Vehicle Goals beyond 1980, 266n
Federal Trade Commission, 163

Firestone Tire and Rubber Company, 146, 147
Fisk, Jim, 69
Flink, James J., 63, 74, 81, 83, 211, 220, 221, 227
Ford, Henry, 63, 74, 80, 81, 82, 83, 85, 86, 121, 256
Ford, Henry II, 79, 109
Ford, President Gerald, 55, 108
Ford Foundation, 243
Ford Motor Company, 57, 81, 85, 86, 88, 95, 98, 104-05, 122, 149, 173, 177, 178, 205, 207, 264; Ford Division, 154; Lincoln-Mercury Division, 149
Ford Times (magazine), 153
Fort Duquesne, 65
Fraser, Douglas, 79, 107-10, 111, 112-14
Future Shock, 239

Garagiola, Joe, 154
Gas stations, 72, 73
Gasoline: price, 237-38, 246, 258; tax, 210; unleaded, 193, 194
"Gasoline Tax and the Automobile Revolution, The," 81
General Motors, 57, 75, 80, 81-82, 85-87, 90, 93, 96, 98, 101, 112, 113, 120, 122, 133, 137-39, 149, 150, 156, 163, 168-70, 177, 220, 221-22, 264; Chevrolet Division, 135-36, 156, 163; creation of, 81-82; GM Corporate, 85; labor costs (1976), 113; management philosophies, 101-03; Motor Holdings, 139; Pontiac Division, 101-03
General Motors Acceptance Corporation, 86
Geological Survey, U.S., 243
Gerstenberg, Richard, 110
Gilberg, Andy, 103-05, 106, 107
Gordon, Dr. Whitney, 58-59
Gordon, Peter, 221
Gould, Jay, 69
Greenberg, Dr. Herbert M., 87
Gregory, Dr. James, 181, 190
"Grosse Pointe Myopians, The," 95-96
Guaranty Securities Company, 86

Haagen-Smit, Dr. Arlie, 204, 205
Haddon, Dr. William, Jr., 167, 170, 175-76
Harrison, David, Jr., 196-97
Haynes, Elwood P., 81
Health, Education and Welfare, Dept. of: Accident Prevention Bureau, 168; National Air Pollution Control Administration, Bureau of Criteria and Standards, 196
"Healthfulness of Motoring, The," 83-84
Heath, Richard, 37, 42, 43-46, 47-48, 51, 55, 57, 59-60
Heilbroner, R. L., 65
Highway Act (1966), 94
Highway Safety, Design and Operations (The Need for a Safer Driving Environment), 210, 213-19
Highways. *See* Roads and Highways
Hill, Phil, 166
Hilton, George W., 221-24
Honda, 101, 188
Hotels, 70-71
Howard, Charles S., 122-23
Hughson, Billy, 121-22

Injuries, automobile, 5, 7
Insolent Chariots, The, 88
Inspection, motor vehicle, 179, 180
Insurance Institute for Highway Safety (IIHS), 175
Interior, U.S. Dept. of, 58
International Association of Chiefs of Police, 164
International Congress of Auto-(motive) Safety (Fourth), 157, 177
Interstate and Defense Highway Act. *See* Roads and Highways, Federal Aid Highway Act
Irvin, Bob, 149, 151

Jeanes, William, 167, 170, 171
Jerome, John, 89-90, 92, 125
Johnson, President Lyndon, 168, 169, 170
Jordan, Philip P., 66-67

Kahn, Helen, 172

Kahn, Herman, 238-39, 240, 241, 243, 252n, 259
Kain, John F., 196-97
Kaiser, Henry, 93
Kaiser Industries, 93
Karts, 46, 47
Keats, John, 88
Kennedy, Senator Robert, 168-69
Kennedy Line, 226
Kettering, C. F. "Boss," 95-96, 99
King, Rick, 111-12, 113-14

Ladies' Home Journal, The, 152
Lankard, Tom, 187
League of American Wheelmen, 69-70
Leasing, car, 147-48
Lee, Don, 122
Lewis, Dr. Richard, 14-20, 29
Licensing, driver, 16
Lienert, Paul, 149
Lindenwold Line, 226
Literary Digest, 83-84
Loofbourrow, Alan, 99-100, 103, 106
Los Angeles Air Pollution Control District, 204
Los Angeles Herald-Examiner, 151
Lynd, Robert S. and Helen M., 32-34, 35, 36, 37-38, 39, 47, 48, 52, 58, 61, 72

McCluggage, Denise, 9-14, 21, 29, 152
McCurry, Robert B., Jr., 153
"Machomobile—Move Over," 12-14
McKinney, Adam, 66-67
McLaughlin, Matthew S., 149
McLaughlin, R. Samuel, 82
McNealy, Bill, 154-55
Madison Avenue, The Advertising Magazine, 9, 12-14, 153-55
Mair, Alex, 101-03
Mass Transit, 20, 22, 23, 228-30, 255, 264-65; [San Francisco] Bay Area (BART), 224-25, 226, 227; Boston, 226; Chicago, 223, 226; Cleveland, 226; Lindenwold Line, 226; Los Angeles, 219-23; Washington, D.C., 226-27, 228-29

Mead, Margaret, 95
Media coverage: consumer-oriented, 150-53; industry, 149-50, 153-55
Mercedes-Benz of North America, 165-66, 187-88
Metropolitan Coach Lines, 222
M-Factor, 64-65, 68
Middletown, 32-34, 48. *See also* Muncie, Ind.
Middletown ("A Study in American Culture"), 32-34, 38, 47
Middletown in Transition, 33, 34, 38, 72
Miller, David, 24-29
Mississippi Valley Historical Review, 81
Mitre Corporation, 193-94
Mobility: automobile and, 63; importance of, 62-65, 69, 76; M-Factor, 64-65, 68
Modal mix, 227-30
Moffatt, Charles A., 177-78
Moldovan, John, 40-60
Monroe, Warren "Snowy," 191
Morris, Dr. David, 51-52, 53-54, 55, 56-57, 58
Morrissey, John, 154
Motels, 71-72
Motor News Analysis, 136-37
Motor Trend (magazine), 101, 152, 155
Motor Vehicle Manufacturers' Association of the U.S., 63, 72
Mott, Charles Stewart, 82
Mumford, Lewis, 219-20, 227
Muncie, Ind., 32, 34-60, 61; Attitude Study, 43; auto accident statistics, 43; auto crime in, 44, 45; autos significance of, 35-36, 40-41, 42, 47-48, 54-60; environmental pollution, 58-59; kart racing in, 46; mass transit, 48-49; and population migration, 53-54; traffic problems, 48-51; Transportation and Land Use Study, 51
Murphy, Thomas, 79, 102, 120
My Years with General Motors, 85

NADA. *See* National Automobile Dealer's Association

Nader, Ralph, 96, 104, 165, 167, 170, 171, 172, 181, 204-05, 217
National Automobile Dealer's Association (NADA), 132-133, 137-138
National City Lines, 220, 222
National Committee on Uniform Laws and Ordinances, 164
National Education Association, National Commission on Safety Education of, 164
National Highway Traffic Safety Administration (Agency; NHTSA), 72, 79, 94, 175, 176, 177, 179, 180, 181, 189, 190, 191; Statistics and Analysis, Office of, 177
National Research Council, Committee on Resources and Man, 243
National Road, 66, 67, 68
National Road, The, 68-69
National Safety Council, 164
National Science Foundation, 52
National Traffic and Motor Safety Act (1966), 171
National Traffic Safety Administration, 174
National Transportation Facts and Trends (Alternative Transportation Futures), 238-40, 245-46, 258-59
"Need for a Safer Driving Environment, The," 210
Neil, Moore Stage Company, 66
New Republic, 67
New York (magazine), 74
New York Times, The, 149, 167, 202n
Next 200 Years, The, 241-48, 257-58
NHTSA. *See* National Highway Traffic Safety Administration

Oakland Tribune, 151
Ohio State University, 198-99
Old Pike, The, 66
OPEC, 50, 74, 94, 190, 238, 242, 244
Ordeal by Hunger, 61-62
Oregon, 210
OTSs. *See* Traffic Safety, Offices of
Ozone, 199-200, 201, 205

Pacific Electric Railway, 220, 221-22, 223-24
Paradise Lost—The Decline of the

Auto-Industrial Age, 85, 87
Parker, Larry, 103, 104-07
Petroleum: industry, 72, 73; shortages, 237-38
Pickard, Jerome, 56
Piersol, Jesse, 66
Pierson, George W., 62, 63-64, 68
Planned obsolescence, 87
Playboy, 152
Pomeroy, Ira, 67
Population Bomb, The, 257
Population Growth and the American Future, Commission on, 53, 56
Population Migrations, 51-53, 63-65, 68, 82-83; mobility, importance of, 62-65, 69-70, 76
President's Committee on Recent Social Trends, 211
Price pack, 127
Prisk, Charles, 217
Product planning, 105
Public Roads, U.S. Office of, 70
Public Works, House Committee on, Subcommittee on Investigations and Review, 209-10, 213-19

Quinn, Tom, 207

Rae, James, 63, 65, 73
Railroads, 69
Randolph, Hugh, 151
Reckless driving, 4, 7
Reed, James Frazier and Margaret, 62
Regulation, auto industry, 161-81
Resources and Man, 243
Reuther, Walter, 108
Ribicoff, Senator Abraham, 161, 166, 168, 169, 170, 171, 205, 217
Riccardo, John, 79, 97, 98, 103
Road & Track (magazine), 152, 155
Road Inquiry, Office of, 70
Road Test (magazine), 152
Roads and highways, 65, 70, 209-19, 256; Cumberland Road, 65; Federal Aid Highway Act, 211; Federal Aid Road Act, 161, 210; Federal Highway Act (1921), 210; Federal Highway Agency, 181; Highway Trust Fund, 212; Interstate Highway Act (1956), 211-12; Interstate system,

209, 210, 211-19
Roche, James, 168-69
Roosevelt, President Franklin D., 211
Rothschild, Emma, 34, 85, 86, 87, 88, 112, 114
Rubin, Irv, 96

Safety: auto, 163-91; highway, 212-19
Salpukis, Agis, 149
Schumacher, E. F., 259-63, 267
Searight, T. B., 66
Seat belts, 173-74, 178-79, 180
Sharma, Dr. Satanand, 188
Shirley Highway Service, 228-29
"Significance of the Frontier in American History," 63
Slaven, John, 155
Sloan, Alfred P., Jr., 75, 80, 85-86, 87
Small cars, 28, 57, 96, 109, 149, 150, 154, 155, 156-57, 189, 190, 234
Small Is Beautiful, 259-63
Small World (magazine), 153
Smith, Gail, 154
Smith, R. P., 148
Smith, Russell, A., 177
Smith, William A., 73
Society, possible futures for, 237-67
Sonosky, Jerry, 165, 166-67, 168, 169-71, 172
South Shore Line, 226
Southern California, University of: Center for Public Affairs, Institute for Public Policy Research, 220-21; Graduate School of Business, Center for Futures Research, 57-58
Southern Pacific Railroad, 222
Speed limit, 55 mph, 102, 190-91
SRI. *See* Stanford Research Institute
Stages, 66-67, 68
Standard Metropolitan Statistical Areas (SMSAs), 51-52, 53, 64, 196
Standards, design and performance, 171-79, 189
Stanford Research Institute (SRI), 52-53, 56-57, 64, 238, 245-46, 254, 258, 263, 264-65
Stanley brothers, 81
Steinem, Gloria, 29
Steward, George R., 61-62

Stratified charge engines, 100-01
Supplementary unemployment benefits (SUBs), 112
System, The, 125-31

"300-Days' Study" (federal), 202n, 266n, 267
Toffler, Alvin, 235, 239, 254
Townsend, Lynn, 96-97, 110
Traffic Safety, (state) Offices of (OTSs), 179-81; California, 178; Nevada, 180
Traffic Safety Act (1966), 94
Transportation, U.S. Dept. of, 79, 94, 104, 172, 178, 179, 238, 258
Transportation Frontier, The, 68
Travel conditions, early, 65-71
Truth-in-lending laws, 131
Tupomaro Escape School. *See* Bondurant, Bob, School of High Performance Driving
Turner, Frederick Jackson, 62-63

United Auto Workers (UAW), 79, 108, 110, 111-12, 114
Unleaded gasoline, 193, 194
Unsafe at Any Speed, 165, 169, 204-05
U.S. Mineral Resources, 243
U.S. News & World Report, 149

Van Buren, President Martin, 67
Vidal, Gore, 194
Vietnam, 74
Volatile highway mixes, 189-90, 247
Volvo, 101, 177, 207-08, 208n
Von Manteuffel, Peter, 166
VW, 155

Wachs, Martin, 228
Wagons, 65
Wall Street Journal, 118, 120, 137-38, 150, 151
Ward's Automotive Reports, 151
Washington, D.C. Metro, 226-27
Washington Monthly, 111
Waters, James, 123
Whitney, George E., 81
Widick, B.J., 110n
Winther, Oscar, 68, 70

Wohl, Martin, 224-25, 226, 227
Women, and autos, 9-14
Woodcock, Leonard, 79, 108, 114
Wylie, Frank, 20-21, 22-24, 29

Yates, Brock, 94-96, 99

Ziegler, Lamar, 36-37, 38, 39, 42, 43,
   48-51, 59
Ziff Davis Publishing Co., 94-95